GENERAL INDEX TO THE REPORTS
OF
THE ARCHAEOLOGICAL SURVEY OF INDIA,

VOLUMES I TO XXIII

GENERAL INDEX TO THE REPORTS
OF
THE ARCHAEOLOGICAL SURVEY OF INDIA,

VOLUMES I TO XXIII,

PUBLISHED UNDER THE SUPERINTENDENCE OF

MAJOR-GENERAL SIR. A. CUNNINGHAM,
C.S.I., K.C.I.E.

BY

VINCENT ARTHUR SMITH,

BENGAL CIVIL SERVICE,
MEMBER OF THE ROYAL ASIATIC SOCIETY, AND OF THE ASIATIC SOCIETY OF BENGAL

WITH A GLOSSARY AND GENERAL TABLE OF CONTENTS.

GYAN

Published by

GYAN

Gyan Publishing House
5, Ansari Road
Daryaganj, New Delhi-110002
Phone: 011-47034999, 9811692060
E-mail: books@gyanbooks.com

Distribution Network
gyanbooks.com
India, USA, Canada, UK, Australia, France

ISBN : 978-81-212-2714-8 (HB)
First Published, 1887

2nd Impression 2021

Printed at: Gyan Press, Delhi.

General Index to the Reports
of
The Archaeological Survey of India
Author: Vincent Arthur Smith

GENERAL INDEX TO THE REPORTS

OF

THE ARCHÆOLOGICAL SURVEY OF INDIA.

VOLUMES I TO XXIII,

PUBLISHED UNDER THE SUPERINTENDENCE OF

MAJOR-GENERAL SIR A. CUNNINGHAM, C.S.I., K.C.I.E.

BY

VINCENT ARTHUR SMITH,
BENGAL CIVIL SERVICE,
MEMBER OF THE ROYAL ASIATIC SOCIETY, AND OF THE ASIATIC SOCIETY OF BENGAL.

WITH A GLOSSARY AND GENERAL TABLE OF CONTENTS.

CALCUTTA:
PRINTED BY THE SUPERINTENDENT OF GOVERNMENT PRINTING, INDIA.
1887.

CONTENTS.

PAGE

Preface . . . v
General Table of Contents . . . vii
List of Abbreviations . . . xix
General Index . . . 1
Glossary . . . 199

PREFACE.

EVERY one who has had occasion to consult the Reports of the Archæological Survey of India, published under the superintendence of Major-General Sir A. Cunningham, must have felt the want of a General Index to the long series of twenty-three volumes. The Reports contain a vast mass of valuable information, but it is presented in such an undigested form that much of it is practically inaccessible. Each volume is certainly provided with an Index, but these Indices are, with two exceptions, extremely meagre, and of very little service. With the approval of General Cunningham I undertook the task of compiling an adequate General Index, and have now completed it to the best of my ability.

I cannot hope that my work will be regarded as perfect, but there can be no doubt that it will add greatly to the value of the Reports; and I trust that, in consideration of the assistance it will render to all students of Indian Archæology, its faults may be forgiven.

No Index of reasonable size could give references to every proper name mentioned, or every topic discussed in the Reports, but I have endeavoured, so far as my limited knowledge of Archæology would permit, to include in my Index every name or subject which an archæologist would be likely to look for, and to give each entry in the form or forms most likely to be convenient. Names in dynastic lists about which nothing is known, except their occurrence in such lists, will not usually be found in the Index. They must be looked for by means of the references to the dynasties concerned.

Some of the more complex headings, such as that of Coins, bring together in a compendious form a very large number of facts which were of little interest or value when scattered through twenty-three volumes. The classification of the entries under such headings has cost me much thought and labour, which will, it is hoped, be justified by the result.

The crude and unscientific speculations of General Cunningham's assistants, which waste so much space in several volumes of the Reports, have been passed over very lightly, and the Index gives few indications of their existence.

The spelling of proper names in the Reports is rather arbitrary and lax, and I have necessarily been compelled to follow it. Alternative spellings will, how-

ever, be found very often in the Index, and I do not think there will be any difficulty in tracing names.

I have not attempted to distinguish the various letters of closely similar sound by elaborate diacritical marks, as is done in the pages of the Indian Antiquary. So far as the text with which I was dealing would permit, the spelling of proper names is in accordance with the practice followed for some years past in official publications of the Indian Government. A long vowel is marked by an accent, unaccented a is pronounced as in the word America, and all other vowels as in Italian.

One of the most serious defects in the Reports is the omission in general to state the civil territorial division of the country in which the place under discussion is situate. The bewildered reader is, for instance, told that an obscure mound of ruins named Atranjí-Kherá is 4 miles south of Karsána, 8 miles to the north of Eyta (*sic*), 15 miles to the south of Soron, and 43 miles to the north-west of Sankisa. It is not easy from such a description to make out where Atranjí-Kherá is, or to discover any mention of it that may exist in other books or official records. The mound is really in the Etá District of the North-Western Provinces, and the moment this information is afforded anything that may exist on record about the place is readily traceable.

I have accordingly remedied this defect by specifying in almost every case the State or Province and the District in which each site mentioned in the Index is included. The obtaining of this information has involved much tedious search in maps and gazetteers, but in a very few instances I have been unable to fix with precision the position of the places described. My European readers will please observe that the word District is used in the technical sense, and means the unit of civil government administered by a District Officer, who is known variously as Magistrate and Collector, or Deputy Commissioner, or Superintendent.

Most of the words belonging to Oriental languages which occur in the Reports are readily intelligible to readers who have resided in India, but, for those who have not enjoyed that advantage, such words may require explanation. I have therefore compiled a Glossary which explains all such words, so far as the meanings are concerned which attach to them in the text.

A General Table of Contents has been prefixed.

V. A. SMITH.

GENERAL TABLE OF CONTENTS.

VOLUME I.

PART I.

	PAGE
Preface, containing Lord Canning's minute on the antiquities of Upper India	I—VIII
Introduction, containing an account of the progress of Indian Archæology up to 1861 A.D.	I—XLIII
Report of operations during 1861-62, in Bihár and S. E. portions of the N.-W. P. by Major-General Cunningham (pp. 1—130)—	
1. Gayá	1
2. Buddha-Gayá	4
3. Bakror	12
4. Punáwa	13
5. Kurkihár, or Kukkutapáda-giri	14
6. Giryek, or Indra-sila-guha	16
7. Rágír, or Rájagriha	20
8. Barágaon or Nálanda	28
9. Bihár	36
10. Ghosráwa	38
11. Titaráwa	39
12. Aphsar	40
13. Barábár	*ib*
14. Dharáwat	53
15. Besárh or Vaisáli	55
16. Kesariya	64
17. Lauriyá Ara-Ráj	67
18. Lauriyá Navandgarh	68
19. Padaraona, or Páwá	74
20. Kasiá, or Kusinagara	76
21. Khukhundo, or Kishkinda-pura	85
22. Kahaon, or Kakubharati	91
23. Hathiyá-dih	95
24. Bhitarí	96
25. Banáras and Sárnáth	103

PART II.

Report of operations during 1862-63 in Punjáb, N.-W. P., and Oudh, by Major-General Cunningham (pages 131—358)—	
1. Delhi	131
2. Mathurá	231
3. Khálsi	244
4. Madáwar, or Madipur	248
5. Káshípur, or Govisana	251
6. Rámnagar, or Ahichhatra	255
7. Soron, or Surakshetra	265
8. Atranjíkhera, or Pilosana	268
9. Sankisa, or Sangkasya	271
10. Kanoj, or Kanyákubja	279
11. Kákupur, or Ayuto	293
12. Daundiákherá, or Hayamukha	296
13. Alláhábád, or Prayága	296
14. Kosam or Kosámbi	301
15. Sultánpur, or Kusapura	313
16. Dhopápapura	315
17. Ajudhya, or Sáketa	317
18. Hátila, or Asokpur	327
19. Sáhet-Máhet, or Srávastí	330
20. Tánda	348
21. Nímsar	350
22. Bárikhar	351
23. Dewal	352
24. Parasuá-kot	357
25. Bilai-kherá	358
26. Kábar	*ib.*

VOLUME II.

PART I.

Report of operations during 1863-64 by Major-General Cunningham—	
(A)—Ethnology (pages 1—82).	
Takkas	6
Megs, or Mekei	11
Other tribes	13
Aryas.	
Janjuhas and Awáns	17
Bhatis	19

VOLUME II—*contd.*

	PAGE
Later Turanians.	
Gákars	22
Káthi and Bálas	33
Sobú	37
Indo-Scythians.	
Su, or Sagaraukae	44
Medi, or Meds	51
Zanthii, Iatii, or Játs	54
Yuchi, or Tochari	61
Little Yuchi, or Kator	73
Ephthalites, or White Huns	75
(B).—Antiquities of Punjáb and the northern extremity of the N.-W. P. (pages 82—239)—	
Antiquities, General Remarks	82
1. Peshâwar, or Parasháwara	87
2. Pushkalávatí, or Peukelaotis	89
3. Palodheri, or Varusha	90
4. Ohind, or Utakhanda	92
5. Láhor, or Sálatura	95
6. Aornos	*ib.*
7. Taxila, or Takshasila	111
8. Hasan Abdál	135
9. Baoti Pind	139
10. Balar	142
11. Bádarpur	144
12. Jáoli	146
13. Tarnáwa	147
14. Kurmál	149
15. Ráwal-pindi or Gájípur	151
16. Mánikyála	152
17. Sakhrabastí	172
18. Diláwar, or Bukephala	173
19. Mong, or Nikaea	186
20. Katás, or Katáksha	188
21. Sangalawála Tiba, or Sangala	192
22. Asarur, or Táki	200
23. Ran-si, or Nara-sinha	202
24. Amba Kápi	203
25. Sarhind	205
26. Thánesar, or Stháneswara	212
27. Amín	223
28. Pehoa, or Prithudaka	224
29. Sugh, or Srughna	226
30. Haridwár, or Gangádwára	231
31. Moradhwaj	237
32. Chaturbhuj	238

PART II.

Report of operations during 1864-65 (pages 241—459) in Rájputána, Central India, and Bundelkhand—	
1. Bairát, or Vairáta	242
2. Amber	250
3. Dhundhár, or Jaypur	251
4. Ajmer, or Ajayamera	252
5. Chandrávatí, or Jhálra Pátan	263
6. Dhamnár	270
7. Kholvi	280
1. Sárangpur	288
9. Mhau Maidán	292
10. Jharkon, or Bajrang-garh	294
11. Máyána, or Máyapura	301
12. Kulháras	302
13. Ranod, or Narod	303
14. Nalapura, or Narwár	307
15. Himatgarh	328
16. Gwáliár, or Gwalior	330
17. Núrábád	397
18. Kutwár, or Kamantalpuri	*ib.*
19. Suhaniya	399
20. Burí Chánderí	401
21. Chánderí	404
22. Khajuráho, or Khajuráya	412
23. Mahoba, or Mahotsava-nagara	439

VOLUME III.

Introduction containing instructions to assistants of Archæological Survey	III—XIII
Report of operations during 1871-72 in N.-W. P. and Bihár, by Major-General Cunningham (pages 1—164)—	
1. Various styles of Hindu and Muhammadan architecture	2
2. Mathurá	13
3. Bithá	46
4. Garhwá	53
5. Latiyá	61
6. Akhandha	63
7. Baghsar, or Buxar	64
8. Mahására, or Masár	66
9. Árámnagar, or Árá	72
10. Buddha Gayá	79
11. Prágbodhi, or Mora Mountain	105
12. Gayá	107
13. Yashtivana, or Jethian	139
14. Old Rájagriha, or Kuságarapura	140
15. Indrasila guho, or Giryek	145
16. Kapotika Monastery	150
17. Rajaona, or Rajjhána	151
18. Kiyul and Birdában	156
19. Jaynagar	159
20. Nongarh	160
21. Indappe	162
Postscript	163

VOLUME IV.

	PAGE
Preface by Major-General Cunningham	I—XIV
Note by Mr. J. D Beglar	XV—XVII
Report of operations during 1871-72 at Delhi, by Mr. J. D. Beglar	1—91
Report of operations during 1871-72 at Agra, by Mr. A. C. L. Carlleyle	93—247

VOLUME V.

	PAGE
Report of operations during 1872-73 in Panjáb, by Major-General Cunningham—Introduction	V—VIII
1. Yusufzai District	1
2. Sháhbáz-garhi	8
3. Takht-i-Bahi	23
4. Sahri-Bahlol	36
5. Jamál-garhi	46
6. Kharkai	53
7. Sáwal-dher	55
8. Nográm	*ib.*
9. Inscriptions from Yusufzai	57
10. Khairábád	64
11. Sháh-dheri, or Taxila	66
12. Mánikyála	75
13. Antiquities of the Salt-Range	79
14. Mallot	85
15. Ketás	90
16. Kutánwála-pind	93
17. Maira	*ib.*
18. Plains of the Punjáb	94
19. Jobnáthnagar	96
20. Shorkot	97
21. Bavanni	103
22. Harapá	105
23. Depálpur	109
24. Tulamba	111
25. Multán	114
26. Tushám	136
27. Hisár Pillar	140
28. Delhi Pillars	142
29. Jálandhara	145
30. Patháпkot	153
31. Kot-Kángra	155
32. Jwála-Mukhi	168
33. Kanhiâra	175
34. Châri	177
35. Kíragráma	178
36. Asapuri	183
Appendix A.—Indo-Persian and Indo-Grecian styles of architecture	185 196
Appendix B.—List of Sculptures from Yusufzai	197-202

VOLUME VI.

	PAGE
Introduction by Major-General Cunningham	III, IV
Report of Tour in Eastern Rájputána and Agra district, N.-W. P., during 1871-72 and 1872-73, by Mr. A. C. L. Carlleyle (pages 1—253)—	
1. Mountain Ranges of Rájputána	1
2. Achnera	5
3. Kherá	13
4. Rúpbás	16
5. Jágner	24
6. Satmás	33
7. Baiáná	40
8. Santípur, or Vijayamandargarh	54
9. Sikandra	74
10. Máchâri, or Sânchári	77
11. Bairát	91
12. Deosá	104
13. Nain, or Nai	109
14. Chátsu	116
15. Shivdungar	121
16. Thoda, or Thore	124
17. Bághera, or Vyághra	136
18. Vísalpur	152
19. Dhand, or Ghár	160
20. Nágar, or Karkota Nágara	162
21. Nágarí, or Tambávatí Nágarí	196
22. Morá	227
23. Bijoli	234

VOLUME VII.

	PAGE
Preface by Major-General Cunningham	V—VII
Report of Tour in Bundelkhand and Málwa or Central India, during 1871-72, by Mr. J. D. Beglar (pages 1—102)—	
1. Ballabgarh	1
2. Hodal	2
3. Dotánáh	2
4. Chátah	3
5. Brindában	*ib.*
6. Jait	4
7. Bateswar	5
8. Bhind	11

VOLUME VII—*contd.*

	PAGE
9. Jálaun	13
10. Orai	*ib.*
11. Kúnch	20
12. Akori	21
13. Khajuráhá	41
14. Rorá	23
15. Mahoba	24
16. Ráhilya	26
17. Makarbái	*ib.*
18. Chhatrpur	27
19. Jaitpur	28
20. Gúrsarai	30
21. Irich	32
22. Deokalí	36
23. Sirswágarh	*ib.*
24. Lahár	37
25. Indurke	38
26. Danui (Dinai)	39
27. Manyágarh	42
28. Panná	45
29. Ajaygarh	46
30. Mahiyar	50
31. Jabalpur	53
32. Hattá	36
33. Rúpnáth	58
34. Damoh	59
35. Garhákota	*ib.*
36. Ráhatgarh	60
37. Pathári	64
38. Udaypur	81
39. Eran	88
40. Gyáraspur	60

Report of Tour in Central Provinces during 1873-74, by Mr. J. D. Beglar (pages 103—246)—

	PAGE
1. Mandlá	103
2. Rámnagar	106
3. Ghansor	107
4. Rámtek	109
5. Nágpur	115
6. Umrer	118
7. Bhiwápur	121
8. Pauni	122
9. Deotek	123
10. Panori	125
11. Ármori	*ib.*
12. Thánegaon	126
13. Wairágarh	127
14. Tipágarh	130
15. Bálod	133
16. Sorar	137
17. Gowror	138
18. Dhamtarí	142
19. Sehwá	145
20. Deokhut	146
21. Murpár	147
22. Rájam	148
23. Sonábirá	156
24. Haranpáp	*ib.*
25. Khalári	*ib.*
26. Khoprá	158
27. Mahásamand	159
28. Árang	*ib.*
29. Ráyapura	165
30. Sirpur	168
31. Náráyanpura	193
32. Kurwái	196
33. Báludá	*ib.*
34. Khárod	201
35. Pámgarh	204
36. Bachhaudgarh	211
37. Akaltárá	*ib.*
38. Kotgarh	212
39. Kotmi	213
40. Biláspur	*ib.*
41. Ratanpur	214
42. Júná Shahr	216
43. Páli	217
44. Láphágarh	219
45. Chhattísghar	224
46. Ajmírgarh	226
47. Amarkantak	227
48. Son Mundá	236
49. Dhanpur	237
50. Pipariá	238
51. Anuppur	*ib.*
52. Sámantpur	*ib.*
33. Jamui	239
54. Singhpur	*ib.*
55. Sohágpur	*ib.*

VOLUME VIII.

Preface by Major-General Cunningham	V—VIII
Note by Mr. J. D. Beglar	IX—XXI

Report of a Tour through the Bengal Provinces (*i. e.*, Bihár, Chutiá Nágpur, and Bengal Proper), by Mr. J. D. Beglar in 1872-73 (pages 1—207)—

1. Patna, or Pátaliputra	1
2. Tilára, or Tiládaka	34
3. Barábár Hills	35
4. Dharáwat	37
5. Kauwá-Dol	40
6. Barábár Caves	41
7. Járu	44
8. Mirápur, Nádera	45
9. Gowror	*ib.*
10. Batháni Hill	46
11. Islámpur	47
12. Lát	*ib.*
13. Old lines of Road	48
14. List of old places	51

VOLUME VIII—*contd.*

	PAGE
15. Kispá	53
16. Baráwáng and Konch	54
17. Páli	61
18. Utrain	62
19. Sihári and Deokut	*ib.*
20. Gunariyá	63
21. Umgá and Deo	*ib.*
22. Bishanpur Ghenjan	*ib.*
23. Pái Bígha	*ib.*
24 Matka Hill, Chilor, &c.	64
25. Hasanpur Káko	*ib.*
26. Ner and Bela	65
27. Hilsá	66
28. Buddha-Gayá	*ib.*
29. Bakror	74
30. Seonagar, Ongári, Dápthu	*ib.*
31. Bihár	*ib.*
32. Soh	77
33. Páwápuri	*ib.*
34. Chandimau	78
35. Sháhpur-átmá	*ib.*
36. Barágaon	*ib.*
37. Siláo	83
38. Barágaon	84
39. Rájgír, or Rájagriha	85
40. Mokámá	101
41. Mári	*ib.*
42. Báwan Gangá	102
43. Hasrá	104
44. Bishanpur-Tandwá	105
45. Sítámarhi cave	106
46. Bárat	107
47. Ghosráwá, Titráwá	108
48. Párvati	*ib.*
49. Aphsand (Aphsar)	114
50. Satgáon and Ektárá	115
51. Roh	*ib.*
52. Shekhpurá	116
53. Sikandrá and Premáyá	*ib.*
54. Lakhi Sarái	116
55. Balgudar	117
56. Jaynagar	*ib.*
57. Nongarh	118
58. Indáppe	120
59. Naulakhágarh	*ib.*
60. Kherhi	128
61. Bhágalpur	129
62. Jethur	130
63. Mandár Hill	*ib.*
64. Baidyanáth	137
65. Shádipur, Seuri	146
66. Lábhpur, Jamwa Kandi and Nagor	*ib.*
67. Mangalpur and Bhimgarh	149
68. Barákar	150
69. Kalyáneswari	154
70. Pándrá	155
71. Katrás	156
72. Chechgaongarh	157
73. Bilonja	160
74. Tugri	*ib.*
75. Bhátbinor	161
76. Alwárá and Dáriká	*ib.*
77. Párá	162
78. Bándá	168
79. Telkuppi	169
80. Pachet	178
81. Khelái Chandi	182
82. Chora	*ib.*
83. Puralya	*ib.*
84. Balrámpur	183
85. Burám	184
86. Dulmi (Dalmi)	186
87. Ichágarh	188
88. Sufáran	189
89. Deoli	*ib.*
90. Suissá	190
91. Dalmi and Barhá Bazár	191
92. Gandwá	192
93. Pákbirrá	193
94. Dhádki Tanr	195
95. Tuisámá	196
96. Budhhpur	197
97. Chatna	198
98. Ekteswar	200
99. Sonátapan	*ib.*
100. Bahulárá	202
101. Chhinpur	203
102. Bishanpur	*ib.*
103. Húglí	206

VOLUME IX.

Report of Tours in Central Provinces and parts of Baghelkhand and Central India during 1873-74 and 1874-75, by Major-General Cunningham—

Preface	v—ix
1. Lál Pahár, or Chhattrí Pahár	1
2. Bhárhut	2
3. Sankargarh	4
4. Uchahara	5
5. Kho, the old capital of Uchahara	6
6. Kári Tálai, or Karnpur	7
7. Bhúbhara Pillar	8
8. Pataini Deví Temple	31
9. Mahiyar	33
10. Bilharí	34
11. Rúpnáth Rock Inscription	38
12. Amoda	39
13. Bahuriband	39
14. Tigowá	41
15. Majholí	48

VOLUME IX—*contd.*

	PAGE
16. Singorgarh	48
17. Tewar, or Tripura	54
18. Bherá Ghát	60
19. Khandwá	113
20. Burhánpur	115
21. Asírgarh	118
22. Bhándak	121
23. Ghorpet	136
24. Chánda	136
25. Keljhar	140
26. Rájgarh	141
27. Márkhanda	142
28. Gonds, or Gaudas	150

VOLUME X.

Report of Tours in the Alláhábád District, Bundelkhand, and Málwa or Central India, during 1874-75 and 1876-77, by Major-General Cunningham—

Preface (discussion of Gupta era)	v—viii
1. Kosam, or Kosámbi	1
2. Bithá and Deoriyá	5
3. Garhwá	9
4. Kakarári	15
5. Lokhri	15
6. Khajuráho	16
7. Jatkara	22
8. Kuailo	27
9. Garh-pahra	28
10. Rahatgarh	30
11. Gyáraspur	31
12. Bhílsá	34
13. Besnagar	36
14. Udaygiri, or Udayagiri	46
15. Sánchi	56
16. Udaypur, or Udayapura	65
17. Pathári	69
18. Báro, or Barnagar	71
19. Eran, or Erakaina	76
20. Dudahi	90
21. Chandpur	96
22. Madanpur	98
23. Deogarh	100
Appendix (discussion of Gupta era)	111—128

VOLUME XI.

Report of a Tour in the Gangetic Provinces, *viz.*, parts of the North-Western Provinces, Oudh, and Bihár, during 1875-76 and 1877-78, by Major-General Cunningham—

Introduction	v—vi
1. Badaon	7
2. Kampila	11
3. Bilsar, or Bilsanda	13
4. Sankisa	22
5. Pakna-Bihár	31
6. Pádham	38
7. Bhítargaon	40
8. Paraolí	46
9. Rár	*ib.*
10. Newal, or Navadevakula	*ib.*
11. Sanchán-kot	53
12. Pátan-Bihár	54
13. Baksar Ghát	57
14. Dálmau	59
15. Singror, or Sringa-víra-pura	62
16. Tusáram Bihár	63
17. Gaura	70
18. Tandwa	*ib.*
19. Srávastí	78
20. Pachran	100
21. Koron-dih, or Kolpur	101
22. Jaunpur	102
23. Chunár, or Charanádrigarh	126
24. Belkhara	128
25. Bhuilí and Hetunpur	130
26. Sahsarám	135
27. Umgá, or Mungá	140
28. Bodh-Gayá	141
29. Pátaliputra, or Patna	151
30. Hilsa	163
31. Teládha, or Telára	164
32. Chandi-mau, or Kalyánpur	169
33. Pawápuri	170
34. Ghosráwá	171
35. Tetráwa	182
36. Dand Bihár	185

VOLUME XII.

Report of Tours in the Central Doáb and Gorakhpur, *scil.* in parts of the North Western Provinces, during 1874-75 and 1875-76, by Mr. A. C. L. Carlleyle—

Introduction (by Major-General Cunningham)	iii—v
Lákhanu or Lakhno	1
Tuksán	2
Gohána Kherá	3
Bajera Kherá	7
Sahegarh Kherá and Nagaria Kherá	9
Qasbah Jaláli and Nilanti	12
Sánkara	15

VOLUME XII—*contd.*

	PAGE
Sambhal	24
Ahár	27
Indor, or Indrapura	36
Kundanpura mound	67
Sculptures from well in Temple	72
Ahírpura mound	79
Vaidyapura mound	80
Bhuilá and Kapilavástu	82
Nagar Khás	83
Site of Kapilavástu	108
Bhuilá	112
Bhuilá Dih	142
Identification of various sites	157
Site of massacre of Sakyas	172
Site where shadow of tree stood still	175
Birth-place of Krakuchanda	177
Khemrájpur, or Kshemavatí	182
Birth-place of Kanaka Muni	184
Sara-Kúpa, or "Arrow well"	187
River of Oil, and Lumbini Garden	189
Koli, or Vyághrapura	211
Rámagrama	215
Maneya	223

VOLUME XIII.

port of Tours in the South-Eastern provinces (*scil.* parts of Rewá or Bagnelkhand, Central Provinces, Orissa, and Tributary Native States) during 874-75 and 1875-76, by Mr. J. D. Beg- par—

roduction (by Major-General Cunningham)	III
1. Akha	1
2. Mádhogarh, Rámpur, Baijnáth	*ib.*
3. Umri, Karwahi, Amarpatan	2
4. Mahori, Kariá Pátan	*ib.*
5. Tálá, Sukulgaon, Makundpur	3
6. Makundpur 2nd	5
7. Bágar	*ib.*
8. Durgápur	*ib.*
9. Chandrehe	6
10. Gobri and Karundi	13
11. Dhamarsen	14
12. Majholi	15
13. Bardhi	*ib.*
14. Saipur, Agori Khas	16
15. Kakarsiba	19
16. Márá	20
17. Rámgarh Hill	31
18. Chhita Likhni	55
19. Benusagar	69
20. Kesnagarh	71
21. Lálgarh, Bhimchula	72
22. Gulka	*ib.*
23. Párasnáth, Bishangarh	73
24. Dumduma, Kichang	74
25. Udaypur	77
26. Rájnagar, Juangs	77
27. Vaitarani Tirath, and Keonjhar	78
28. Deogaon	78
29. Khandagiri	79
30. Udayagiri	91
31. Dhauli	95
32. Rudrapur, Satyábadi	98
33. Khurda	99
34. Kantilla	100
35. Táradeví, Sebaksai	*ib.*
36. Maglajuri, Chandeswar	*ib.*
37. Sunakhalla	102
38. Bhánpur	*ib.*
39. Gumsar	111
40. Nyagarh, Jaugada	112
41. Raolapálle	116
42. Aska	*ib.*
43. Malti	117
44. Bod	118
45. Chandrapur	119
46. Sonpur, Hot Springs	120
47. Bamni, Rajapadar	120
48. Pátna	126
49. Ránipur Jurál	128
50. Sinni	137
51. Ghoral	138
52. Udaypur	*ib.*
53. Kunira	*ib.*
54. Phuljor	143
55. Saranghar	*ib.*
56. Pujári Páli	144
57. Arbhar	145
58. Chanderpur	*ib.*
59. Turturia	146
60. Kosgain	153

VOLUME XIV.

ɔort of Tour in the Punjáb during 1878-9, by Major-General Cunningham—

face	III—V
1. Mánikyála	1
2. Ráma-ká-dheri	7
3. Sháh-dheri, or Taxila	8
4. Chása-dheri, or Fatehjang	24
5. Mári and Kálábágh	25
6. Káfir-kot of Til Rájá	26
7. Rám-kund	28
8. Rokri	29
9. Ván-Bachrán	32

VOLUME XIV—*contd.*

	PAGE
10. Amb	33
11. Bherá, or Bhedá	35
12. Vijhi, or Sabz-pind	40
13. Jhelam	41
14. Sohdara	43
15. Siálkot	44
16. Parsarur	46
17. Nara-sinha, or Ran-si	47
18. The Bágh-bachchhá mounds	48
19. Chinê, or Chinapate	53
20. Sultánpur, or Tamasa Vana	55
21. Dallá	58
22. Nakodar	58
23. Núrmahal	62
24. Sunet, or Sunit	65
25. Janer	67
26. Panchapura, or Pinjor	70
27. Sádhora	72
28. Kapál-mochan	75
29. Topra	78
30. Sirsáwa	79
31. Kurukshetra	86
32. Rájapuri, or Rajaori	106
33. Champa, or Barmáwar	109
34. Audumbara, or Núrpur	115
35. Mandi	119
36. The Kunindas	125
37. Autonomous coins of N. India	135

VOLUME XV.

Report of Tour in Bihár and Northern Bengal during 1879-80, by Major-General Cunningham—

Preface	III—VI
1. Patna	1
2. Kurkihár	4
3. Párbati	6
4. Aphsar	10
5. Sháhpur	11
6. Shekhpura	12
7. Rajjána	13
8. Mongír	15
9. Bhimband	18
10. Singi-Rikhi	19
11. Jáhngira	20
12. Bhágalpur	31
13. Kahalgaon	34
14. Patharghatta	36
15. Kánkjol	37
16. Gaur	39
17. The citadel of Gaur	50
18. The city of Gaur	57
19. The suburbs of Gaur	70
20. Máldah	77
21. Hazrat Panduá	79
22. Devthala	94
23. Devíkot	95
24. Khetlál	100
25. Bhásu Bihár	102
26. Mahásthán	104
27. Pahárpur	117
28. Jogí-guphá	120
29. Amári, or Amai	121
30. Ghátnagar	122
31. Debar Dighi	*ib.*
32. Panduá	123
33. Dhákká	127
34. Bikrampur	131
35. Sunárgaon, or Suvarna-grama	135
36. Notes on the History of Bengal	145
Appendix.—The hot springs of Tuttila Panee	179—182

VOLUME XVI.

Reports of Tours in North and South Bihár during 1880-81, by Major-General Cunningham (pages 1—81, with preface, pages III—IX), and by Mr. H. B. W. Garrick (pages 83—140)—

General Cunningham's Tour—

Preface	III—IX
1. Tírhút, or Tírabhukti	1
2. Hájípur	5
3. Besárh, or Vaisáli	6
4. Bakhrá	12
5. Kesariyá	16
6. Ságar-dih	19
7. Sítá-kúnd	22
8. Bediban	25
9. Sárongarh	26
10. Kasturia	*ib.*
11. Harwá-Barwá	27
12. Deokallí	29
13. Subhegarh	30
14. Andhára	32
15. Sítá-Marhi	34
16. Katrá	35
17. Káko, or Husenpur Káko	36
18. Dharáwat	39
19. Kauwá-dol	46
20. Pret-silá	50
21. Páli	51
22. Koch, or Konch	52
23. Deo-Márkanda	59
24. Karath	61
25. Mahádeopur	62
26. Deo-Barnárak	64

VOLUME XVI—*contd.*

	PAGE
Mr. Garrick's Tour—	
1. Hájípur	84
2. Besárh, or Vaisáli	89
3. Chak Rám Dás	91
4. Bakhrá	92
5. Sharaf-ud-dín-pur	93
6. Sowrát, or Sawráth	94
7. Sítá-Marhi, or Mahila	97
8. Andhára or Andhárí	99
9. Sugowli	99
10. Singásuni	100
11. Dhokráha	103
12. Lauriyá-Navandgarh	104
13. Chandkígarh	109
14. Rámpurwá, or Pipariyá	110
15. Rámnagar	117
16. Baguhaghát	118
17. Padaraona, or Parowna	188
18. Kasiá, or Kusinagara	120
19. Tarkulwa Thána	125
20. Khukhundo, or Khukuno	127
21. Kahaon	122
22. Bhágalpur	130
23. Khairágarh	131
24. Amarpur	132
25. Gayá	133
26. Buddha-Gayá	133
27. Rohtak (in Panjáb)	136

VOLUME XVII.

Report of a Tour in the Central Provinces and Lower Gangetic Doab (*scil.* part of the North-Western Provinces) during 1881-82, by Major-General Cunningham—	
Preface	III—V
1. Mahodha	1
2. Murmári	*ib.*
3. Dongargarh	2
4. Drúg, or Siva-dúrgga	3
5. Deo-Baloda	4
6. Rájim	6
7. Árang	20
8. Nawagaon	22
9. Sírpur, or Srípura	23
10. Kunwara	31
11. Simga	33
12. Kawarda	34
13. Boram Deo	*ib.*
14. Sahaspur	42
15. Kankáli	44
16. Râmnagar	46
17. Mandala	54
18. Arvi	55
19. Samlai Gadi	59
20. Sambalpur Fort	61
21. Pátna	63
22. Kusaleswara	63
23. Ráni Jhoria	64
24. Titirlagarh	67
25. Pujáripali in Sárangarh	68
26. Mahá-Kosala, or Chhattisgarh	68
27. Karrá	88
28. Aphui	95
29. Hathgaon, or Hastigráma	96
30. Hanswa, or Hasapura	98
31. Asní, or Aswiní-Kumára	99
32. Makanpur	102
33. Mathurá	107
34. The Sauras, or Savara Aborigines	112
35. Demon worship, or deified ghosts	139

VOLUME XVIII.

Report of a Tour in the Gorakhpur District, North-Western Provinces, during 1875-76 and 1876-77, by Mr. A. C. L. Carlleyle—	
Preface (by Major-General Cunningham)	III & IV
1. Khirnípur	1
2. Rámpur Deoriyá, or Rámagráma	3
3. Maneya, and the Anoma River	10
4. Ruins at Maneya	22
5. The three stúpas { 1. Chandaka's Return; 2. Cut hair; 3. Changed Garments }	27
6. City of the Moriyas	31
7. Rudrapur, and its neighbourhood	41
8. Banyan Forest, and Mithabel	52
9. Ruins near Bhopa	54
10. Kusinagara	55
11. Old river channels	97
12. Colossal Nirvána Statue	99
13. Páwá, or Chetiyaon and Fájila	101
14. Ruins at Fájila or Fazilnagar	111
15. Other ancient sites	114

VOLUME XIX.

	PAGE
Report of a Tour through Bihár, Central India (*scil.* Bagheklhand or Rewá in this case); Pesháwar and Yusufzai (*scil.* parts of the Panjáb), during 1881-82, by Mr. H. B. W. Garrick—	
Preface (by Major-General Cunningham)	III & IV
1. Deo Márkandih	2
2. Mahádeopur	14
3. Deo Barunárak	17
4. Garhani	21
5. Bhojpur	23
6. Dildárnagar	23
7. Darauli	25
8. Rámgarh	27
9. Vaidyanáth	*ib.*
10. Hanumánganj	48
11. Barmáyan	49
12. Dumraon	59
13. Benares	60
14. Bihtá	*ib.*
15. Seorájpur-Badgarh	62
16. Ghumán, Koh-Chaukhandi	63
17. Bhawáni	65
18. Jhirná	68
19. Kakariri	71
20. Bhirpur (Birpur)	73
21. Rupaoli Tola	79
22. Rewá	*ib.*
23. Nipánia	84
24. Gurgi-Masán	85
25. Chandara	90
26. Explorations in Gandhára	91
27. Chársada	96
28. Shahr-i-Naparsan	107
29. Jamálgarhi	110
30. Ismasgarh	111
31. Sáwaldhi or Thareli	116
32. Sháhbázgarhi	119
33. Garhi Umarzai	124
34. Kotki, or Uria	126
35. Ránigat	128
36. Jángira, or Jahángira	131
37. Takkái Bála	133
38. Ruhmia, or Hájí Sháh	137

VOLUME XX.

	PAGE
Report of a Tour in Gwáliár, Eastern Ráj-putána, and parts of the North-Western Provinces and Panjáb during 1882-83, by Major-General Cunningham—	
Preface	III—VIII
1. Eastern Rájputána	1
2. The Yaduvansís	5
3. The Nikumbhas	8
4. The Khánzádas	10
5. The Mevs, or Meos	22
Mathurá—	
6. Mathurá	30
7. Parkham	39
8. Mahwan	41
9. Mahában	42
10. Lohban	46
11. Páli Kherá	47
12. Morá	48
13. Anyor	49
14. Kota	*ib*
15. Chaumukha	52
16. Tumaula	53
Bharatpur—	
17. Kamán, or Kadamba-vana	54
18. Bayána, or Payámpuri	60
19. Sikandra	79
20. Vijaymandirgarh	81
21. Tahangarh	88
22. Dhandora	92
23. Khánwa	93
24. Rúpbás	98
Gwáliár—	
25. Dubkund	99
26. Kadwai	105
27. Pároli	105
28. Parávali	107
29. Kutwál	112
30. Dholpur	*ib.*
Alwar—	
31. Tejára	114
32. Sarhata	118
33. Bahádurpur	119
34. Alwar	120
35. Rájgarh	121
36. Talao	122
37. Páránagar	124
Gurgaon—	
38. Fírozpur Jhirka	127
39. Kotilá	129
40. Indor	133
41. Palah	135
42. Sohna	*ib.*
43. Bhonsi	137
44. Gurgaon	138
Delhi—	
45. Iron Pillar at Mahrauli	139
46. Mahipálpur, Sultán Ghári	142
47. Begampur, Masjid and Tomb	146
48. Tomb of Kabír-ud-dín Auliyá	147
49. Chor Minár	149
50. Tomb of Fíroz Sháh	151
51. Sháhpur—small Masjid	153
52. Kotila, Tomb of Mubárak Sayyid	*ib.*
53. Khairpur, Jámi Masjid	155
54. Okhala	160

VOLUME XXI.

PART I (PAGES 1—137).

	PAGE
Report of a Tour in Alláhábád district, Bundelkhand, Rewá, and parts of the Panjáb, during 1883-84, by Major-General Cunningham—	
Preface	III—VI
1. Kosam, or Kausámbi	1
2. Rithora	4
3. Bar-Dewal	4
4. Rikhian caves	7
5. Chillá	8
6. Chitr-kúta	10
7. Gupta Godávari	13
8. Gonda, or Gora	13
9. Rásin, or Rájavásiní	15
10. Márphá	18
11. Bilhariyá	19
12. Kálanjar Fort	20
13. Kálanjar Inscriptions	33
14. Ajaygarh Fort	46
15. AjaygarhInscriptions	48
16. Bachon, or Bachaund	54
17. Khajuráha	55
18. Khajuráha Inscriptions	63
19. Maniyágarh	69
20. Mahoba Inscriptions	70
21. Dáhi copper-plate	74
22. Gobari	76
23. Ráypur	76
24. The Chandela kingdom	77
25. Map of N.-W. India by Ptolemy	90
26. Náchna, or Kúthara	95
27. Jasso	99
28. Chhotá Deori	100
29. Marhiá	*ib.*
30. Bargaon	101
31. Simrá	*ib.*
32. Besáni	*ib.*
33. Baghelkhand, or Rewá	103
34. Piáwan	112
35. Álhá Ghát	114
36. Kevati-kund	115
37. Ginjá Hill	119
38. Katká Obelisk	120
39. Haliyá	121
40. Dibhor	124
41. Adesar Hill	125
42. Tura	126
43. Ahugi	*ib.*
44. Bardi and Bhopári	128
45. Durgá-kho	128
46. Bhuilí	130
47. Seopur, near Mirzápur	130
48. Kálpí, on the Jumna	131
49. Sultánpur, in Jálandhar	133
50. Chíní	134
51. Chamba	*ib.*

PART II (PAGES 141—179).*

Report of a Tour in Rewá, Bundelkhand, Málwa, and Gwáliár, during 1884-85, by Major-General Cunningham—	
1. Kevatí-kund, or Keonti	141
2. Rewá, or Baghelkhand	143
3. Gurgi-Masáun	149
4. Baijnáth	154
5. Ráypur-Kothi	156
6. Kiyán, or Ken River	156
7. Parainí	158
8. Suror	*ib.*
9. Chhotí Deorí	*ib.*
10. Simrá	*ib.*
11. Rithí	160
12. Nánd-chánd	*ib.*
13. Bargaon	*ib.*
14. Kundalpur	166
15. Hindoriá	167
16. Damoh	168
17. Biyá-kund	169
18. Saurai	170
19. Madanpur	171
20. Lalitpur	175
21. Surahar	176
22. Jhaloni	*ib.*
23. Terahi	*ib.*
24. Rájapur	178

VOLUME XXII.

Report of Tours, during 1877-80, in Gorakhpur and neighbouring districts of North-Western Provinces, and in Sáran and Champáran districts of Bengal, by Mr. A. C. L. Carlleyle—	
Preface (by Major-General Cunningham)	III—IV
General Summary—	
1. Rámagráma	2
2. Maneya	*ib*
3. Anoma	3
4. Three *stúpas*	5
5. City of the Moriyas	7
6. Rúdrapur	9
7. The Bar Tree Forests and Mithabel	13

* Several of the places described in Part I are again described in Part II.)

VOLUME XXII—*contd.*

	PAGE
8. Bhopa	15
9. Kusinagara	16
10. Pawá	29
11. Lauriyá Navandgarh . .	35
Report for 1877-78—	
12. Mounds, near Lauriyá . .	35
13. Mounds, near Harhi . .	47
14. Jánkí kot, or Jánkí Garh .	49
15. New Edict Pillar of Asoka .	51
Report for 1878-79—	
16. Concluding notice of the Gorakhpur district . .	57
17. Dighwa Dubaoli in Sáran district	72
18. Cherán, Sáran district .	73
19. Na-lo-yen, or Náráyana (Narainpur)	75
20. The Asylum *stúpa,* conversion of man-eating demons .	76
21. The Drona *stúpa* or Kumbhán *stúpa*	77
22. The Dharmáranya (and Dhamaoli) at Baliyá (Balliá) .	81
23. Other ancient sites on the Ganges between Baliyá and Gházípur	86
24. Capital of the kingdom of "Chen- chu," or "Lord of Battles"	88
Report for 1879-80—	
25. Gházípur	94
26. Old sites to the west of Gházípur	95
27. Masaon Dih, Joharganj, and Krelulendrapura . . .	95
28. Chandraotí, or Chandrávatí .	104
29. Chiraya-kot	105
30. Gárha-ka-kot	*ib*
31. Khairá Dih	106
32. Bairánt or Vairánta . .	107
33. Hingtar, or Hengutar, and Dhánapur	171

VOLUME XXIII.

Report of a Tour in the Panjáb and Rájputána, during 1883-84, by Mr. H. B. W. Garrick—	
1. Pírkhánah	1
2. Bakhtu	2
3. Bhatinda, Tiranda, or Govindgarh	*ib*
4. Sirsá or Sirse-pattan . .	8
5. Fatehábád	11
6. Hánsi, Asá, or Amba . .	13
7. Tushám	19
8. Loháru	25
9. Nárnaul	26
10. Bairát	29
11. Ambír	31
12. Jaypur	33
13. Ájmer	34
14. Nágaur or Nágapuri . .	48
15. Gavan	72
16. Mandor	73
17. Jodhpur	85
18. Páli	*ib*
19. Nadola	91
20. Júná Kherá	96
21. Náthdwára	99
22. Chitor	101
23. Nimtor	124
24. Jhalrápátan, or Chandrávati .	125
25. Mokanddwára	131
26. Khatkar-Bhimgaj . . .	135
27. Bhimgaj	137

ABBREVIATIONS.

A. H.	Anno Hijræ.
C. I.	Central India.
C. P.	Central Provinces.
N.-W. P.	North-Western Provinces.
R.	River.
S.	Samvat (samvatsara).

GENERAL INDEX.

	VOL.	PAGE.	PLATE.
A			
Abár Scythians—			
Supposed wide diffusion of—	II	29, 32	. . .
Identified with Su Horde of Chinese authors . .	”	48	. . .
Abdagases, King—			
Nephew of Gondophares, and reigned in Panjáb .	”	60	. . .
Abhisára—			
A district in Panjáb, occupied by Gákar tribe . .	”	23, 29	. . .
Abisares, King—			
Reigned in N. Panjáb in time of Alexander . .	”	23, 28	. . .
Abriyán on Jhelam R—			
The ancient capital of the Gákars	”	29, 31	. . .
Perhaps = Euthymedia or Sagala of Ptolemy . .	”	153, 173	. . .
Abú Bakr Kandahárí—			
Tomb of, at Bayána	XX	60, 77	. . .
Abú Rihán—			
Discussion of account of Gupta era by—	IX	20	. . .
Accadian race—			
Probably represented in India by the Brahuis and Dravidians	”	160	. . .
Adisadra of Ptolemy—			
= Ahichhatra in Barelí District, N.-W. P. . . .	I	255	. . .
Adisathra town, of Ptolemy—			
Probably = Bidisá or Besnagar, in Bhopál State, Central India	XXI	93	. . .

	Vol.	Page.	Plate.
Adisathri, country of—			
Identified with kingdom of Chedí	IX	56	. . .
„ „ Mahá Kosala or Chhattísgarh	XVII	69, 71	. . .
	XXI	93	. . .
Aditya Sena Deva, King of Magadha—			
Flourished in 7th century, A.D.	XV	163	. . .
Inscriptions of, at Mandár and Sháhpur	„	12, 164	XI.
	XVI	60, 79	. . .
Mentioned in inscription from Nepál	„	80	. . .
Adi Varáha coins—			
See **Varáha coins.**			
Adraistæ of Arrian—			
Perhaps = Yaudheya tribe	XIV	142	. . .
Afghán architecture—			
Described	III	9	. . .
Afrásiyáb of Turán—			
Gákar traditions of—	II	29, 31	. . .
Agara of Ptolemy—			
Perhaps = Ságar in C. P.	XXI	93	. . .
Agathocles, Bactrian King—			
Coins of, copied from Indian types	XIV	19	X.
Agnimitra Sunga, King of Magadha—			
A Brahmanist, not Buddhist	I	Intr. xxxi	. . .
Confounded by Stevenson and Taylor with a petty Buddhist Chief of Maháráshtra	„	„ xxxii	. . .
Fought the Yavanas on the Indus	II	41	. . .
Coin of, found at Bhuilá Dih	XII	165	. . .
Agra, in Agra District, N.-W. P.—			
Old bed of Jumna near—	IV	98	. . .
First occupied by the Lodí Dynasty as a capital	„	„	. . .
Báradarí of Sikandar Lodí at—	„	99	. . .
Fort at, built by Sikandar Lodí, altered and added to by Akbar	„	xiv	. . .
Site of Bábar's garden palace at—	„	100, 105	. . .
Humáyún's mosque at—	„	100	XII.
Site of old city, east of—	„	103	. . .
Great well near *Dargáh* of Kamál Khán at—	„	111	. . .
Akbar's camping-ground at—	„	112	. . .

	Vol.	Page.	Plate.
Agra, in Agra District, N.-W. P—*contd.*			
Inscription of Akbar on Delhi gate of Fort at—	IV	113	. . .
City walls of—	„	116, 194	. . .
Akbar's mosque at—	„	119	XII.
Remains of palaces of Bírbal near—	„	120	. . .
Inscribed boundary stone near—	„	121	. . .
Remains of Mausoleum of Jodh Báí near—	„	„	. . .
Ládli Bágh and Mausoleum of Ládli Begam near—	„	122	. . .
Salímgarh in Fort at—	„	124	. . .
Palace at, ascribed to Jahángír, but really the work of Ibráhím Lodí, described	„	XII, 124	XIII.
Inscriptions on Jahángír's black marble throne at—	„	132	. . .
Jahángír's bath at—	„	135	. . .
Mausoleum of Itimád-ud-Doula at—	„	137	. . .
Palace of Sháhjahán at—	„	142	. . .
Díwán-ám and Nágína mosque at—	„	144	. . .
Motí mosque at—	„	145	XV.
Inscription on Motí mosque at—	„	154	. . .
Idgáh of Sháhjahán at—	„	156	XIV.
Motí Bágh mosque at—	„	157	„
Date and cost of Tájmahal at—	„	159	. . .
Newal Ganj at—	„	161	. . .
Chíní-ká-Roza Mausoleum at—	„	163	XVI.
Jámí mosque at—	„	170	. . .
Kalán or Great mosque at—	„	„	XVII.
Mosque of Sháh Wiláyat at—	„	174	. . .
Mukhannisán, or Eunuchs' mosque, at—	„	178	. . .
Mahtáb Khán-ká-Bágh at—	„	180	. . .
Red stone horse near—	„	183	. . .
Guru-ká-tál near—	„	184	. . .
Minor buildings near—	„	186	. . .
Mausoleum of Fíroz Khán near—	„	188	. . .
Sundry tombs near—	„	192	. . .
Mubárak Manzil at—	„	195	. . .
Tomb of Shaháb-ul-Alláh at—	„	196	. . .
Baths of Alláh Vardí Khán at—	„	197	. . .
Arám or Rámbágh at—	„	199	. . .
Remains of sundry palaces near—	„	200	. . .
Chhatrí of Jeswant Singh at—	„	202	. . .
Burhiyá-Tál near—	„	207	. . .
Agra District, N.-W. P.—			
Sundry ancient sites in—	„	210—215	. . .
Ahár, in Bulandshahr District, N.-W. P.—			
Anciently named Kundilpur	XII	27	. . .
Inscription of Mahípála Deva at—	„	36	. . .
Plan of temple at—	„	. . .	V.

	Vol.	Page.	Plate.
Ahichhatra or Rámnagar, in Barelí District, N.-W. P.—			
The capital of Northern Panchála = Adisadra of Ptolemy	I	255	. . .
Description of ruins at—	„	256	XLIII, XLIV
Inscriptions in Gupta characters at— . . .	„	263	XLIV.
Ahír caste—			
Certainly not of Indo-Scythian origin; is absent from Panjáb	II	81	. . .
Ahírwára Province—			
Extent of—	„	300	. . .
Ahmad Nialtigín—			
Attacked Benares in A.D. 1033	VIII	116	. . .
Ahugi, in Mirzápur District, N.-W. P.—			
Ruined mediæval temples at—	XXI	127	. . .
Aii of Ptolemy—			
Perhaps = Avam (? Avu) of Sháhbázgarhi inscription	V	20	. . .
Ajátasatru, King of Magadha—			
Chronology of reign of—	VIII	2	. . .
Held first Buddhist synod	III	142	. . .
Founded Pátaliputra according to the Buddhists .	VIII	2	. . .
	XI	151	. . .
Removed relics of Buddha from Kusinagara . .	XVIII	75	. . .
Ajayapura—			
A name of Bakror near Gayá	I	13	. . .
Ajaygarh (Ajaigharh) in Ajaygarh State, Bundelkhand—			
One of the eight Chandel Forts	VII	46	. . .
Called Jayapura-dúrga in inscriptions	XXI	„	. . .
Described	„	47	XI.
Inscriptions of Chandel period at—	VII	46	. . .
	XXI	48—54	XII—XV.
Ajmer, in Ajmer-Mhairwára District, Rájputána—			
Founded by Ajaypál Chauhán	II	253	. . .
Historical notices of—	„	255	. . .
Great mosque at—	„	258	LXXIII.
Inscriptions on mosque at—	„	259 *Note*	. . .
		261, 262	LXXIV.
Minár of „ „	XXIII	36	X.

	Vol.	Page.	Plate.
Ajmer in Ajmer-Mhairwárá District, Rájputána—*contd.*			
Ána Ságar at, named after Arnna Rájá	X	99	. . .
Criticism on restoration of mosque at— . . .	XXIII	35	. . .
Gates of—	,,	39	. . .
Hindu buildings at Táragarh near—	,,	42	. . .
Tombs at—	,,	47	. . .
Sir Thomas Roe's account of—	,,	48	. . .
Ajudhia City—			
See **Ayodhya City.**			
Akbar, Emperor—			
Tradition of birth of, at Bándhogarh in Rewá State .	XVII	100	. . .
	XXI	109	. . .
Founded Alláhábád Fort, A.D. 1572	I	298	. . .
Changed name of Parsháwar to Pesháwar . .	II	87	. . .
Altered and added to Sikandar Lodí's fort at Ágrá .	IV	xiv	
Asírgarh gold medal of—	IX	118	XIX.
Akbarábád—			
Muhammadan name of Agrá	IV	93	. . .
Akesines R—			
Course of—	II	38	. . .
Akhandha—			
Old name of Dildárnagar in Gházípur District, N.-W. P.	III	63	. . .
Ruins of temples of Siva at—	,,	,,	XXII.
Akorí, near Orai, in Jálaun District, N.-W. P.—			
Jayastambha, formerly existing at—	VII	39	. . .
Alasadda, birth-place of King Milinda—			
Probably = Alexandria Opiané, north of Kábul .	II	197	. . .
Alá-ud-dín Khiljí, Emperor—			
Made additions to Kutb mosque at Delhi . . .	I	188	. . .
Improved Kutb Mínár at Delhi	,,	204 *Note*	. . .
Gateway of, at Delhi	,,	,,	
Mínár of, at Delhi	,,	205	. . .
Palace of 1,000 pillars at Delhi, built by— . .	,,	207	. . .
Alexander the Great—			
Route of, illustrated by Chinese pilgrims . . .	II	82	LII.

	Vol.	Page.	Plate.
Alexander the Great—*contd.*			
Campaign in B.C. 327 and 326 of, described by Strabo, Curtius, and Arrian	II	83	. . .
Various opinions as to site of battle between Porus and—	„	173, 180, 184, 187	LXVII.
Attack on Sangala by—	„	198—200	. . .
Alexandria Opiané, N. of Kábul—			
Probably = Alasadda, birth-place of King Milinda .	„	197	. . .
Alexandria Soriané—			
Probably = **Shorkot**, *q.v.*	V	99	. . .
Álhá and Udal, Banáphar Chiefs—			
Legends of—	II	455	. . .
	VII	13	. . .
	IX	152	. . .
Dwelling-house at Chillá ascribed to—	XXI	8	V.
Álhá Ghát, in Rewá State, Baghelkhand—			
Inscription of Nara Sinha Deva of Chedí at— . .	„	114	XXVIII.
Alláhábád in Alláhábád District, N.-W. P.—			
So named by Sháhjahán; named Iláhábás by Akbar, A.D. 1572	I	297	. . .
Akshay bat tree at—	„	„	. . .
Pillar with inscriptions of Asoka, Samudra Gupta, Jahángír, &c., at—	„	298	. . .
Popular tradition as to Prayág name of—	„	300	. . .
Alms bowl of Buddha—			
See **Buddha.**			
Alphabet, Arian—			
See **Ario-Pálí alphabet.**			
Alphabet, ancient Nágrí—			
Asoka's inscription form of, must have been preceded by an earlier alphabet	XXII	IV	. . .
Form of letter *n* is best test of age of— . . .	III	38, 48	. . .
Indo-Scythian and Gupta forms of—	„	37	. . .
	IX	21—26	. . .
Comparison of forms of, in Gupta, Ráipur, and Rájim inscriptions	XVII	. . .	VI.
Gupta form of, still used by Baniyás in Panjáb Hill States	XIV	121	. . .
'Box-headed' form of, used in some inscriptions of early Gupta dynasty	XXI	97	. . .

	Vol.	Page.	Plate.
Alphabet, ancient Nágrí—*contd.*			
'Square-headed' or *chitravarna* form of, used in many Chandel inscriptions	XXI	72	. . .
Takárí cursive form of, used in Káshmír and Kángrá	II	9	. . .
	V	182	. . .
'Shell-character' or 'flourished' form of, used in N. India in 7th and 8th centuries, A.D.	III	154	XLV.
Ditto, example of, at Bhágalpur	VIII	129	. . .
Ditto, ditto, at Gondwá	,,	192	. . .
Ditto, ditto, at Lauriyá-Araráj	I	67	. . .
Ditto, ditto, at Rájgír	VIII	86	. . .
Ditto, ditto, at Besārh (Vaisáli)	I	60	. . .
Altamsh—			
See **Iltitmish, Emperor.**			
Alwar, in Alwar State, Rájputána—			
Said to have been founded by Nikumbhas	XX	120	. . .
Muhammadan tombs at—	,,	121	. . .
Amakapis or Amakatis of Ptolemy—			
Probably = Ambakápi in Lahore District	II	69, 205	. . .
	XIV	48	. . .
Amanda or Amandra—			
The name given by Pliny to the Taxila district; perhaps = Awánkárí	II	6, 112	. . .
Amara Deva—			
Forged inscription ascribed to—	I	6	. . .
	VIII	58, *Note*	. . .
Amarakúta of Kálídása—			
Probably = Amarkantak	VII	227	. . .
Amarávatí stúpa—			
Date of—	I	Intr. XXIII	. . .
Amarkantak, in Sohágpur District, C. P.—			
Believed to be source of Son and Narbadá rivers, and probably = Amarakúta of Kálídása	VII	227	. . .
Architecture of Karan Mandir temple at—	,,	228—9	XX, XXI.
Other temples at—	,,	230—235	. . .
Short inscriptions, one dated S. 922, at—	,,	233—4	. . .
Amb, in Salt Range, Panjáb—			
Temples in Káshmír style at—	XIV	33	XV.

	Vol.	Page.	Plate.
Amba-kápi, in Lahore District, Panjáb—			
Legend concerning three brothers at, which probably refers to Kanishka, etc.	II	153, 203—5	. . .
Probably = Amakatis or Amakapis of Ptolemy .	"	69, 205	. . .
Mounds along Bágh-bachchhá river at— . . .	XIV	48, 52	XVII.
Ambar=Ohind—			
See **Ohind.**			
Amber in Jaipur State, Rájputána—			
An ancient town	II	250	. . .
Amin in Ambála (Umballa) District, Panjáb—			
Ancient site with temple of sun at—	"	223	. . .
Amogha-bhúti, King of Kuninda—			
Two coins of, found at Sunit near Lúdiána . .	XIV	65	. . .
Silver and copper coins of, described . . .	"	134, 139	XXXI.
Anang Pál I., Tomar—			
Rebuilt Delhi, probably in A.D. 736 . . .	I	141—4	. . .
Anang Pál II., Tomar—			
Rebuilt Delhi about A.D. 1052	"	152	. . .
Erected Lálkot at Delhi	"	180	XXXVI.
Traditions of sons of—	"	153	. . .
Inscription of, on Iron Pillar, dated S. 1109 = A.D. 1052	"	174	. . .
Anang Pál III., Tomar—			
Defeated by Vísala Deva Chauhán, in A.D. 1151 or 1152	"	150	. . .
Ananta Varmma, King of Magadha—			
Placed Hindu images in Barábár caves . . .	"	52	. . .
Andhára in Muzaffarpur District, Bengal—			
Worship of meteorite at—	XVI	32	. . .
Andhra dynasty—			
Puranic chronology of, untenable	I	Intr. XXXIV	. . .
Proposed chronology of—	V	20—1	. . .
Anga, kingdom of—			
= Bhágalpur District, in Bengal	I	52	. . .
Champánagar was capital of—	XV	31	. . .
Aniruddha, first cousin of Buddha—			
Share of, in Buddha's obsequies	I	83	. . .

	Vol.	Page.	Plate.
Anoma R. of Buddhist tradition—			
= Kúdawá Nála, in Bastí District, N.-W. P.	XII	224	. . .
	XVIII	13	. . .
	XXII	3, 111	. . .
Antarála country—			
The region east of Rewá	IX	89	. . .
Antiochus the Great—			
Made treaty on Indus with Sophagasenas Maurya	II	41	. . .
Anyor, in Mathurá District, N.-W. P.—			
Ancient statue of Buddha at—	XX	49	. . .
Aornos—			
Opinions of Court, Lœwenthal, Abbott, and Cunningham concerning site of—	II	96—111	LV, LVI.
Name of, perhaps derived from Rájá Vara (Varni)	"	97	. . .
Exaggerated Greek accounts of—	"	103, 110	. . .
Possible positions for—	"	106	. . .
Apápapuri—			
Ancient name of Páwá in Patna District, Bengal	XI	170	. . .
Aparánta country—			
Probably Northern Sindh and part of Western Rájputána	XIV	137	. . .
Copper coins of, obtained in Rájputána	"	136	XXXI.
Aparni Scythians of Strabo—			
Speculations concerning—	II	29,49	. . .
Aphsar, in Patna District, Bengal—			
Inscription of later Guptas discovered by Kittoe at—	I	40	. . .
	IX	27	. . .
	XV	11	. . .
	XVI	79	. . .
Apollodotus, King of Bactria—			
Coins of, found at Pushkar, near Ájmer	VI	205	. . .
Apollonius of Tyana—			
Alleged visit of, to King Phraates of Taxila between 42 and 45 A.D.	II	83, 113	. . .
Árá (Arrah), in Sháhábád District, Bengal—			
Identified with Hwen Thsang's 'Place of the Demons of the Desert.' Legends of—	III	73	. . .
Also named Árámnagar	"	70, 76	. . .
Anciently named Ekachakra or Chakrapura	"	73, 76	. . .

	Vol.	Page.	Plate.
Arachosia—			
= Kophene, with capital named Kophes . . .	II	45	. . .
Arakan, King of—			
Author of Burmese inscription at Buddha Gayá .	III	102	. . .
Árámnagar—			
A name of Árá (Arrah) in Sháhábád District . .	III	70, 76	. . .
Arang, in Ráipur District, C. P.—			
Ancient city of—	VII	159	. . .
	XVII	20	. . .
Three principal temples at—	VII	160-163	XVI, XVII.
Numerous Jain remains at—	„	164	. . .
Long broken inscription at—	XVII	20	. . .
Short early inscriptions at—	„	21	XI.
History unknown of—	„	22	. . .
Araráj—			
See **Lauriyá-Araráj**			
Aráshtras of Mahábhárata—			
Perhaps = Yaudheya tribe	XIV	142	. . .
Arch, Indian (Hindu)—			
Discussion as to structure and date of, in great temple at Buddha Gayá	III	84	. . .
	VIII	66	. . .
At Konch in Gayá District, Bengal	„	54, 55	. . .
In temple at Nongarh overlaid by a *stúpa* . . .	„	119	. . .
Proofs and examples of early use of— . . .	XI	43, 143	. . .
In common use in fourth and fifth centuries, A.D. .	XVI	Pref. VIII.	. . .
Archæological remains—			
Chronological classification of—	III	1	. . .
Archæological Survey—			
Plan of—	I	Pref. III-VII	. . .
	III	IV	. . .
Instruction to assistants of—	„	V	. . .
Archaic period—			
Remains of—	„	2	. . .
Architecture—			
Mr. Beglar's theories as to laws of proportion in Indian—	VIII	66—73	. . .
Styles of, in N.-W. India	V	VII, 185, 189	. . .

	Vol.	Page.	Plate.
Architecture, Gupta Style of—			
See **Gupta style of architecture.**			
Architecture, Hindu—			
Six periods of—	III	2	. . . .
Architecture, Indo-Greek and Indo-Persian—			
Described	V	APP. A.	. . . .
Architecture, Káshmír style of—			
Characteristics of—	II	189	. . . .
Architecture, Muhammadan—			
Eight periods of—	III	7	. . . .
Ariana—			
Date of Scythian and Yuchi conquests of—	II	54	. . . .
Ario-Pálí alphabet—			
Deciphered by Masson, Prinsep, and Cunningham	I	Intr. VIII, XXXVII, XL.	. . . .
Used in all Yusufzai inscriptions: disused about 100 A.D.	V	7, 187	. . . .
Value of numerals in—	,,	61	. . . .
Ario-Pálí inscriptions—			
From Mánikyála	II	160, 162	LXIII.
On oil lamp found at Ráwalpindí, now in British Museum	,,	152	. . . .
From Sháhdheri (Taxila)	,,	124—135	LIX.
	V	67	. . . .
At Maira in Salt Range	,,	84	XXVIII.
Collection of, from Yusufzai	,,	57—84	XVI.
Aruna, Rájá—			
Grandfather of Prithí Ráj	X	99	. . . .
Arrah—			
See **Ará, in Sháhábád District, Bengal.**			
Arsakes—			
Brother of King Abisares in time of Alexander	II	23, 28	. . . .
Arsakes, King—			
A predecessor of Gondophares	,,	61	. . . .
Artabanus III. of Parthia—			
Contemporary with Gondophares	V	60	. . . .

	Vol.	Page.	Plate.
Arvi, in Nágpur District, C. P.—			
Early copper-plate inscriptions obtained at Ráipur erroneously said to come from—	XVII	55—59	XXIV, XXV.
Árya-Párswika—			
A Buddhist teacher at Peshávar, *circa* A.D. 1 . .	II	89	. . .
Ásaf Khán—			
Attack by, on Queen Dúrgávatí, A.D. 1563 . .	IX	50	. . .
Asala Deva, Raja of Narwár—			
Dated coins and inscriptions of—	II	315	. . .
Asapuri, in Sháhábád District, Bengal—			
Temple of Deví and modern inscriptions at— . .	V	183	. . .
Asarur, in Gujránwála District, Panjáb—			
Anciently called Udamnagar = Pimprama of Alexander	II	200	LXIX.
Extensive ruins at—	V	64	. . .
Stúpa of Asoka at—	II	202	. . .
Was the capital of Panjáb in Hwen Thsang's time, under name of Tse-kia (Chekia, Dhaka, Taki)	„	41, 193, 200	. . .
	V	113	. . .
Asi Nála—			
A rivulet under Benares	I	104	. . .
Asiani of Trogus—			
Probably = Kuei-shwang tribe of Yuchi or Tochari .	II	43, 64	. . .
Asiatic Society of Bengal—			
Founded in 1784 by Sir W. Jones	I	Intr. I	. . .
Asirgarh, in Nimár District, C. P.—			
Gold medal struck by Akbar at—	IX	118	XIX.
Description of fortress of—	„	119	„
Muhammadan inscriptions at—	„	120	. . .
Perhaps = Ozoabis of Ptolemy	„	121	. . .
Aska, in Ganjám District, Madras—			
Inscriptions from—	XIII	116	. . .
Ásni, in Fatehpur District, N.-W. P.—			
The treasure city of Jai Chand	XVII	100	. . .

	Vol.	Page.	Plate.
Asoka, Emperor—			
Conqueror and Viceroy of Taxila	II	112, 113	. .
Story of Kunála, eldest son of—	"	149	. . .
Púrna Varmma, last descendant of—	III	81, 135	. . .
Probably became acquainted with Greek art at Taxila .	"	97	. . .
Disposition of edict inscriptions of, along ancient lines of road	XVI	112, *Note*	. . .
	XXII	55	. . .
Rock inscription at Bairát of—	II	247	. . .
	VI	98	. . .
Inscriptions of 12th and 19th years of, in Barábár caves	I	45—48	XX.
'Golden' edict pillar of, brought from Topra to Delhi by Fíroz Sháh	"	161	. . .
	XIV	78	. . .
Corrections in readings of edict inscriptions on above .	I	165	. . .
Edict pillar of, at Delhi, brought from Mírat (Meerut) by Fíroz Sháh	"	167	. . .
Imperfection of inscription on above	"	169	. . .
Edict inscription of, at Jaugada in Ganjám District .	XIII	113	. . .
Ditto, at Khálsi	I	245	XLI.
Ditto, on Lauriyá-Navandgarh pillar .	"	73	. . .
Ditto, on Rámpurwa pillar . . .	XVI	110, VIII	XXVIII.
	XXII	51	VI, VII.
Ditto, at Rúpnáth	VII	59	. . .
	IX	38	. . .
Ditto, at Sháhbázgarhi (Kapurdagiri)	V	8, 19—22	. . .
Site of *stúpa* built by, at Rájgír	I	24	. . .
A *stúpa* of, at Vaisáli	"	62	. . .
Stúpas of, at Kusinagara	"	82, 85	. . .
Tower erected by, in the Deer-Park near Benares .	"	112	. . .
Great *stúpa* built by, at Pushkalávati	II	90	. . .
Erected 'head gift' *stúpa* at Taxila	"	117	. . .
Buildings of, at Buddha Gayá	III	80, 96	. . .
Works of, at Pátaliputra	XI	151, 158	. . .
Asokpur—			
See **Hátila or Asokpur, in Gonda District, Oudh** . .	. .	. .	. . .
Aspa Varmma—			
Named on coins of Azas	I	Intr. XXXVII.	. . .
Atarkin—			
A Muhammadan Saint	XXIII	51, *Note.*	. . .
Atranjí-Kherá in Etá District, N.-W. P.—			
Perhaps = Hwen Thsang's Pi-lo-shanna . . .	I	269*	. . .

* *See* Vol. XI, 15, where this identification is given up.

	Vol.	Page.	Plate.
Attak (Attock), in Ráwal Pindi District, Panjáb—			
Called Atak-Banáras by Abúl Fazl. Fort at, built by Akbar. Is not ancient Udakhanda	II	93	. . .
Audumbara (Odumbara)—			
Ancient name of Núrpur State in Panjáb and its capital Pathánkot	XIV	116	. . .
Coins bearing name of above	V	154	. . .
	XIV	116, 136	XXXI.
Also ancient name of Peninsula of Kachchh, = country of the Odonbeores of Pliny	V	155	. . .
	XIV	135, 136	. . .
Also a name of province surrounding Kánkjol opposite Gaur in Bengal	XV	38	. . .
Auhadí family—			
Rulers of Bayána in 15th century, A.D.	XX	63, 65	. . .
Aundhá Kherá—			
See **Batesar—**	. .	. . .	. . .
Aurangzeb, Emperor—			
Destroyed great temple at Mathurá	I	235	. . .
Avalokiteswara, Bodhisatwa—			
Statue of, at Dharáwat in Gayá District, Bengal .	„	54	. . .
Avam (? Avu) country—			
Mentioned in Sháhbázgarhi inscription, = ? Aii of Ptolemy	V	20	. . .
Avantidesa—			
=Ujjain, *q. v.*	XIII	17	. . .
Awán tribe—			
In western parts of Salt Range	II	„	. . .
	V	80, 81	. . .
Awánkárí, in Panjáb—			
Perhaps = Amanda or Amandra of Pliny	II	6, 112	. . .
Ayodhya (Ajodhia) City in Fyzábád District, Oudh—			
Identified by some writers with Hwen Thsang's Ayuto;	I	294	. . .
= Sha-chi of Fa-Hian, Visákhá of Hwen Thsang, and Sáketá of Hindus	„	317	. . .
Also named Baretá	„	327	. . .
Traditions of—	„	321	. . .

	Vol.	Page.	Plate.
Ayodhya (Ajodhia), City in Fyzábád District, Oudh—*contd.*—			
No ancient buildings now exist at—	I	322	. . .
Suggested identifications of Buddhist sites at— . .	,,	324	XLIX.
According to tradition restored by Vikramáditya of Ujjain	XI	98	. . .
Ayodhya Kingdom—			
Divided into Uttara-Kosala, and Banaodha . .	I	327	. . .
Ayumukha (Hayamukha) of Hwen Thsang—			
Probably = either Tusáran-Bihár in Partábgarh, or Singror in Alláhábád District	XI	68, 69	. . .
Ayuto of Hwen Thsang—			
Identified by some writers with Ajodhia . . .	I	294	. . .
Azam Shah of Bengal—			
Tomb of, at Sunárgáon	XV	139	. . .
Azes (Azas), King—			
Coins of, with name of Aspa Varmma Strategasa on reverse	I	Intr. XXXVII	. . .
Coins of, under *vihár* at Sháhdheri	V	72, 190	. . .
Belonged to Su tribe	II	46	. . .
Azes and Azilises, Kings—			
Immediate successors of Moga in N.-W. Panjáb . .	,,	59	. . .
Azilises, King—			
One type of coinage of, adopted by Saudása . .	III	40	. . .
Azím, Prince—			
Son of Akbar; gave his name to Azímábád or Patna .	VIII	34	. . .
Azímábád—			
Muhammadan name of Patna	,,	,,	. . .
B			
Bábá Wali—			
Panjáb legends of—	I	136	. . .
Bábar—			
Site of garden palace at Agra of—	IV	100, 105	. . .
Mosque with inscriptionof, at Sambhal . . .	XII	24	. . .
Great battle at Khanwá between Sanga and— . .	XX	93	. . .

	Vol.	Page.	Plate.
Bábhan—			
Synonymous with **Bhuinhár**, *q.v.*	XV	147	. . .
Babhru Váhana, Rájá—			
A legendary person in C. P.	XVII	30	. . .
Bachaund (Bachon) in Ajaygarh State, Bundelkhand—			
Sculptures and inscription at—	XXI	54	. . .
Báchhal Clan—			
Succeeded by Katahriya Clan in Eastern Rohilkhand in A.D. 1174	I	356	. . .
Badaon—			
Muhammadan capital of Katehar (Rohilkhand) for four centuries	XI	1, 2	. . .
Iltitmish, first governor of—	"	1	. . .
Included in dominions of Mahípála Tomara, Rájá of Delhi	"	"	. . .
Later history of—	"	2	. . .
List of ancient Muhammadan buildings at— . . .	"	4	. . .
Jámi Masjid of Iltitmish at—	"	5	II—IV.
Tombs at—	"	8	. . .
Badarpur, N.-E. of Sháhdheri (Taxil)—			
Great *stúpa* at—	II	144	. . .
Skeleton found in great *stúpa* at—	"	145	. . .
Bágar-des—			
The desert country west of Hánsi, now in Bikaner and Baháwalpur States	XIV	81	. . .
Bágdi Province—			
= Samatata of Hwen Thsang and Samudra Gupta. Also named Bháti. Boundaries and chief cities of—	XV	146	. . .
Bágh-bachchha R., in Lahore District, Panjáb—			
Mounds near—	XIV	48	XVII.
Baghel dynasty of Rewá—			
Rose in 12th century, A.D.	IX	113	. . .
Baghelkhand—			
See **Rewá State.**			
Bághera, in Jaypur State, Rájputána—			
Formerly called Vasantpur and other names . .	VI	136	. . .
Ádi Varáha coins found at—	"	137	. . .

	Vol.	Page.	Plate.
Bághera, in Jaypur State, Rájputána—*contd.*			
Legends of Rájá Chandra Sena at—	VI	138	. . .
'Marriage pillar' at—	"	143	XVI.
Temple of Varáha Avatár at—	"	145	. . .
Baghsar—			
See **Buxar.**			
Bagraha District—			
See **Bogra District.**			
Bágrám—			
See **Ránígat.**			
Bahádur Náhar—			
Founder of ruling family of Khánzádas of Mewát .	XX	15—17	. . .
Bahádurpur, in Alwar State, Rájputána—			
Jain inscription, dated S. 1573 = 1516 A.D., at— .	"	119	. . .
Baháwalpur State, in Panjáb—			
Partly corresponds with ancient Bágar-des . .	XIV	81	. . .
Báhika country—			
= Jálandhar District	V	148	. . .
Báhika tribe—			
= **Madra tribe,** *q.v.*	II	195	. . .
Bahraich, in Bahraich District, Oudh—			
Tomb of Sálár Masaúd at—	I	330, *Note.*	. . .
Bahulára, in Bánkurá District, Bengal—			
Fine brick temple at—	VIII	202	. . .
Bahuriband, in Jabalpur District, C. P.—			
Probably = Tholobana of Ptolemy	IX	40, 57	VIII.
	XXI	93	. . .
Baijnáth (Vaidyanáth)—			
Temple of, at Kiragráma in Kángra Valley . .	V	178	. . .
Baijnáth (Vaidyanáth), in Sháhábád District, Bengal—			
Frequented by pilgrims	VIII	137	. . .
Plans of group of temples at—	"	138	IX.
Thirteen inscriptions at—	"	140	. . .
Some Buddhist remains at—	"	141	. . .

	Vol.	Page.	Plate.
Baijnáth (Vaidyanáth), in Sháhábád District, Bengal—*contd.*			
Known as Deogarh-Baijnáth	XVIII	141	. . .
Ancient temple at—	XIX	29	. . .
Inscription of Madana Pála Deva at—	”	30	XI.
Inscription of Magardhwaja Jogí at—	”	31	X.
List of ancient sites near—	”	35	. . .
Baijnáth in Rewá—			
Temples and sculptures at—	XXI	154	. . .
Bairánt, in Benares District, N,-W. P.—			
Site of an ancient city	XXII	110	XIII.
List of 101 ancient coins found at—	”	114	. . .
Miscellaneous antiquities from—	”	115	. . .
Stone implements from—	”	116	. . .
Masons' marks on bricks at—	”	118	. . .
Bairát, city in Alwar State, Rájputána—			
The capital of *Matsya-desa*	II	244	. . .
	XX	2	. . .
Extensive ruins at—	II	245	. . .
Copper mines at—	”	”	. . .
Described by Hwen Thsang, A.D. 634 . . .	”	246	. . .
Destroyed by Mahmúd of Ghazní	”	247	. . .
Asoka's inscription from—	”	247—48	. . .
Very ancient coins found at—	”	249	. . .
Traditions of Rájá Viráta and Rájá Vena Chakravartí at—	VI	91	. . .
Rock inscription of Asoka at—	”	98	. . .
Ancient tomb at—	”	100	. . .
Removal of an inscription from, in A.D. 1834 . .	XXIII	31	. . .
Bairát (Vairáta) country in Rájputána—			
Anciently a kingdom	II	242	. . .
Naráyana or Naráyanpur, capital of— . . .	”	243	. . .
Bais Rájpúts—			
Claim descent from Sáliváhana	I	280	. . .
Daundiá Kherá, capital of—	”	296	. . .
Instead of Brahmans attend on great temple at Rájim, C. P.	XVII	9	. . .
Baiswárá—			
The Bais country in Southern Oudh	I	280	. . .
Bajranggarh—			
See **Jharkon in Málwa.**	. . .		

	Vol.	Page.	Plate.
Bakhra near Besárh, in Muzaffarpur District, Bengal—			
=Part of ancient **Vaisáli**, *q.v.*	I	56	...
Weight of lion-pillar at—	XVI	12	...
Further details of ruins at—	„	13	V.
Bakkula, Buddhist Saint—			
Legend of—	I	303	...
Bakra Gupta—			
A misreading for **Chandra Gupta II.**, *q.v.*	IX	24	...
Bakror, near Buddha Gayá—			
Numerous lac seals found in *stúpa* at—	I	12	...
Sandstone pillar at, in part removed to Sáhibganj or New Gayá	„	13	...
Anciently named Ajayapura	„	„	...
Baksar Ghát in Rái Barelí District, Oudh—			
A place of pilgrimage	XI	57	...
Scene of massacre of English in mutiny	„	58	...
Bála tribe—			
Related to the Káthi of the Panjáb, and probably ruled Síndh in 6th century A.D.	II	34	...
May be identical with the Malli of Multán	„	35	...
Balabhi—			
See **Valabhi.**			
Báláditya (I.), King of Magadha—			
Great *vihár* at Nálanda built by—	I	34	...
Date of, discussed	III	95	...
Báláditya (II.), King of Magadha—			
Conquered Mihirkul of Sangala	II	197	...
Balai-Kherá, in Pílibhít District, N.-W. P.—			
An ancient site	I	358	...
Balanti-purgon of Ptolemy—			
Probably = Bándhogarh in Rewá State	IX	56	...
	XVII	69	...
Balar near Sháhdheri (Taxila), in Ráwalpindí District, Panjáb—			
Great *stúpa* at—	II	142—144	LXI.
Other Buddhist ruins at—	„	144	...

	Vol.	Page.	Plate.
Balban, Emperor—			
See **Ulúgh Khán.**			
Ballál Sena, Rájá—			
Founded Gaur	XV	41	. . .
Balliá (Baliyá) District, N.-W. P.—			
Ancient sites in	XXII	86	. . .
Bálmer in Jodhpur State, Rájputána—			
=Pilomalo, capital of Gurjjara in time of Hwen Thsang	II	70	. . .
Bálnáth peak—			
In Tila Range in Panjáb	"	177	. . .
Bálod, in Ráipur District, C. P.—			
Various ruins at—	VII	133—137	XV.
Inscription in ruined temple at—	"	136	. . .
Very ancient inscribed *Satí* pillar at— . . .	"	137	. . .
Bána—			
Extracts from '*Harsha-charita*' by—	IX	154	. . .
Banaodha—			
=Oudh, south of the Ghágrá R.	I	327	. . .
Banáras—			
See **Benares.**			
Banás, R., a tributary of the Son—			
=Sanskrit Parnása, and Panassa of Ptolemy . .	VIII	15	. . .
	IX	57	. . .
Banásur—			
An old name of **Bayána**, *q.v.*	VI	40	. . .
Bándhogarh in Rewá State—			
Probably = Balantipurgon of Ptolemy	IX	56	. . .
	XVII	69	. . .
Identified with the fortress of Dalaki-wa-Malaki .	XXI	104	. . .
Muhammadan attacks on—	"	107	. . .
Story of Akbar's birth at—	"	109	. . .
Banga Province—			
Boundaries and chief cities of—	XV	145	. . .
Bangála—			
A name of Dhákka (Dacca) in 16th and 17th centuries	"	127	. . .
Bángarmau—			
See **Newal and Bángarmau.**			

	Vol.	Page.	Plate.
Bánnagar, in Dinájpur District, Bengal—			
Also called **Devíkot,** *q.v.*	XV	95	. . .
Baotí Pind, E. of Hasan Abdál, in Ráwalpindí District, Panjáb—			
Buddhist ruins at—	II	139—142	LX.
Ancient coins and *lapis lazuli* found at—	"	141	. . .
Barábár hills, in Gayá District, Bengal—			
Map of—	I	. . .	XVIII.
Four caves in—	"	44	XIX.
Inscriptions of Asoka in caves at—	"	45—48	XX.
Mr. Beglar's identification of Buddha's hill at—	VIII	36	. . .
Barágaon, in Patna District, Bengal—			
Certainly = **Nálanda,** *q.v.*	I	28	. . .
Said by local Bráhmans to have been named Kundilpur	"	"	. . .
Description of ruins of—	"	29	XVI.
Masons' marks at—	"	30	. . .
Great Buddhist temple of Báláditya at—	"	34	. . .
	III	94	. . .
Statues and inscriptions at—	I	35	. . .
Tanks at—	"	36	. . .
Legend of headless statue at—	VIII	79	. . .
Bárah Chhetra, in Bastí District, N.-W. P.—			
Identified with Vyághrapura or Koli of Buddhist tradition	XII	213	. . .
Barahat—			
See **Bhárhut.**			
Barákar, in Mánbhúm District, Bengal—			
Sundry temples at—	"	150—154	VI, XIV, XVIII.
Baran (Bárán)—			
Ancient name of Bulandshahr	XIV	147	. . .
Coins of Gomitra of—	"	"	XXXI.
May also = Báranáwa in Mírath (Meerut) District	"	148	. . .
Barárí, in Sháhpur District, Panjáb—			
Capital of Rájá Chobnath *See* **Bhurárí.**	II	37	. . .
Bardaotis of Ptolemy—			
= Bhárhut	XXI	92	. . .

	Vol.	Page.	Plate.
Bar-Dewal, in Bándá District, N.-W. P.—			
Fine temple at—	XXI	4	III, IV.
Barendra—			
See **Varendra.**			
Baretá—			
Later Hindu name of **Ayodhya City,** *q.v.* . . .	I	329	. . .
Bargaon, in Damoh District, C. P.—			
Kalachuri inscription and temples at— . . .	XXI	101—163	XXXVIII, XXXIX.
Bargújar Rájás of Máchárí, in Alwar—			
Genealogy of—	VI	79	. . .
Barmáwar, in Chamba State, Panjáb—			
Temples of wood and stone at, dated A.D. 1417 .	XIV	110	. . .
Inscriptions of—	„	110—112	XXVIII.
Barmáyan—			
Name of a Jogini (Yogini)	XXIII	57	. . .
Barmáyan in Balliá District, N.-W. P.—			
Buddhist remains at—	XIX	50	XII—XIV.
Barmé—			
Earlier name of **Uchahara,** *q.v.*	IX	5	. . .
Barna (Varana) Nadí—			
A small river under Benares	I	10	. . .
Báro or Barnagar, in Bhopál Agency, Central India—			
Inscription at, dated Samvat 933	X	74	. . .
Satí pillars and other remains at—	„	72, 75	. . .
Plundered by Chhatarsál Bundela	„	76	. . .
Legends of—	„	71	. . .
Barrows—			
See **Tumuli.**			
Bastí District, N.-W. P.—			
Ancient Buddhist sites in—	XII	82 to end	
	XVIII	1	I.
Batan-Kaisara of Ptolemy—			
Perhaps = Thánesar	II	212	. . .

	Vol.	Page.	Plate.
Batesar in Agra District, N.-W. P.—			
Formerly called Surapur or Surajpur	IV	222	. . .
List of Hindu, Jain, and Buddhist sculptures found near—	"	240	. . .
Legends of—	VII	6	. . .
Jain statues at—	"	8, 9	. . .
Bathani hill in Patna District, Bengal—			
? = Banthawa or Pandhawa hill of Buddhist legend .	VIII	46	. . .
Bavanni near Montgomery in Montgomery District, Panjáb—			
Fort at—	V	103	XXXI.
Báwan Garhi—			
See **Kasaundhi Garhi in Agra District.**			
Bayána in Bharatpur State, Rájputána—			
Anciently named Banásur	VI	40	. . .
Other names of—	XX	61, 62	. . .
Ukha Mandir mosque at—	VI	50	IV, V.
	XX	71	XIII, XV.
Minár at—	VI	51	. . .
	XX	73	. . .
Inscription, dated S. 1100 at—	VI	52	VI.
	XX	62, 77	. . .
A place of much importance previous to time of Lodí dynasty	VI	53	. . .
Attacked by Muhammad bin Sám	XX	62	. . .
Held by Auhadí family in 15th century A.D. . .	"	63	. . .
Genealogy of Auhadí family of—	"	65	. . .
Held by Bahlol Lodí in A.H. 878	"	67	. . .
Nágrí inscription of Khán Khánán Farmuli, dated A. D. 1496 at—	"	"	XVII.
Teaching of Shekh Iláhi Mahdawí in reign of Islám Sháh at—	"	68	. . .
Permanently annexed by Akbar	"	"	. . .
Passed under rule of the Játs on break-up of Mughal Empire	"	68	. . .
Traditions of Játs of—	II	54	. . .
Jhálar Baoli at, with inscriptions of Kutb-ud-dín Mubárak Sháh, dated A.H. 718 = A.D. 1318 .	"	69	XV, XVI.
Tughra inscription of Alá-ud-dín Muhammad at— .	XX	72	XIV.
Minor mosques at—	"	75	. . .
Kázís' mosque with inscription of Alá-ud-dín Khiljí, dated A.H. 705 = 1305 A.D. at—	"	76	XIV.

	Vol.	Page.	Plate.
Bayána in Bharatpur State, Rájputána—*contd.*			
Sundry tombs at—	XX	78	. . .
Gindoria well with inscription, dated S. 1503 = 1446 A. D. at—	"	79	XVII.
Tomb of Abúbakr Kandhárí at—	"	60, 77	. . .
Báz Bahádur of Málwá—			
Story of love of Rúpmatí and—	II	289	. . .
Rare square copper coins of—	"	292	. . .
Bázár in Yusufzai, Panjáb—			
Perhaps = Bazaria of Greek writers	"	101	. . .
Bazaria of Greek writers—			
Identified with Bázár in Yusufzai	"	"	. . .
with Sháhbázgarhi	V	18	. . .
Bazodeo, King—			
See **Vásudeva, King.**			
Bediban near Motihári, in Champáran District, Bengal—			
Muhammadan inscription worshipped by Hindus at— .	XVI	25	IV.
Begampur, near Delhi—			
Tomb of Kabír-ud-dín Auliya near—	XX	147	XXXIII.
Chor Minár or 'Thieves' Pillar' near—	"	149	XXXIV.
Beglar, Mr. J. D.—			
Retractation by, of erroneous views respecting Kutb Mosque and Mínár	IV	xv	. . .
Architectural theories of—	VIII	66—73	. . .
Belá in Gayá District, Bengal—			
Hindu and Buddhist statues at—	"	65	. . .
Belkhara in Mirzápur District, N.-W. P.—			
Inscription, dated S. 1253 = A.D. 1196, probably of son of Rájá Jaya Chandra at—	XI	129	XXXVIII.
Bellew, Dr.—			
Account of Yusufzai by—	V	5, 24, *Note*	. . .
Belo, Chandel Rájá—			
Singorgarh traditions of—	IX	50	. . .
Ben, Rájá Chakravarttí—			
Perhaps = Wema Kadphises	XII	37	. . .
Mentioned in Vishnu Purána	I	65	. . .

	Vol.	Page.	Plate.
Ben, Rájá Chakravartti—*contd.*			
Traditional founder of Kesariyá *stúpa* . . .	I	65	. . .
of Atranjí Kherá in Etá District .	„	269	. . .
of Indor Kherá in Bulandshahr District	XII	37	. .
of fort at Haridwár . . .	II	233	. . .
Alwar traditions of—	VI	85, 91	. . .
Central Provinces traditions of—	IX	49	. . .
Benares in Benares District, N.-W. P.—			
Famous as locality of first exposition of law of Buddha	I	103	. . .
Position of city of—	„	104	XXXI.
Benares, Sárnáth near—			
Buddhist remains at—	„	105—107	XXXII.
Great Dhamek *stúpa* at—	„	107—113	. . .
Derivation of name Dhamek	„	113	. . .
Inscription of Mahípála Deva, dated Samvat 1083, from—	„	114	. . .
Messrs. Kittoe's, Thomas', and Hall's further excavations at—	„	116, 126	XXXII.
Chaukandi mound *stúpa* at, mentioned by Hwen Thsang	„	117	. . .
Buddhist seals found in immense numbers at— . .	„	119	. . .
Sculptures found at, in 1835-36, by Cunningham .	„	120, 122	. . .
Vihár discovered at same time at—	„	121	XXXIII.
Shrine of the ? Buddhist Triad at—	„	„	. . .
Bas relief with inscription of donor named Hari Gupta at—	„	123	XXXIV.
Buildings excavated at, by Cunningham, have all disappeared	„	124	XXXIII.
Ruins of an ? hospital at—	„	125	. . .
Stone umbrellas at—	„	„	. . .
Traces of destruction by fire at,—perhaps burnt by Ahmad Niáltigín	„	126, 128	. . .
	VIII	16	. . .
Inscribed seal, &c., from, now in College Museum .	I	129	. . .
Further excavations not now desirable at— . .	„	„	. . .
Various inscriptions found at—	„	. . . .	XXXIV.
Bengal—			
Map of—	XV	. . . .	I.
Notes on history of—	„	145—177	. . .
Anciently divided into four Provinces, *viz.*, Barendra, Banga, Rárh, and Bágdi	„	145	. . .
List of early Muhammadan Governors of— . .	„	169	. . .
Muhammadan kings of, 1286 to 1537 A.D. . . .	„	172	. . .

	Vol.	Page.	Plate.
Bengal—*contd.*			
Embassies to China from, in A.D. 1408-09 and 1414 .	XV	173	. . .
Errors in chronology of historians of— . . .	"	"	. . .
Conquered by Sher Sháh, A.D. 1537-38 . . .	"	177	. . .
Bengal, Eastern—			
Great changes in courses of rivers of—	"	v	. . .
Bengal, Ránchi Frontier Agency of—			
List of ancient sites in—	XIII	66	. . .
Bengálí-Patháп architecture—			
Described	III	10	. . .
Besání in Panná State, Bundelkhand—			
Inscription, dated in intercalary month at— . .	XXI	102	XXVII.
Besárh (Besádh) in Muzaffarpur District, Bengal—			
= Ancient **Vaisálí**	I	55	. . .
Besnagar in Bhopál State, Central India—			
Description of site of—	X	36	XII.
= Chetiyagiri, = Wessanagara	"	37	. . .
Legend of Rájá Rukmangada at—	"	"	. . .
Kinds of coins found at—	"	"	. . .
Inscribed Buddhist railing at—	"	38	XIII.
Sculptures of Gupta period at—	"	41	. . .
Crocodile and 'fan-palm' pillars at—	"	42	XIV.
Kalpa-drúm capital at—	"	43	XV.
Colossal female statue at—	"	44	. . .
Buddhist remains near—	"	46	. . .
Probably = Adisathra town of Ptolemy, = Bidisa .	XXI	93	. . .
Bettigi, country of—			
= Vákátaka (Bhándak in C. P.)	IX	56	. . .
	XXI	94	. . .
Bhábru Váhan, Rájá—			
A legendary person of Sirpur in C. P.	VII	192	. . .
Bhadári, (Barári or Bhurárí) ruined city in Sháhpur District, Panjáb—			
Traditional capital of Rájá Chobnáth	II	37, 40	. . .
Bhágalpur in Bhágalpur District, Bengal—			
Ancient subterranean passage at—	XV	31	. . .
Buddhist legend connected with—	"	33	. . .

	Vol.	Page.	Plate.
Bhágalpur District in Bengal—*contd.*			
= Ancient kingdom of Anga	I	52	. . .
Anciently named Champá	XV	33	. . .
Bhágalpur in Gorakhpur District, N.-W. P.—			
Inscribed pillar at—	XVI	130	XXX, XXXI.
	XXII	60	. . .
Bhagwán Lal Indrají, Pandit—			
Remarks on inscriptions of Jívita Gupta and those from Nepál by—	XVI	73, *etseq.*	. . .
Bhagwánganj in Patna District, Bengal—			
Stúpa at—	VIII	18	. . .
Bhándak in Chándá District, C. P.—			
Site of city was capital of Province of Vákátaka .	IX	122,137	XXI.
Buddhist caves in Wijásan hill near—	„	124	XXI, XXII.
Early imperfect inscriptions at—	„	126	. . .
Long Buddhist inscription from—	„	127,137	. . .
Brahmanical temples at—	„	129	XXIII, XIV.
Snake worship at—	„	131	. . .
Bhánu Gupta—			
Mentioned in inscription, dated Samvat 191 at Eran .	X	89	. . .
Bhánu Varmma, Yaudheya (?)—			
Coin of—	XIV	144	. . .
Bhar tribe—			
Oudh legends of—	XI	67	. . .
Rájá of Sultánpur in Oudh belonged to, in time of Alá-ud-dín Khiljí	I	314	. . .
Formerly occupied south-west of Bastí District, N.-W. Provinces	XII	89	. .
Tradition makes Rájá Karna Deva Kalachuri of Chedí belong to—	XXI	149	. . .
Bhárhut (Barahat) in Nágaudh State, Baghelkhand—			
Indo-Persian architecture at—	V	188	. . .
Inscription of Kalachuri dynasty at—	IX	1, 94	. . .
Buddhist temple at, with additions of date *circa* 1100 A.D.	„	3	. . .
= Bardaotis of Ptolemy	XXI	92	. . .
Bhásu-Bihár in Bogra District, Bengal—			
Identified with Po-shi-po of Hwen Thsang . .	XV	102	. . .
Buddhist remains at—	„	103	. . .
Tank of Rájá Sasángka at—	„	102	. . .

	Vol.	Page.	Plate.
Bhateswar—			
See **Batesar in Agra District.**			
Bhati (or Bháti) tribe—			
In Central and Eastern Panjáb are Yádava Aryans	II	19	. . .
Comprise both Hindus and Musalmáns	„	22	. . .
Tod's account of—	XXIII	4	. . .
Bhati Province—			
Another name of Bágdi	XV	146	. . .
Bhátia of Utbi—			
= Bhera on Jhelam river	XIV	36	. . .
Bhatinda in Patiála State, Panjáb—			
Govindgarh fort at—	XXIII	2	. . .
Also known as Tiranda	„	2,7	. . .
Legends of—	„	4	. . .
Minor Muhammadan inscriptions at—	„	6	. . .
Death of Rájá Jaipál at—	„	7	. . .
Early Nágrí inscription at—	„	8	XXVII.
Bhattah (Bhath, or Bhath-ghorah)—			
Muhammadan name of Rewá State	XXI	110, 154	. . .
Bhattáraka, Senapati of Valabhi—			
Date and silver coins of—	IX	20, 28	V.
Bháu Dájí, Dr.—			
Archæological works of—	I	Intr. XXXIII	. . .
Mistakes of, as to the queens of Gupta dynasty, and chronology of Káshmír and Valabhi	„	„ XXXIV	. . .
Mistaken reading by, of Gilika as = Greek in Asoka's edict	„	„ XXXV	. . .
Bháva, Rájá—			
Inscription of, on Iron Pillar at Delhi	„	170	. . .
Bhávabhuti—			
Described Padmavatí = Narwár	II	308, 318	. . .
Bhelsá—			
See **Bhílsá.**			
Bherá in Sháhpur District, Panjáb—			
Modern city founded by Sher Sháh in 1540 A.D.	XIV	35	. . .
Perhaps referred to by Virgil and Vibius Sequester	„	36	. . .
= Bhátia of Utbi	„	„	. . .
Incidents in later history of—	„	38	. . .

	Vol.	Page.	Plate.
Bherá Ghát in Jabalpur District, C. P.—			
A sacred spot	IX	60	. . .
Temple of *Chaunsat Jogínís* at—	,,	61	XII—XVI.
Bhika Pahárí—			
A ward of Patna city	VIII	IX	. . .
Bhilla (Bhíl)—			
In Kathá-Sarita-Sâgar synonymous with Pulinda and Savara	XVII	139	. . .
Bhílsa in Bhopál State, Central India—*			
Etymology of name of—	X	34	. . .
Probably founded during Gupta period	,,	35	. . .
Bhíma Deva, King of Gándhára—			
Coins of, extremely rare	V	83	. . .
Bhíma Sena, King—			
Silver coins of—	IX	26	V.
Painted inscription of, at Girija Hill, dated S. 52 .	XXI	119	XXX.
Bhímband in Mongír District, in Bengal—			
Hot springs at—	XV	19	. . .
Bhímnagar—			
Another name for Kángra town	V	156	. . .
Bhítargaon in Cawnpore District, N.-W. P.—			
Ancient brick temple at—	XI	40	XIV—XVII.
Hindu arch in ,, ...	,,	42	. . .
Terra-cotta ornaments at—	,,	44	XVI, XVII.
Bhitarí in Gházípur District, N.-W. P.—			
An ancient Hindu town	I	96	. . .
Pillar with inscription concerning Skanda Gupta at— .	,,	38, *Note*, 97—99, 101	XVII, XXX.
Indo-Sassanian coins of 8th or 9th century from— .	,,	97	. . .
Elephant and *chaitya* copper coin from— . . .	,,	,,	. . .
Bricks inscribed with name of Kumára Gupta at— .	,,	,,	XXX.
Sculptures of Gupta period at—	,,	99, 100	. . .
Excavations by Mr. C. Horne at—	,,	100, 103	. . .
Bhoja Deva, King of Northern India—			
Inscription of reign of, dated Samvat 919 and Saka 784, at Deogarh in Lalitpur	X	101	XXXIII.

* The Imperial Gazetteer places Bhílsá in Bhopál, but Mr. Fleet (*Corpus. Inscr. Ind. III, p. 22*) states that it is the principal town of the Bhílsa subdivision of the Iságarh District in the Gwálior State, otherwise known as Sindia's dominions.

	Vol.	Page.	Plate.
Bhoja Deva, King of Northern India—*contd.*			
Mentioned in Rájá Tárangini and inscriptions of Gwáliár and Pahewa (Pehoa)	X	101	. . .
Ruled over all Northern India in 9th century A.D.	„	102	. . .
Inscription of, at Pehoa (Pahewa), dated Samvat 276	II	224	. . .
Gwáliár inscription of, dated S. 933=A. D. 876.	„	335, 355	. . .
Seems to be mentioned in inscription at Rájim, C. P.	XVII	15	. . .
Bhoja tribe—			
Mentioned in Sháhbázgarhi inscription and in Mahábhárata and Puránas	V	20	. . .
Bhonsi in Gurgaon District, Panjáb—			
Mosque at—	XX	137	. . .
Bhúbhara (Búmara) in Nágaudh State, Baghelkhand—			
Inscription of Rájá Hastin, &c., from—	IX	8	. . .
Bhuilá Dih in Bastí District, N.-W. P.—			
= Kapilavástu	XII	IV, 82	. . .
Maps of neighourhood of—	„	. . .	VIII—X.
General description of—	„	143	. . .
Discovery of supposed bed chamber of Mahá-Máyá at—	„	168	XI.
Pottery found at—	„	145	XII.
Indo-Scythian and other ancient coins found at and near—	„	145,153,164	. . .
Ancient causeways at—	„	152, 154	. . .
Kot, an ancient fort north of—	„	155	. . .
Various sites around, identified with those mentioned in Buddhist legend as around Kapilavástu	„	IV,112,157, 172	. . .
Bhuilí in Mirzápur District, N.-W. P.—			
Nágrí inscriptions in cave, and sculptured obelisks at—	XI	131	XXXVIII.
Inscription of Kutb-ud-dín Mubárak Khiljí at—	XXI	130	. . .
Bhuinhár caste—			
In Bengal and Bihár	V	115	. . .
Not to be confounded with Bhuiyás	XVII	134	. . .
Bhuinhárs, Bárah—			
Bengal traditions of—	XV	147	. . .
Bhuiyás (Bhúmiyas)—			
The most numerous Kolian tribe of aborigines	XVII	133	. . .
Not to be confounded with Bhuinhárs	„	134	. . .
Characteristics of—	„	135	. . .

	Vol.	Page.	Plate.
Bhuksa tribe—			
Mr. E. Colvin's account of—	XII	136	. . .
Bhurárí (Bhadrárí) in Sháhpur District, Panjáb—			
Ruins at—	V	96	. . .
See **Barárí.**			
Bidisa—			
See **Besnagar.**			
Bihár—			
Four places of this name in Gangetic Provinces	XI	31	. . .
Bihár (Dand-Bihár) in Patna District, Bengal—			
Name of = *Vihára*	I	36	. . .
Only extant Buddhist remains at, are votive *stúpas* and broken statues	,,	37	. . .
Pillar with Gupta inscriptions inside the fort at—	,,	37,38,*Note.*	XVII.
Christian (? Armenian) tombs at—	,,	38	. . .
Cyclopean walls of fort at—	,,	,,	. . .
Formerly known as Dand Bihár, and Súba-Bihár	VIII	75	. . .
Seems to be ancient Udandapura or Otantapura	,,	,,	. . .
	XI	185,191	. . .
Also probably named Yasovarmmapura or Jaspur	III	135	. . .
	VIII	76	. . .
The capital of Magadha in 1200 A.D.	XI	185	. . .
Topography of—	,,	186	. . .
Bihár Province—			
= Ancient Magadha	,,	185	. . .
List of ancient sites in—	VIII	52	. . .
Tradition of emigration of Chamárs from, to Chhattísgarh in Central Provinces	VII	225	. . .
Bíjápur in Kaládgi District, Bombay—			
Described by Sykes, Fergusson, &c.	I	Intr. iv	. . .
Bijaymandirgarh—			
See **Vijayamandirgarh.**			
Bijolí in Mewár (Udaipur) State, Rájputána—			
Also named Morakúro and Ahaichpur.	VI	234	. . .
Temples at—	,,	235	. . .
Mediæval inscriptions at—	,,	238	. . .
Satí inscription, dated S. 1232 = A.D. 1175 at—	,,	239	. . .
Ancient inscription supposed to exist at—	,,	251	. . .
Bikaner State, Rájputána—			
Partly corresponds with ancient Bágar-des	XIV	81	. . .

	Vol.	Page.	Plate.
Bikrampur near Dhákká—			
The capital of the early and of the latest Sena Rájás	XV	132, 167	. . .
Ruins of palace of Ballál Sen at—	„	132	. . .
Legends of tomb at—	„	133	XXXV.
Bilharí in Jabalpur District, C. P.—			
Formerly named Puphávatí or Pushpávatí	IX	34	. . .
Traditions of Lakshman Singh Parihár at—	„	35	. . .
Temples at—	„	36	VII
Legend of Mádhavánala and Kám Kandalá at—	„	37	. . .
= Bridama of Ptolemy	„	57	. . .
	XXI	93	. . .
Bilan Deo—			
An alias of **Anang Pál I.**, *q.v.*	I	141	. . .
Biláspur in Bilàspur District, C. P.—			
Inscriptions from Malhár and Ratanpur formerly at—	VII	214	. . .
Stone from Kosgain inscribed on both faces, and inscribed statue at—	„	„	. . .
Bilhariyá in Bándá District, N.-W. P.—			
Temples at—	XXI	19	. . .
Bilsar (Bilsand) in Etá District, N.-W. P.—			
= Pi-lo-shan-na of Hwen Thsang	XI	15	. . .
= Tilsanda, &c,, of Muhammadan authors	„	22	. . .
Remains of monastery, &c., at—	„	16	V.
Square pillars of Gupta temple at—	„	17	VI.
Pillars with inscriptions of Kumára Gupta at—	„	18	VIII.
Carved bricks from—	„	21	VII.
Bimbisára, King of Magadha—			
Also named Srenika	I	23	. . .
Founded second city of Rájagriha	„	„	. . .
Said to have resided at Nálanda	„	28	. . .
Binagara of Ptolemy—			
= Thatha in Síndh	II	46	. . .
Bindusára, King of Magadha—			
Rebellion of Taxila against—	„	112	. . .
Bírbal, Rájá—			
Palaçes of, at Agra	IV	120	. . .
Originally named Mahesh Dás, and born at Kálpí	XXI	131	. . .

	Vol.	Page.	Plate.
Birpur (Bhirpur in ?) Rewá State, Baghelkhand—			
Ancient temple at—	XIX	73	XV—XVII.
Bishanpur in Bánkurá District, Bengal—			
Numerous late temples at—	VIII	203	. . .
Inscriptions, dated in Malla era at—	,,	,,	. . .
in either Bengal or local era at—	,,	205	. . .
at, combined with those from Pachet and Chátná	,,	,,	. . .
The 'Ras Mancha' at—	,,	206	. . .
Bishanpur Ghenjan in Gayá District, Bengal—			
Buddhist creed inscriptions at—	,,	63	. . .
Bishanpur Tandwá in Gayá District, Bengal—			
Inscribed Buddhist statues at—	,,	105	. . .
Identified at one time by Cunningham with Udandapura	,,	75	. . .
Bitbhaya-pattana—			
Ancient name of **Bithá in Alláhábád District**, *q.v.*—	. .	. . .	. . .
Bithá and Deoriyá in Alláhábád District, N.-W. P.—			
= Ancient Bitbhaya-paṭṭana	III	47	XVII.
Buddhist inscriptions from—	,,	,,	XVIII.
Ruins of extensive city at—	,,	49	. . .
Glazed pottery found at—	,,	51	. . .
Stone stools found at—	,,	52	. . .
Buddhist and Brahmanical sculptures at—	X	6	III.
Inscriptions of Kumára Gupta (Imperial) on statue and obelisk near—	,,	7	IV.
Three inscriptions of 9th century near—	,,	,,	,,
Bithanda of Ferishta—			
Perhaps = Ohind on Indus	II	93	. . .
Certainly = **Bilsar**, *q.v.*	XI	22	. . .
Biyá-Kund in Bijáwar State, Bundelkhand—			
A holy place	XXI	169	. . .
Blochmann, Mr.—			
Contributions to history of Bengal by—	XV	168	. . .
Divides Muhammadan period in Bengal into five parts	,,	169	. . .
Bod in Orissa—			
Temples at—	XIII	118	XVIII.

	Vol.	Page.	Plate.
Boddika—			
= *Pádika*, a coin , = ¼ *Kársha*, = obolus . . .	XI	176	. . .
Bodh-Gayá—			
See **Buddha-Gayá.**			
Bodhi-tree, the (*Bodhi-drúm*)—			
See **Buddha-Gayá.**			
Bodosamar State, Orissa—			
Temples in—	XIII	140	. . .
Bogra (Bagraha) District, Bengal—			
Red soil of—	XV	113	. . .
Bolingæ, country of (Ptolemy)—			
= Rewá State	XXI	92	. . .
Boram Deo in Biláspur District, C. P.—			
Inscription, dated S. 1608 = A.D. 1551 at— . .	XVII	34	. . .
Temple of Boram Deo at, with five inscriptions . .	„	35, 42	XXI, XXII.
Inscription of Magardhwaja Jogí at—	„	36	„
Satí monument, dated S. 1422 = A.D. 1365 at— . .	„	37	„
Brick temple of peculiar plan at—	„	38	XXI.
Other temples at—	„	39	XXIII.
Inscription, dated Vikrama Saka 1406 at— . . .	„	40	. . .
Satí pillars with date in Vikrama Samvat and 60 years Jupiter's cycle at—	„	41	. . .
Brahmá—			
Temple of, at Dudahi in Lalitpur	X	93	XXII.
at Khajuráho	XXI	57	. . .
Colossal statue of, at Garhwá	III	56	. . .
Bráhmana Deva Yaudheya—			
Coins of—	XIV	143	. . .
Brahmanism—			
Early introduced in Yusufzai	V	7	. . .
Brahmans, Maithila—			
Divided into four sections by Rájá Hara Sinha . .	XVI	4	. . .
Brahui Race—			
Probably a remnant of the Accadians	IX	160	. . .

	VOL.	PAGE.	PLATE.
Brass—			
Images in Chambá State, Panjáb	XIV	109	. . .
Brick—			
Characteristics of early architecture of N. India in, illustrated by Bhítargaon example	XI	42	. . .
The material of buildings in Panjáb plains . . .	V	95	. . .
Hindu arches at Konch in Bihár constructed of— .	VIII	54, 55	. . .
Bricks—			
At Bhitarí inscribed with name of Kumára Gupta .	I	97	. . .
Bricks, moulded—			
Characteristic of ruins in Panjáb plains	V	100	XXX.
Inscriptions on, at Shorkot	,,	102	,,
At Tulamba, &c., in Panjáb	,,	113	XXXV.
Bridama of Ptolemy—			
=Bilahrí in Jabalpur District, C. P.	IX	57	. . .
	XXI	93	. . .
Broadley, Mr.—			
Destructive researches of, at Nálanda	VIII	88	. . .
Buchanan Hamilton, Dr.—			
Statistical and archæological work of—	I	Intr. III, IV	. . .
Budaon—			
See **Badaon.**			
Buddha—			
Resided for a time at Vaisáli	,,	63	. . .
Death and obsequies of, at Kusinagara	,,	8	. . .
First expounded his doctrine at Benares	,,	103	. . .
Statues of, at or near Benares	,,	104, 113	. . .
Duration of residence of, at Srávastí and Sáketa .	,,	319	. . .
Legend of body offering of—	II	54	. . .
History of reputed alms-bowl of—	,,	87	. . .
	XVI	8—12	III.
Early images of, in Indo-Scythian sculptures and coins, and at Srávastí	V	VII	. . .
	XI	84, 86	. . .
Early statue of, at Anyor in Mathurá District . .	XX	49	. . .
Buddha-Gayá (Bodh-Gayá) in Gayá District, Bengal—			
Described by Fa-Hian and Hwen Thsang . . .	I	4, 7	. . .

	Vol.	Page.	Plate.
Buddha-Gayá (Bodh-Gayá) in Gayá District, Bengal—*contd.*			
Bodhi-drúm at, destroyed by Sasángka, and renewed by Púrna Varmma	I	5	. . .
	III	80, 81	. . .
Ruined fort of Amara Sinha, &c., at—	I	11	. . .
Few extant inscriptions at—	"	12	VI.
Rude stone circles near—.	VIII	66	. . .
Stúpa of Asoka originally on site of great temple at—.	I	6	. . .
Forged inscription of Amara Deva, said to have been found at—	"	"	. . .
	VIII	58, *Note*	. . .
Identification of sundry sites at—	XI	147	XL.
Further discoveries in 1880 at—	XVI	Pref. III	. . .
Traces of Greek art at—	III	97, 100	XXVII–XXIX.
Great temple at—			
Plan of—	I	5	IV, V.
	III	82	XXV.
Buddha-pad stone at—	I	9	VII.
Inscribed Buddhist railing round and near— . .	"	10, *Note*	VII—XI.
	III	86—98	XXVI, & XXVIII–XXX.
Date of—	I	Intr. XL	. . .
	III	90—95	. . .
	XI	146	. . .
Date of vaults and arches in—	III	84	. . .
	VIII	66—72	. . .
	XI	141	. . .
Model *stúpas* found at—	III	87	. . .
Burmese inscription, dated A.D. 1305 at— . . .	I	8	. . .
	III	102	XXXII.
Modern Burmese inscriptions at—	"	105	"
Ornamentation of—.	"	96, 104	XXVII, XXXI.
Details of structure of—	VIII	67, 73	. . .
Buddhism—			
Antagonism of sects of—	I	251	. . .
Destroyed at Mathurá between A.D. 634 and 1017 .	"	237	. . .
Relation to Jainism of—	X	63	. . .
The four great sites famous in early history of— . .	XVIII	3	. . .
Persecuted by King Pushpamitra	II	41	. . .
Proofs from Hindu writers of Brahmanical persecution of—	XX	103	. . .
Revival of, probably in reign of Harsha Varddhana of Kanauj	XI	98	. . .
Was dominant religion in Magadha from 8th century A.D. to Muhammadan conquest	III	119	. . .
	XX	103	. . .

	Vol.	Page.	Plate.
Buddhism—*contd.*			
Later history of, *circa* 800 A.D., illustrated by inscriptions from Ghosráwa in Bihár	I	38	. . .
Existed at Mahoba in Bundelkhand in 11th or 12th century A.D.	II	445	. . .
In Kángra Valley traceable at Chári only . . .	V	178	. . .
Buddhist Creed—			
Hodgson's and Burnouf's translations of— . .	I	111	. . .
Buddhist Railing—			
At Buddha-Gayá	"	10	VII—XI.
	III	86—98	XXVI & XXVIII—XXX.
At Mathurá and elsewhere	"	23	VIII—X.
May be a development of the rude stone circle . .	I	Intr. xxx	. . .
Buddhist Satraps—			
See **Satraps, Buddhist**—	. .	. . .	. . .
Buddhist Synod—			
See **Synod, Buddhist**	. .	. . .	. . .
Buddhpur in Singhbhúm—			
Jain, &c., remains at—	VIII	197	. . .
Budha Gupta, King—			
Dated silver coins of—	IX	21, 25	V.
Inscribed pillar of, at Eran	X	81	XXV, XXVI.
Bukephala—			
Probably = either Jalálpur, or Diláwar (Dáráp ur) .	II	175, 186	. . .
Bulandshahr, in Bulandshahr District, N.-W. P.—			
Anciently named Baran	XIV	147	. . .
Bundelkhand—			
Named Jejákabhukti in inscriptions, and perhaps = Sandrabatis of Ptolemy	X	23, 99	. . .
	XXI	VI, 57, 58, 92, 173.	. . .
Map of—	VII	. . .	XXII.
Women's costume in—	"	57	. . .
Burám in Mánbhúm District, Bengal—			
Temples at—	VIII	184—186	XIX.

	Vol.	Page.	Plate.
Burhánpur in Gwáliár State, Central India—			
Mosques at—	IX	115	XVII, XVIII.
Burmese—			
Eras	VIII	2, 3	. . .
Inscriptions at Buddha Gayá	I	8, 9	. . .
	III	102, 105	XXXII.
Buxar (Baghsar) in Sháhábád District, Bengal—			
Not = Mahására	"	65	. . .
Byána—			
See **Bayána in Bharatpur State.**			

C

	Vol.	Page.	Plate.
Cairns, sepulchral—			
In Agra District	VI	13, 33	II.
Calamina—			
Traditionary locality of martyrdom of Saint Thomas, and perhaps = Minnagar of the Periplus . .	II	60	. . .
	V	"	. . .
Canning, Lord—			
Minute on Archæology in Upper India by— . .	I	Pref. I—III	. . .
Capitals—			
Form of, a test of age of buildings	X	61, 64	XXII.
Cardinal points—			
Deviation of Gupta and certain other ancient buildings from, a mark of antiquity	XI	72, 82	. . .
Carlleyle, A. C., Mr.—			
Discovered Asoka pillar at Rampurwá . . .	XVI	Pref. VIII	. . .
	XXII	51	. . .
Researches and restorations at Kasiá of— . .	XVI	124, *Note*	. . .
	XXII	16-29, 58	III, IV.
Cashmere—			
See **Káshmír**	. . .	. . .	. . .
Celt—			
Copper, found at Mathurá	III	16	II.
See **Stone implements.**			

	Vol.	Page.	Plate.
Central Provinces—			
Coins scarce in eastern parts of—	VII	160	. . .
Chach, Rájá of Sindh—			
Captured Multán about A.D. 650	V	114	. . .
Chach-Hazára—			
Modern name of Taxila District	II	115	. . .
Cháhada Deva, Rájá of Narwár—			
Dated coins of—	„	314	. . .
Conflict of, with Násir-ud-dín, King of Delhi, 1251 A.D.	„	315	. . .
Cháhara Deva—			
A younger brother of Prithí Ráj Chauhán . . .	I	157	. . .
Chakrapura—			
An ancient name of Árá (Arrah)	III	73	. . .
Chakravarttí Ràjá—			
Memorial of, at cross-roads	I	66	. . .
Chalpáni R. in Yusufzai—			
=Malamantos of Arrian	V	3	. . .
Chálukya Dynasty—			
Probably began in A.D. 318	I	Intr. xxix	. . .
Conquered a branch of the Kalachuri Haihayas in 6th and 7th centuries A.D.	IX	77	. . .
	XVII	83	. . .
Vikramáditya of, defeated Harsha Vardhana . .	I	281	. . .
Inscriptions of, in C. P.	VII	141	. . .
Chambá (Champá) State in Panjáb—			
Inscriptions on brass images at Barmáwar, &c., in— .	XIV	109	XXVIII.
Rájás of—	„	114	. . .
Three inscriptions on copper, and one on stone in— .	XXI	135	. . .
Champá—			
Ancient name of Bhágalpur in Bengal . . .	XV	33	. . .
Champánagar in Bhágalpur District, Bengal—			
Capital of ancient kingdom of Anga . . .	„	31	. . .
Champáran District, Bengal—			
Included in ancient Mithila	XVI	34	. . .
Unexplored ancient sites in—	XXII	50	. . .

	Vol.	Page.	Plate.
Champávatí—			
Alleged ancient name of Chátsú in Jaypur State .	VI	116	. . .
Champávatí R.—			
Chándan R. in Bengal	VIII	130	. . .
Chand Ráisá poem—			
Brief account of—	I	159	. . .
Historical errors of—	IX	153	. . .
	X	91	. . .
Chándá in Chándá District, C.P.—			
Founded by Ballál Sáh Gond about A. D. 1450 .	IX	136	. . .
Curious sculptures at—	„	138	. . .
Chandaka, *Stúpa* of—			
At Maháthán in Bastí District	XXII	III, 5	. . .
Chándan R. in Bengal—			
=Ancient Champávatí R.	VIII	130	. . .
Chandel (Chandella) clan—			
Migrations of sections of—	XXI	90	. . .
Chandel (Chandella) dynasty of Bundelkhand—			
Capitals of, at Khajuráho and Mahoba	II	412, 439	. . .
Legend of origin of—	„	445	. . .
Traditional dates for foundation of—	„	446	. . .
Annalists' list of—	„	449	. . .
Eight forts of—	VII	21	. . .
Traditions of Rájá Belo of—	IX	50	. . .
Sumer Singh of—	X	66	. . .
Jálandhar of—	„	91	. . .
Occupation of Deogarh by—	„	103	. . .
Conquered by Prithví Rájá in 1239 S.	„	100	. . .
Devalabdhi, grandson of Yaso Varmma, a Prince of—	„	95	. . .
Revised lists of Kings of—	II	451	. . .
	X	24	. . .
	XXI	78	. . .
Coinage of, described	II	458	. . .
	X	25	X.
Extent of dominions of—	XXI	77	. . .
List of inscriptions connected with—	II	448	. . .
	XXI	81	IX—XXIII.
Chitravarna, or square-headed, character used in inscriptions of—	„	72	. . .
History of—	II	451	. . .
	XXI	83, 90	. . .

	Vol.	Page.	Plate.
Chanderí (New) in Gwáliár State, C. I.—			
Fortress of—	II	404	XCIII.
Kírat-Ságar lake at—	,,	405	. . .
Rock-cut gateway at—	,,	406	XCIV.
Muhammadan attacks on—	,,	407	. . .
Later history of—	,,	411	. . .
Chanderí (Old) in Gwáliár State, C. I.—			
History and description of—	,,	402	XCII.
Chandeswar in Katák District, Orissa—			
Temples at—	XIII	101	XIX.
Chandi Mau in Patna District, Bengal—			
Remains at, described by Broadley	VIII	78	. . .
Inscription of King Ráma Pála Deva, dated S. 12 at—	XI	169	. . .
Chandpur in Lalitpur District, N.-W. P.—			
Remains at, both Jain and Brahmanical . . .	X	96	. . .
Inscribed boar, dated S. 1207, and inscribed monolith at—	,,	97	XXXII.
Chandra Deva Ráthor, Rájá—			
Wrested Kanauj from Tomar dynasty about A.D. 1050	I	151	. . .
Chandra Gupta of Kosala—			
Mentioned in Sirpur inscription	XVII	17	. . .
Chandra Gupta Maurya—			
= Sandracottus of Greek writers	I	Intr. I.	. . .
Kingdom of, extended to Indus	II	41	. . .
Chandra Gupta I. (Early or Imperial Gupta Dynasty)—			
Gold coins of, with legends Kumárí Deví and 'Lichchhavayah'	I	Intr. XXXIV	. . .
Traditions possibly referring to—	XI	99	. . .
Chandra Gupta II. (Early or Imperial Gupta) Dynasty—			
Inscriptions of, at Udayagiri	X	49, 51	XIX.
Inscription, dated Samvat 131 of, at Sánchi . .	,,	59	. . .
Inscription probably of reign of, at Garhwá . .	III	55	XX.
Description of silver coins of—	IX	23	V.
Coin of reign of, found at Sultánganj with one of Swámi Rudra Sinha (Sena)	X	127	*
	XV	30	. . .
Gold coin of, found near Mahásthán in Bengal . .	,,	116	. . .

* In text this coin is erroneously ascribed to Chandra Gupta I.

	Vol.	Page.	Plate.
Chandra Sena, Rájá—			
Legends of—	VI	138	. . .
Chandrabhága R.—			
= Chenáb R.	II	193	. . .
Chandrávatí in Jhaláwár State, Rájputána—			
=Modern Jhálrá Pátan, and probably = Sandrabatis of Ptolemy	"	264, 270	. . .
Cast copper, and square silver coins found at—	"	"	. . .
Ruins at—	"	265	LXXV.
Inscription at, said by Tod to be dated in S. 748	"	"	. . .
Principal temple at—	"	266	LXXVI.
Pilgrims' records on temple at—	"	268	. . .
Inscription of 9th or 10th century A.D. at—	"	269	LXXVI.
Chandrehí in Rewá State, Baghelkhand—			
Temple and palace at—	XIII	6, 11	I—IV.
Chandrikápuri—			
A later name of Srávastí	XI	98	. . .
Character—			
See **Alphabet.**			
Charanádrigarh—			
See **Chunar in Mirzápur District.**			
Chárí in Kángra District, Panjáb—			
Temple and late Buddhist inscription at—	V	177, 178	XLII.
Charms—			
Used in demon-worship	XVII	149	. . .
Chársada or Hashtnagar near Peshávar, Panjáb—			
= Pushkalávatí, = Peukalaotis	II	90	. . .
Remains of ancient city at and near—	XIX	96—110	XXI, XXII.
Chása, or Fatehjang in Ráwal Pindi District, Panjáb—			
An ancient site	XIV	24	. . .
Chátna in Bánkurá District, Bengal—			
Inscriptions, dated Saka 1476 at—	VIII	199	. . .
Chátsú in Jaypur State, Rájputána—			
Kutila inscription at—	VI	116	. . .
Anciently named Champávatí	"	"	. . .

	Vol.	Page.	Plate.
Chaturbhuj in Tarái District, N.-W. P.—			
Extensive ruins not yet explored at—	II	239	. . .
Chauhán clan—			
Legends of origin of—	„	253	. . .
Chauhán Dynasty of Ajmerand Delhi—			
Lists of—	I	158	. . .
Chaumuhá in Mathurá District N.-W. P.—			
Buddhist remains at—	XX	52	. . .
Chaunsat Joginís—			
See **Joginis sixty-four.**			
Chechgaongarh in Chutiá Nagpur, Bengal—			
Fine temples and Jain inscription at—	VIII	157—159	. . .
Chedí era—			
See **Kalachuri (or Chedí) era.**			
Chedí, Kingdom of—			
Mr. Beglar's speculations concerning—	„	126	. . .
Mentioned in Mahábhárata	„	125	. . .
	IX	54, 76	. . .
Perhaps mentioned by Hwen Thsang	„	55	. . .
corresponds to Ptolemy's country of the Adisathri	„	56	. . .
Coins of Kalachuri dynasty of—	X	25	x.
Titles of Kalachuri (Haihaya) Kings of—	XVII	71	. . .
In 12th century apparently divided into two—	„	„	
Ratanpur, capital of northern section, and Tripuri of Dáhal, or western section of—	„	72	. . .
Distinct dynasties at different times in—	„	73	. . .
Traditional division of, about 1000 A.D. into principalities of Láphá and Ráipur	„	75	. . .
Inscriptions and genealogy of Haihaya Kings of, from 1000 to 1140 A.D.	„	75, 76	. . .
Division of northern section into two probably took place about 1400 A.D.	„	77	. . .
Full genealogy of Haihaya Rájás of Ratanpur or northern section of—	„	78	. . .
Genealogy of Haihaya Rájás of Ráipur section of—	„	80	. . .
Conquest of Kírtti Varmma Chandel by Karna Deva, King of—	II	453	. . .

	Vol.	Page.	Plate.
Chenáb R.—			
= Ancient Chandrabhága R.	II	193	. . .
Formerly joined Jhelam about 50 miles above present junction	"	38	. . .
Cheon in Gayá District, Bengal—			
Ruins at—	VIII	63, 64	. . .
Cherán in Sáran District, Bengal—			
An ancient site with inscription of Husen Sháh, King of Bengal	XXII	74, 79	. . .
Chero (Cheru) tribe—			
Traditions of, in Sháhábád District	XVI	60	. . .
in Sáran District	XXII	75	. . .
Conquered by Saura tribe in Sháhábád and Benares, A.D. 499	XVII	131, 132	. . .
Chetiyagiri of the Mahávanso—			
= Modern Besnagar	X	37	. . .
Chetiyaon in Gorakhpur District, N.-W.P.—			
Identified with Páwá of Buddhist legend . . .	XVIII	102	. . .
Ancient sites near—	XXII	35	v.
Chhattisgarh (*or*-ghar) Division in C. P.—			
Tradition of emigration of Chamárs from Bihár to— .	VII	225	. . .
The ancient Mahá Kosala	XVII	68	. . .
Probably = Ptolemy's country of the Adisathri . .	XXI	93	. . .
Chhorra in Mánbhúm District, Bengal—			
Ruins at—	VIII	182	. . .
Chhotá Deorí in (?) Panná State, Bundelkhand—			
Kalachuri inscription at—.	XXI	100, 158	XXVIII.
Chhotá Gandak R.—			
= Hirana *or* Hiranyavatí R.	VIII	25	. . .
Chillá in Alláhábád District, N.-W.P.—			
Ancient dwelling-house ascribed to Álhá and Udal at—	XXI	8	v.
China—			
Embassies between Bengal and, in 1408—15 A.D. .	XV	172	. . .

	Vol.	Page.	Plate.
Chíné in Amritsar District, Panjáb—			
= Chi-na-pote of Hwen Thsang	XIV	53	XVIII.
Ancient statue of Vishnu at—	XXI	134	. . .
Chinese—			
Accounts of Indo-Scythians	III	44	. . .
Chinese hostages of Kanishka—			
Resided at Chíné near Amritsar	XIV	53	. . .
Introduced pears and peaches into India . . .	"	54	. . .
Chistí—			
A family of Muhammadan saints	I	230	. . .
Chitaolí in Gwáliár State, Central India—			
Inscription of Rám Des Parihár at—	II	378	. . .
Chitor in Udaipur State, Rájputána—			
Coins of Sibi country found at—	XIV	146	XXXI.
Dr. Stratton's account of—	XXIII	101	. . .
Two long inscriptions at—	"	111	XXI, XXII.
Tod's account of—	"	107	. . .
Pillar of victory at—	"	113	XXIII.
Arabic inscriptions on above	"	116	. . .
Jain tower (*Chhotá Kirtain*) at—	"	117	. . .
Mokaljí temple at—	"	118	XXIV.
Sculptures of above	"	121	. . .
Singár Chaurí at—	"	123	XXV.
Chitrakúta (Chitrakot) hill in Bándá District, N.-W. P.—			
Described	XXI	10	. . .
Is the Chitrakuta of the Rámáyana	"	12*	. . .
Chitrángadápura, ancient capital of Chedi—			
Probably = Sageda metropolis of Ptolemy, = Sirpur or Srípura	XVII	69, 70	. . .
	XXI	93	. . .
Chobia of Ferishta—			
Sobii, Sobæ, or Sibæ of Greek and Roman writers .	II	27	. . .
Chobnáth Rájà—			
Capital of, at Barári (Bhurári) in Sháhpur District, Panjáb	"	37	. . .
Name of, perhaps Graecized as Sopeithes . . .	"	40	. . .

* For an erroneous identification by Mr. Beglar see XIII, 50.

	Vol.	Page.	Plate.
Chola (Choda) country—			
Mentioned in Sháhbázgarhi inscription of Asoka .	V	20	. . .
Cholera—			
Popularly ascribed to displeasure of Hardaur Lála .	XVII	163	. . .
Christian—			
Cemetery and chapel at Narwár	II	322	. . .
Chronology—			
See **Era.**			
Chunár (Charanádrigarh) in Mirzápur District, N.-W. P.—			
Ancient pilgrims' inscriptions near—	XI	127	XXXVIII.
	XXI	128	XXXII.
Chu-sha-si-lo (Chutyasira)—			
Fa-Hian's name for **Taxila**, *q.v.*	II	114	. . .
Cidaritæ, of Priscus—			
Probably = Katár tribe and people of Chitrál . .	„	79	. . .
Circles, rude stone—			
Found in hilly parts of districts of Delhi, Mirzápur, and Orissa, and in Shorapur District, Bombay .	I	Intr. xxx	. . .
At Deosá in Jaypur State	VI	104–108	XII.
Near Buddha Gayá ascribed to Kols . . .	VIII	66	. . .
Used in Rájputána for game of *táhar* or *ewáro* .	XXIII	49	. . .
Clisobora—			
See **Klisobora.**			
Coins, early Indian—			
Scale of weights of—	X	78	. . .
	XIV	17	. . .
Existed before invasion of Alexander the Great . .	„	„	. . .
Coins, classes of, found—			
At Bhurári in Sháhpur District, Panjáb . . .	V	96	. . .
Harapá in Montgomery District, Panjáb . .	„	108	. . .
Kosam (Kosámbi)	X	4	. . .
Mathurá	XX	37	. . .
Sankisa	XI	25	. . .
Sháhdheri (Taxila)	XIV	16	IX, X.
Shorkot in Jhang District, Panjáb	V	99	. . .
In Yusufzai country	„	6	. . .

	Vol.	Page.	Plate.
Coins, analysis of lists of—			
101 from Bairánt in Benares District . . .	XXII	114	. . . .
90 from Besnagar	X	37	. . . .
197 „ Bhon in the Salt Range	V	93	. . . .
150 „ Indor Khera	XII	40	. . . .
184 „ Janer in Fírozpur District	XIV	69	. . . .
61 „ Masaon Dih in Gházípur District . . .	XXII	103	. . . .
145 „ Nágarí in Mewár	VI	200	. . . .
85 „ Sultánpur in Jálandhar District . . .	XIV	57	. . . .
576 „ Sunit near Ludhiána	„	65	. . . .
Coins, autonomous, of ancient India—			
Description of ten kinds of—	„	135—151	XXXI.
From Pathánkot, with legend 'Odumbara' . .	„	„	. . . .
	V	154	XXXI.
Coins, ancient square—			
Four classes of, all found at Eran	X	77	XXIV.
Coins, ancient cast or moulded—			
From Bairát	II	249	. . . .
Chandrávatí	„	264	. . . .
Eran	X	77	. . . .
Indor Kherá	XII	41	. . . .
Coins, ancient die-struck—			
From Sháhdheri (Taxila) both of single and double die types	XIV	17—22	X.
From Eran, some being inscribed	X	79, 80	XXIV.
Coins, punch-marked—			
Antiquity of—	I	70	. . . .
	II	229,264,288	. . . .
Classified by Mr. Carlleyle	VI	213—220	. . . .
Description of Eran forms of—	X	77	XXIV.
Weights of —	XIV	16	. . . .
Found at Nágar and Nágarí in Jaypur State . .	VI	179—198	. . . .
At Indor Kherá	XII	40 *	. . . .
Coins, inscribed Kádasa, with snake—			
From Western Panjáb	II	10	. . . .
	VI	167	. . . .
Coins of the Tochari and of Kapisa—			
Described by Hwen Thsang	II	79	. . . .
Coins of Buddhist Satraps—			
Description and find-spots of—	III	39, 40	. . . .
	XI	25, 28	. . . .
	XII	41	. . . .
	XIV	57	. . . .

* Punch-marked coins are so common that it has not been thought worth while to index all the notices of their find-spots.

	Vol.	Page.	Plate.
Coins, of Multán—			
With figure of Sun-god	V	121—123	XXXVIII.
Coins, of Azes, Gondophares, Arsaces, &c.—			
Discussion of arrangement of—	II	59—61	. . .
Coins, Indo-Sassanian—			
From Bhitarí in Gházípur District	I	97	. . .
Indor Kherá	XII	44, 68	. . .
Nágarí and Chitor in Mewár	VI	200, 207	. . .
Description of degraded forms of—	XI	176	. . .
Coins, Indo-Scythian (early, of Su horde)—			
Divisible into three classes	II	58	. . .
Coins, Indo-Scythian (later)			
Range of find-spots of—	XI	67	. . .
Of the Kadphises Kings	II	67, 69	. . .
From Bairát	,,	249	. . .
Bhuilá in Basti District	XII	165	. . .
Depálpur in Panjáb	V	110	. . .
Indor Kherá in Bulandshahr District	XII	43	. . .
Jaugada in Ganjám District	XIII	116	. . .
Kanhiára near Kángra	V	177	. . .
Khairá Dih in Balliá District	XXII	108	. . .
Sahegarh in Alígarh District	XII	10	. . .
Sahri-Bahlol in Yusufzai	V	45	. . .
Coins, of Hindu Kings of Kábul—			
Common in Yusufzai and Panjáb	,,	45,83,156	. . .
Coins, of Kángra—			
Names on—	,,	152	. . .
Coins, Roman—			
Sold in large quantities at Ráwal Pindí	II	148	. . .
Found in No. 2 *stúpa* at Mánikyála	,,	162	. . .
Singhbhúm District, Bengal	XIII	72	. . .
Colebrooke, H.			
Importance of essays of—	I	Intr. III	. . .
Condochates R. of Pliny—			
= Candak R.	VIII	VI	. . .
Constantine, Emperor—			
Coins of, found in Singhbhúm District, Bengal	XIII	72	. . .

	Vol.	Page.	Plate.
Copper—			
Used as a bolt in Rámpurwá pillar of Asoka	XVI	113	. . .
Copper celt—			
Found at Mathurá	III	16	.
Copper Mines—			
At Bairát in Rájputána	II	245	. . .
Court, General—			
Excavated *stúpa* at Máni kyála	"	161	. . .
Cowries—			
Used in Indian currency	X	78	. . .
	XIV	17	. . .
Sole deposit in Ságardih *stúpa*	XVI	Pref. VII	. . .
Found in earthen barrow at Lauriyá	"	104	. . .
Creed, Buddhist—			
Translation of, by Hodgson and Burnouf	I	111	. . .
Crocodile—			
Symbol of Ganges river	X	49	. . .
Cromlech—			
See **Dolmen and Circles, rude stone.**	. . .	. . .	. . .
Cross-roads—			
The proper site for memorial to a Chakravarttí Rájá	I	66	. . .
Cunningham, Major-General Sir A.—			
Memorandum by, on establishment of Archæological Survey Department	I	Pref. iii-vii	. . .
List of writings of, on Indian antiquities to 1870	"	Intr. XXXVI	. . .
Retracts former opinion as to certain Kings of Magadha following the Guptas	"	" XL	. . .
Began work as Archæological Surveyor in 1861	"	" XLI	. . .
Cutis (? Cuphis) of Pliny—			
= Kophes, capital of Arachosia	II	45	. . .
D.			
Dacæ and Dahæ of Strabo—			
Speculations concerning—	II	48	. . .
Dacca—			
See **Dhákká.**			

	Vol.	Page.	Plate.
Dáhai—			
A name of kingdom of **Chedí**, *q.v.*	IX XXI	106 IV	. . . . . .
Dáhi in Bijáwar State, Bundelkhánd—			
Copperplate inscription of Víra Varmma Chandel from—	II XXI	455 74	. . . . . .
Dahmerí (Dahmbeorí)—			
= Audumbara, = Núrpur State, in Panjáb . .	XIV	116	. . .
Dalaki-wa-malaki, Ráná—			
Perhaps chief of Kosámbi	XVII	91	. . .
Identified with Dalakeswar and Malakeswar, Baghel chiefs of Bándhogarh	II XXI	445 103	. . . . . .
Dallá-Sultánpur—			
See **Sultánpur (Dallá) in Jálandhar District.**			
Dálmau in Rái Barelí District, Oudh—			
Legends of—	XI	60	. . .
Dalmi—			
See **Dulmi in Mánbhum District, Bengal.**			
Damoh in Damoh District, C. P.—			
Inscriptions at—	XXI	168	. . .
Dand-Bihár—			
Ancient name of **Bihar City,** *q.v.*	VIII	75	. . .
Dángí Rájputs—			
A clan near Ságar	X	28	. . .
Daniell, F.—			
Drawings of Pagodas at Mahámallaipur by— . .	I	Intr. vi	. . .
Dantalok, Mount—of Hwen Thsang—			
= Kárámár hill at Shahbázgarhi	V	17	. . .
Danui—			
A mis-spelling for **Dinai in Hamírpur District,** *q.v.*			
Dápthu in Patna District, Bengal—			
Remains at, described byBuc hanan and Broadley .	VIII	74	. . .
Dárápur—			
See **Diláwar (Dárápur) in Jhelam District, Panjáb.**			

	Vol.	Page.	Plate.
Daraulí in Sháhábád District, Bengal—			
Obelisks at—	XIX	25	...
Imperfect inscription at—	"	26	...
Darbhanga District, Bengal—			
Included in ancient Mithila	XVI	34	...
Daryápur-Parvatí in Patna District, Bengal—			
Buddhist remains at—	VIII	108	...
Hill called Garh Paráwat at—	"	113	...
Hoard of gold coins found near—	"	110	...
Dasaratha, grandson of Asoka—			
Inscriptions of, in Nágárjuní caves	I	49—51	XX.
Dasaratha Játaka—			
The basis of the story of the Rámáyana	XXI	11	...
Dasárna territory—			
Position of—	XX	2	...
Date of buildings—			
Indications of, from coins, masons' marks, and pilgrims' records	V	72	...
Daundiá Kherá in Unao District, Oudh—			
Capital of the Bais Rájputs	I	296	...
Davis, Samuel—			
Wrote on Hindu astronomy and the Jovian Cycle	"	Intr. ii	...
Debar Dighi in Dinájpur District, Bengal—			
A tank probably constructed by Rájá Deva Pála, with a pillar, perhaps of Asoka, at—	XV	122	...
Deer-park of Buddhist legend—			
At Sárnáth, near Benares	I	106, 107	...
Delhi—			
Extent of ruins of—	"	132	XXXV.
Seven forts of old—	"	134	...
Distinct from Indraprastha	"	"	...
Traditions of foundation of—	"	137	...
Rebuilt by Anang Pál Tomar, A.D. 736	"	144	...
Not a capital previous to 736 A.D.	"	145	...
Probably included in kingdom of Kanauj, A.D. 915	"	146	...
List of Tomar dynasty of—	"	148	...

	Vol.	Page.	Plate.
Delhi—*contd.*			
Rebuilt by Anang Pál II., about A.D. 1052 . .	I	152	. . . .
Lál kot of Anang Pál II., at—	„	152, 180	XXXVI.
Captured by Chauháns about A.D. 1151 . . .	„	156	. . .
Lists of Chauhán dynasty of—	„	158	. . .
Captured by Muhammadans, A.D. 1191 . . .	„	160 *Note*	. . .
Two edict pillars of Asoka at—	„	161—167	. . .
	V	143	XLI.
	XIV	78	. . .
Iron pillar at—*	I	169	. . .
Inscription of Rájá Dháva (Bháva) on Iron pillar at—	„	140, 170	. . .
Other inscriptions on Iron pillar at—.	„	175	. . .
Legends concerning ditto at—.	XX	129—142	. . .
27 temples destroyed to build Kutb mosque at— .	I	178	. . .
	IV	v	. . .
Fort of Rái Pithorá at—	I	183	. . .
Kutb mosque at, described	„	185—189	. . .
Controversy as to Hindu or Muhammadan origin of Kutb Mínár at—	„	189	. . .
	IV	x, xv	. . .
Dimensions of Kutb minár at—	I	193—204	. . .
Tomb of Emperor Iltitmish at—	„	204	. . .
Alá-ud-dín's gateway at—	„	„	. . .
Alá-ud-dín's *minár* at—	„	205	. . .
Identification of fort of Siri, and Alá-ud-dín's palace of 1,000 pillars at, with Sháhpur	„	207	. . .
Fort of Tughlakábád at—	„	212	. . .
Tomb of Tughlak Sháh at—	„	213	. . .
Fort of Ádilábád or Muhammadábád at— . . .	„	217	. . .
Jahánpanáh fortifications and 52 gates of— . .	„	218	. . .
City of Fírúzábád at—	„	219	. . .
Black mosque at—	„	220	. . .
Citadel known as Shergarh or Purána Kila at— . .	„	221	. . .
Fort of Salímgarh at—	„	223	. . .
Tomb of Humáyún at—	„	„	. . .
City of Sháhjahánábád at—	„	224	. . .
Statues of Chitor chiefs mounted on elephants at— .	„	225	. . .
Plans and sections of buildings at—	IV	. . . .	I—X.
List of noticeable buildings at—	„	78	. . .
Minor remains near—	I	230	. . .
	XX	142—161	. . .
Tomb of Fíroz Sháh Tughlak near—	„	151	XXXIV.
Demon-worship in Northern India—			
Originated among the aboriginal races	XVII	132	. . .
Now practised by all classes of Hindus	„	140	. . .
Definition of—	„	141	. . .

* The Iron Pillar is situated in village of Meharauli (Mihirapuri). (*Corpus Inscr. Ind. III, p. 139.*)

	Vol.	Page.	Plate.
Demon-worship in Northern India—*contd.*			
Ceremonies of—	XVII	144	. . .
Instances of—	„	143, 145, 148	. . .
Shrines of—	„	146	XXXIV.
Charms used in—	„	149	. . .
Antiquity of—	„	157	. . .
Gúgá Chauhán, Harshu Bábá, and Hardaur Lála, most conspicuous examples of—	„	158	. . .
Deo-Balodá in Ráipur District, C. P.—			
Saiva temple at—	„	4	III.
Deo-Barnárak in Sháhábád District, Bengal—			
Anciently named Várunika-gráma	XVI	64	. . .
Monolith of Gupta period at—	„	65	XXIV.
	XIX	20	. . .
Brick temples at—	XVI	68	XXII, XXIII.
	XIX	20	IV—VIII.
Inscription of Jívita Gupta at—	XVI	68, 73	XXIV—XXVI.
Sculptures at—	„	71	. . .
Worship of sun at—	„	72	. . .
Deogarh in Lalitpur District, N.-W. P.—			
Description of—	X	100	. . .
Inscription of Bhoja Deva, dated Samvat 933 and Saka 784 at—	„	101	XXXIII.
Short inscription in Gupta characters at—	„	102	. . .
Inscription of Kírtti Varmma Chandel, dated Samvat 1154 at—	„	„	„
Sundry mediæval Jain temples at—	X	104	. . .
Temple in late Gupta style at—	„	„	XXXIV—XXXVI.
Deogarh—Baijnáth—			
See **Baijnáth (Vaidyanath) in Sháhábád District, Bengal.**			
Deokalli in Muzaffarpur District, Bengal—			
Old temple at—	XVI	29	. . .
Deokhat in Ráipur District, C. P.—			
Temples and sculptures at—	VII	146	. . .
Deoli near Sápharan in Bengal—			
Jain remains at—	VIII	189	. . .
Deo-Márkanda in Sháhábád District, Bengal—			
Age of temples at—	XVI	60	. . .
Descriptions of temples at—	„	61	XIX, XX.
Ancient temple at—	XIX	8	II.

	Vol.	Page.	Plate.
Deoriyá in Allahabad District—			
See **Bithá and Deoriyá—**			
Deosá in Jaypur State, Rájputána—			
Stone circles and ancient tombs at—	VI	104—108	XII.
Deotek in Chándá District, C. P.—			
Inscriptions at—	VII	124	. . .
Deotí in Jaypur State, Rájputána—			
Capital of Bargújar Rájás	VI	83	. . .
Depálpur in ? Lahore District, Panjáb—			
History of, from 13th to 15th century . . .	V	109	XXXIV.
Now nearly deserted		110	. . .
Derí-Sháhán—			
See **Sháhdheri in Ráwal Pindi District, Panjáb.**			
Deva Pála, King of Magadha—			
Inscription of his reign at Ghosráwa	I	38	. . .
	II	89	. . .
	XI	173	. . .
Other inscriptions of—	XV	151	. . .
Deva putra—			
Family title of Indo-Scythian kings	III	42	. . .
Deva Rájá—			
Inscription of, at Pehoa	II	225	. . .
	XIV	101	. . .
Devalabdhi, a Chandel prince—			
Inscriptions of, at Dudahi	X	95	XXXII.
Devikot (Deokot) in Dinájpur District, Bengal—			
Citadel of ancient city of Bánnagar	XV	"	. . .
Muhammadan remains and inscriptions at— . .	"	96—99	XXVIII.
Appears to be Sonitapura of Vishnu Purána. Numerous Hindu remains at—	"	100	. . .
Devthala between Dinájpur and Pandua, Bengal—			
Inscription of Bárbak Sháh A.H. 868 at— . .	XV	94	XXIII.
Statuette of Vishnu from—	"	95	XXVII.
Dewal and Deoriyá in the Pílibhít District, N.-W. P.—			
Site of ancient capital of the Báchhal Rájás . .	I	352	. . .
Inscription of Rájá Lalla, dated S. 1049, A.D. 992 at—	"	"	LI.
Dewalwára in Chándá District, C. P.—			
Caves at—	IX	135	. . .

	Vol.	Page.	Plate.
Dhákká (Dacca) in Dacca District, Bengal—			
Known as Bangála in 16th and 17th centuries . .	XV	127	. . .
Perhaps the *Tagma metropolis* of Ptolemy . .	„	„	. . .
Tomb of Bíbí Perí, daughter of Sháista Khán, at— .	„	128	XXXIV.
Dhamek—			
The proper name of great *stúpa* at Sárnáth . .	I	105	. . .
Suggested derivation of name	„	113	. . .
	III	121	. . .
Dimensions of *stúpa*	I	107, 110	. . .
Slab inscribed with Buddhist creed found in *stúpa* .	„	111	. . .
The *stúpa*, a memorial, not a relic, tower . . .	„	112	
See **Benares, Sárnáth near—**			
Dhamnár in Central India—			
Buddhist caves at—	II	270—276	LXXVII—LXXXI.
Brahmanical rock temples at—	„	276—279	LXXXII, LXXXIII.
Inscription dated S. 1363 = A.D. 1306 at— . .	„	279	. . .
Dhamtarí in Ráipur District, C. P.—			
Group of temples at	VII	143	. . .
Inscribed *satí* pillar and statue at—	„	145	. . .
Dhana Deva—			
Coins of, found at Ayodhyá	I	319	. .
Coins of (?) found at Masáon Dih in Gházípur District	XXII	99	. . .
Dhand or Ghár in Jaypur State, Rájputána—			
A very ancient site	VI	160	. . .
Dhandora in Karaulí State, Rájputána—			
Curious *báolí* at—	XX	92	. . .
Dhanga Deva, Chandel King—			
A powerful prince	II	451	. . .
Khajuráho inscriptions of—	XXI	65—67	XVI.
Dhanpur in Pendra chief's territory, C. P.—			
Extensive Jain and Hindu ruins at—	VII	237	. . .
Dharáwat hills in Gayá District, Bengal—			
Maps of—	I	. . .	XVIII.
	XVI	. . .	XI.

	Vol.	Page.	Plate.
Dharáwat hills in Gayá District, Bengal—*contd.*			
Buddhist remains at—	I	54	. . .
Anciently called Dharmmapura	VIII	39	. . .
Site of Gunamatí monastery	„	„	. . .
	XVI	„	. . .
Ruins of—	VIII	38	. . .
	XVI	40	XII.
Seals and punch-marked coin found at— . . .	„	45	XIII.
Antiquity of—	„	46	. . .
Dharma Pála, King of Bengal—			
Inscription at Buddha Gayá fixing date of— . . .	XV	111	. . .
Dharmáranya in Balliá District, N.-W. P.—			
Perhaps site of a monastery mentioned by Fa-Hian and Hwen Thsang	XXII	84	VIII.
Dhaulí in Katák District, Orissa—			
Asoka's edict inscription at—	XIII	95	. . .
Small early inscription at—	„	96	. . .
Dháva, Rájá—			
A various reading for **Bháva Rájá**, *q.v.*	I	171	. . .
Dholpur in Dholpur State, Rájputána—			
Tomb of Bíbí Zarína near—	XX	113	XXXVII.
Dhopápapapura in Sultánpur District, Oudh—			
A place of pilgrimage on Gumtí river . . .	I	315	. . .
Dhruvabhata—			
Discussion of date of—	IX	16	. . .
Dhundhár—			
Ancient name of Jaypur State	II	251	. . .
Diamond—			
Of Rájá of Gwáliár, probably the Kohinúr . .	„	390	. . .
Diamond mines—			
At Panná in Bundelkhand	VII	45	. . .
At Wairágarh in C. P.	„	129	. . .
Dighwá-Dubaolí in Sáran District, Bengal—			
Pyra midal mounds ascribed to the Cherús at— . .	XXII	73	. . .

	Vol.	Page.	Plate.
Diláwar (Dárápur) in Jhelam District, Panjáb—			
The capital of Karlukí princes	II	19	. . .
Also named Udamnagar or Udinagar	,,	175	. . .
Extensive ruins at—	,,	176	. . .
Ancient coins abundant at—	,,	,,	. . .
Probably Bukephala	,,	186	. . .
Dildárnagar in Ghází́pur District, N.-W. P.—			
Formerly named Akhandha	III	63	. . .
Dillí—			
See **Delhi.**			
Dilwárí in Barelí District, N.-W. P.—			
Inscription of Gupta period at—	I	264	XLIV.
Dinai in Hamírpur District, N.-W. P.—			
Hindu and Jain temples and inscribed Jain statue at—	VII	40	I, IV.
Dínár—			
Used in inscriptions to denote Gupta gold coins . .	III	56	. . .
Dionysius, the Geographer—	X	10, 11, 27	. . .
Date of, probably 300—350 A.D.	II	26	. . .
Dog—			
Worship of, at Lohárú	XXIII	,,	. . .
Dolmens—			
Used as temples at Keljhar in C. P.	IX	140	XXV.
Dom tribe—			
Formerly powerful in Gorakhpur District . . .	XVIII	41	. . .
	XXII	66	. . .
Dongargarh in Ráipur District, C. P.—			
Site of ancient city Kamantípuri	XVII	2	. . .
Dosád—			
See **Dusád Caste.**			
Drachma coin—			
Represented by Indian *dramma*	XI	176	. . .
Was the model of coinage of Chandel and Haihaya kings	X	27	. . .
Drangiana—			
Part of kingdom of Kipin	II	45	. . .

	Vol.	Page.	Plate.
Dravidian Races—			
Affinities of—	IX	159	. . .
Drishadvatí, R.—			
= Modern Rákshí, R.	XIV	88	. . .
Drona stúpa—			
Perhaps situated between Árá and Patna	III	77	. . .
Drúg in Ráipur District, C. P.—			
An ancient Buddhist site, with inscriptions	XVII	3	II.
Dúbkund in Gwáliár State, C. I.—			
Inscription of Vikrama Sinha, dated S. 1145 = A.D. 1088 at—	XX	99	. . .
Jain temple at—	,,	100	XX.
Other inscriptions at—	,,	102	,, XXII.
Dudahi—			
The capital of southern half of Lalitpur District, N.-W. Provinces	X	90	. . .
Ruins at, ascribed to Rájá Jálandhar Chandel	,,	91	. . .
Jain temple of unusual plan and temple of Brahmá at—		93	XXXI.
Pilgrim's inscriptions at—	,,	94	XXXII.
Six inscriptions of Devalabdhi, grandson of Rájá Yaśo Varmma Chandel, at—	,,	95	,,
Second group of temples at—	,,	,,	. . .
Dulhá Deva—			
Worship of—	XVII	166	XXXIV.
Dulmi (Dyápar-Dulmi) in Mánbhúm District, Bengal—			
Numerous remains at—	VIII	186	XVII.
Ancient city at, 4 miles long	,,	188	. . .
Perhaps included in kingdom of Kirná Suvarna, mentioned by Hwen Thsang	,,	51, 191	. . .
Dund—			
A hill tribe west of the Jhelam	II	13	. . .
Durgá-kho in Mirzápur District, N.-W. P.—			
Short inscriptions in caves at—	XXI	128	XXXII.
Durgápur in Rewá State, Baghelkhand—			
Imperfect inscription at—	XIII	6	. . .

	Vol.	Page.	Plate.
Durgávatí, queen of Singorgarh—			
History of—	II IX	458 50	. . . . . .
Dusád (Dosád) caste—			
Legend of Rájá Sales in Tirhút	XVI	28	. . .
of Báwan Gangá in Bihár	VIII	102	. . .
E			
Ekachakra—			
Ancient name of Ará (Arrah)	III	73	. . .
One of the capital cities of India in time of Buddha	„	77, *Note*	. . .
Ekbolima—			
See **Embolima.**			
Ekteswar in Bánkurá District, Bengal—			
Laterite temple at—	VIII	200	. . .
Elápatra, a Nága king—			
Tank of, identified with spring at Hasan Abdál	II	135	. . .
Elephanta caves, in Bombay Harbour—			
Described by Erskine and Burgess	I	Intr. VI	. . .
Elliot, Sir Walter—			
Collected 595 inscriptions in, and elucidated history of, Southern India	„	„ XXIX	. . .
Embolima of Arrian—			
Probably = Ohind, according to Cunningham	II	101—103	. . .
= Amb-balima, 8 miles east of Mahában, according to Abbott	„	102	. . .
Empalathra of Ptolemy—			
Identified with Mahobá	X XXI	99 58, 92	. . . . . .
Ephthalites—			
= White Huns (*q.v.*) Supposed derivation of name	II	77, *Note*	. . .
Era of Balabhi—			
See **Era of Valabhi.**			

	Vol.	Page.	Plate.
Era, Bengali—			
= Saka plus 715, used at Bishanpur in Bengal .	VIII	205	. . .
„ **Burmese—**			
Based on Nirvána of Buddha	„	2, 3	. . .
„ **Chedí—**			
***See* Kalachuri era.**			
„ **Gupta—**			
***See* Gupta era—**			
„ **of Harsha Vardhana—**			
Began A.D. 607	I	282	. . .
„ **Kalachuri—**			
***See* Kalachuri era.**			
„ **of Lakshmana Sena—**			
Began in 1107 A.D.	XV	160	. . .
„ **Lok-kál of Káshmír—**			
= Sástrí era	XXI	36	. . .
„ **Malla—**			
***See* Malla era—**	. .	. . .	. . .
„ **of Nirvána—**			
***See* Nirvana, era of—**			
„ **Saka—**			
Speculations as to origin of—	III	45	. . .
„ **Sástrí—**			
A synonym for Lok-kál of Káshmír . . .	XXI	36	. . .
„ **Valabhi (Balabhi)—**			
Began in A.D. 319	IX	20	. . .
„ **of Vikrama—**			
***See* Vikrama era.**			
Eran (Erakaina) in Ságar District, C. P.—			
Position of, described	X	76	XXIII.
Temples of Gupta period at—	„	81	XXV—XXX.
Inscribed monolith of Budha Gupta at— . . .	VII	88	. . .
	X	81	XXIV.

	Vol.	Page.	Plate.
Eran (Erakaina) in Ságar District, C.P.—*contd.*			
Boar with inscription of Toramána at—	VII	89	. . .
	X	83, 84	. . .
(Varáha) temple at—	,,	,,	XXVII
Toran at—	,,	,,	XXVIII
Temple of Vishnu at—	,,	85	XXV, XXVI, XXIX
Inscribed statue of Vishnu at—	,,	87	. . .
Narsinha temple at—	,,	88	XXV, XXX
Long inscription of Samudra Gupta at— . . .	,,	89	. . .
Inscription of Mádhava and Bhánu Gupta, dated Samvat 191 at—	,,	,,	. . .
Various *satí* monuments near—	,,	89, 90	. . .
Ancient square coins of four classes found at— . .	,,	77	XXIV
Copper coins with name of city, found at— . .	XIV	149	XXXI
Erannoboas, R.—			
Of Pliny and Arrian, = the Son, and not the Gandak .	VIII	VI	. . .
Eukratides, King of Bactria—			
Scythian imitations of *oboli* of—	II	59	. . .
Euphorion—			
Alludes to Maurya Dynasty	I	Intr. XLI	. . .
Eusufzai—			
See **Yusufzai.**			
Euthydemus, King of Bactria—			
Scythian imitations of tetradrachms of—	II	58	. . .
Euthymedia *or* **Sagala of Ptolemy**—			
? = Sakhrá, *or* ? Abriyán	,,	153, 173	. . .
Ewáro—			
A synonym of **táhar,** *q.v.*	. .	. . .	. . .

F

	Vol.	Page.	Plate.
Fa-Hian, Chinese traveller—			
Map of route of—	I	. . .	I
Began his journey in 399 A.D.	II	84	. . .
Gives accurate geographical notes	,,	,,	. . .
Faizábád in Faizábád District, Oudh—			
Capital of early Nawábs of Oudh to 1775 A.D. .	I	321	. . .

	Vol.	Page.	Plate.
Fatehábád in Agra District, N.-W. P.—			
Scene of Aurangzeb's victory over Dárá . . .	IV	195	. . .
Fatehábád in Sirsá District, Panjáb—			
Pillar at, inscribed with genealogy of Fíroz Sháh Tughlak	XXIII	11	II.
Inscription of Humáyún at—	"	"	III.
Humáyún's mosque at—	"	12	IV.
Fatehjang—			
See **Chása, or Fatehjang, in Ráwal Pindi District, Panjáb.**			
Fázilnagar in Gorakhpur District, N.-W. P.—			
Identified with Páwá of Buddhist legend . . .	XVIII	102	. . .
Fergusson, J.—			
Archæological work of—	I	Intr. xix	. . .
		xxiv	. . .
Excessive estimate of value of architectural style as evidence of dates by—	"	" xx	. . .
Correct chronology of mediæval temples of Brahmans and Jains fixed by—	"	" xxii	. . .
Complete and comprehensive classification of Indian styles of architecture by—	"	" "	. . .
Erroneous dates for Kánharí and Kárle caves, and Amarávatí *stúpa* adopted by—	"	" xx	. . .
		xxiii	. . .
The serpent-worship theory of, controverted . .	"	" xxiv	. . .
Erroneous opinion of, respecting date of Buddha Gayá temple	VIII	60, 71	. . .
Fire worship—			
In India	XII	68	. . .
Fíroz Tughlak, emperor—			
Public works at Delhi and elsewhere of—	I	218	. . .
Set up both the Asoka pillars at Delhi . . .	V	143	. . .
Alleged visit to Jwálá-mukhi of—	"	172—175	. . .
Proselytising and intolerance of, in Mewát . . .	XX	11, 14, 132	. . .
Tomb of, near Delhi	"	151	XXXIV.
Inscription of, dated 753 A.H. = A.D. 1352 at Sháhpur near Delhi	"	153	XXXI.
Genealogy of, on pillar at Fatehábád . . .	XXIII	11	II.
Fírozábád—			
A town in Agrá District	IV	192	. . .
A name of Panduá in Máldáh District	XV	80, *Note*	. . .

	Vol.	Page.	Plate.
Fírozábád, at Delhi—			
Described	I	219	. . .
Fírozpur—			
A suburb of Gaur	XV	73	. . .
Fírozpur-Jhirká in Gurgaon District, Panjáb—			
A Mewátí stronghold	XX	127	. . .
Temple in Bengal style at—	"	128	XXVIII.
Flint implements—			
See **Stone implements.**			
Fo-leu-Sha of Fa-Hian—			
= **Peshávar**, *q.v.*	II	87	. . .
Footstools, stone—			
See **Stools, stone.**			
Fyzábád—			
See **Faizábád in Faizábád District, Oudh.**			
G			
Gájípur (Gajnípur)—			
Ancient name of Ráwal Pindí cantonments . .	II	20, 152	. . .
Gákar tribe in N. Panjáb—			
Probably of Scythian origin	"	23	. . .
Perhaps a colony of Abárs, who came from Hyrcania in time of Darius Hystaspes, or earlier . . .	"	31	. . .
Occupied Abhisára district, under a king named Abisares by Greek writers	"	23, 28, 29	. . .
Attacked Mahmúd of Ghazní, A.D. 1008 . . .	"	24	. . .
Probably = Gargaridæ of Dionysius, &c. . . .	"	25	. . .
According to tradition sent into Panjáb by Afrásiyáb of Turán	"	29, 31	. . .
Earliest capital of, at Abriyán on the Jhelam . .	"	" "	. . .
Ganda Deva, Chandel King—			
Submitted to Mahmúd of Ghazní	"	452	. . .
Khajuráho inscription of—	XXI	66, 68	XVIII.
Gandak R.—			
= Condochates of Pliny	VIII	VI	. . .
Changes in channel of—	XVI	I	. . .

	Vol.	Page.	Plate.
Gándhára *or* Lower Kábul Valley—			
Map of—	II	...	LIV.
Ohind capital of, till A.D. 1026	XIV	94	...
Last Hindu dynasty of—	V	82	...
Gangá Ráo—			
Cenotaph of, at Mandor in Jodhpur State	XXIII	75	XVI, XVII.
Gangádwárá—			
A name of Haridwár	II	231	...
Ganges R.—			
Called Holung by a Chinese writer	VIII	XI	...
Falling in of bank of, about 750 A.D.	"	XII	...
Affected by change in course of Son R.	"	XII, 23	...
Statue of, characteristic of Gupta style of architecture	IX	43, 70	...
Crocodile, the symbol of—	X	49	...
Sanctity of northerly bends of—	XV	20	...
Gangetic Provinces—			
Map showing routes of Fa-Hian and Hwen Thsang in—	I	...	I
Gánggeya Deva, King of Chedi—			
Coins of—	IX	106	...
	X	25	X.
Inscription of, at Piáwan in Rewá State	XIX	71	XVIII.
	XXI	113	XXVIII.
Gaorára in Chándá District, C. P.—			
Caves and temples at—	IX	134	XXIII, XXIV.
Garaios R. of Arrian—			
= Panj Kara R. in Yusufzai	V	3	...
Gargaridæ of Dionysius—			
Perhaps = Gákar tribe	II	25	...
Garhá ká Kot—			
An old site in Azamgarh District	XXII	106	XI.
Garhá Mandala in Jabalpur District, C. P., Gond dynasty of—			
Sleeman's list of—	XVII	52	...
Corrected chronology of—	"	51	...
Extent of dominions of—	"	53	...

	Vol.	Page.	Plate.
Garhwá in Alláhábád District, N.-W. P.—			
General description of—	III	53	. . .
Inscriptions of (?) Chandra Gupta and Kumára Gupta at—	"	55	XX.
	X	9, 10	V.
Colossal statues of Brahmá, Vishnu, and Siva, with inscriptions at—	III	56	XX.
Group of Vaishnava statues at—	"	57	. . .
Pilgrims' inscriptions, dated S. 1199 = A.D. 1142, on temple at—	"	58	XXI.
Statue of Rájá on horse-back at—	"	60	. . .
Inscription of Skanda Gupta, dated 140 at— . .	X	11	V.
Architecture and sculpture of Gupta period at— .	"	11—15	VI, VII.
Gauda (Gaura) in Oudh—			
=The Gonda District	I	327	. . .
Probably gave name to Gauda Brahmans and Tágas .	"	328	. . .
Mayúradhwaja and other kings of—	"	329	. . .
Gauda (Gaura), Western—			
Comprised the Betul, Chhindwára, Seoní, and Mandala Districts, C. P.	IX	150	. . .
Also known as Kosala (Western)	"	151	. . .
Notices of, in the Chand-Ráisá	"	152	. . .
Invasion of, by Rájya Vardhana, and Harsha Vardhana of Kanauj	"	154	. . .
Gupta dynasty of, included Sasángka Narendra Gupta	"	156	. . .
Inhabited by Sábaras in time of Sasángka	"	157	. . .
First mentioned in inscription, dated Saka 739 = A.D. 808	XVII	124	. . .
Gaur (Gauda) city in Máldáh District, Bengal—			
Map of—	XV	. . .	XIII.
Capital of the Sen Rájás and the Muhammadan Governors of Bengal	"	39	. . .
Founded by Ballál Sen	"	41	. . .
Named Lakhnautí (Lakshmanavatí) towards end of Hindu rule	"	43	. . .
Described by historian Minháj, who lived there after 1243 A.D.	"	"	. . .
Occupied by Bakhtiyár Khiljí in 1198 A.D. . .	"	"	. . .
Captured by Násir-ud-dín Mahmúd, son of Iltitmish, in 1227 A.D.	"	44	. . .
Inscription of reign of Iltitmish at—	"	45	XX.
Capital of kings of Bengal from 1284 A.D. to 1326 A.D.—	"	46	. . .
Seat of Government transferred from— to Hazrat Pandua by Sikandar	"	"	. . .

	Vol.	Page.	Plate.
Gaur (Gauda) city in Máldáh District, Bengal—*contd.*			
Again made capital of Bengal by Mahmúd I in A.D. 1442	XV	46	. . .
Existing buildings at—belong to century between A.D. 1442 and Sher Sháh	"	"	. . .
Description of ruins of—	"	41, 46 *seqq.*	. . .
No Hindu remains at—	"	42	. . .
Great pestilence in 1575 A.D. at—	"	47	. . .
Gradually deserted after the pestilence	"	48	. . .
Cleared of jungle in 1879 A.D.	"	"	. . .
Three groups of ruins at—	"	49	. . .
The citadel of—described	"	50	XIV.
Kadam-Rasúl mosque at—	"	54	XIX.
So-called 'Jail' at—	"	55	. . .
Inscribed bridge at—	"	57	XX.
Fíroza or Chirágh Mínár at—	"	"	. . .
Chámkatti mosque at—	"	60	XVIII.
Thántipura mosque at—	"	61	XVI, XVII.
Lathan (*Nathan*) mosque at—	"	62	XVIII.
Gunmant mosque at—	"	65	XIX.
Bará Soná mosque at—	"	66	XV.
Kotwálí gate at—	"	69	. . .
Tomb of Shekh Akhi Siráj near—	"	70	. . .
Janjaniya mosque at—	"	73	. . .
Chhotá Soná " "	"	"	. . .
College with inscription of Yúsuf Sháh at— . . .	"	76	XXII.
Muhammadan inscriptions at—	"	. . . .	XX.—XXIII.
Gaura in Partábgarh District, Oudh—			
Temple of Sun of 8th or 9th century A.D. at— . .	XI	70	. . .
Gávan in Jodhpur State, Rájputána—			
Curious stone tower at—	XXIII	72	. . .
Gayá City in Gayá District, Bengal—			
Statues and inscriptions numerous, but no ancient buildings now standing at—	I	1	. . .
Inscription dated in era of Nirváṇa (1819) at— . .	"	1, 3	. . .
	III	126	XXXV.
Long and well-preserved inscription in Krishna Dwárika temple at—	I	3	. . .
Temples of Súrya with inscriptions at—	"	"	. . .
	III	110, 112	XXXIII.
Brahmá-yoni hill near, with sculptures and inscriptions	I	3	. . .
Rámsila hill and temple near, with date 1071 Samvat .	"	4	. . .
Pretsila hill, a place of pilgrimage near— . . .	"	"	. . .
Temple of *Vishnu-pad* at—	III	108	. . .

	Vol.	Page.	Plate.
Gayá City in Gayá District, Bengal—*contd.*			
Akshay-bat and inscription at—	III	111	. . .
Sundry minor inscriptions at—	„	112	. . .
Inscriptions at and near—	I	34	. . .
	III	120—133	XXXV.—XXXIX.
Gayá District—			
Map of parts of—	I	. . .	III.
Gayá Karna Deva, Rájá—			
Of Kalachuri dynasty of Chedi	IX	87, 109	. . .
Gedrosia—			
A part of the kingdom of Kipin	II	45	. . .
Generation—			
Average length of Indian—	IX	101	. . .
Ghansor in Seoni District, C.P.—			
Brahmanical and Jain remains at—	VII	107, 108	. . .
Ghár—			
See **Dhand** *or* **Ghár in Jaypur State**—	. .	. . .	. . .
Ghatotkacha, king—			
Supposed to be mentioned in Tushám inscription	V	138	. . .
Gházípur District, N.-W. P.—			
Some ancient sites in—	XXII	87, 96	. . .
Discussion of Hwen Thsang's route through—	„	88	. . .
Ghazní—			
Minárs at—	I	194	. . .
Ghorí-Pathán, architecture—			
Described	III	8	. . .
Ghorpet in Chándá District, C. P.—			
Ruined temple at—	IX	136	XXIV.
Ghosráwá in Patna District, Bengal—			
Buddhist monastery at—	I	38, 39	. . .
	XI	171	XLIII.
Important Buddhist inscription of Deva Pála at—	I	38	. . .
	II	89	. . .
	XI	173	. . .
Sculptures found at—	„	175	. . .
Coins of Srí Vigraha [Pála] from—	„	174	. . .
of late Indo-Sassanian type from—	„	175	. . .

	Vol.	Page.	Plate.
Gilding—			
On buildings at Mánikyála	II	157, 171	. . .
On sculptures at Jamálgarhi, &c.	V	28, 46, 49	. . .
Ginjá Hill in Alláhábád District, N.-W. P.—			
Painted inscription in Indo-Scythian style at— . .	XXI	119	XXX.
Girivraja, the capital of Rájá Járasandha—			
A name of **Rájagriha,** *q.v.*	I	21	. . .
	III	141	. . .
Ditto, in Panjáb—			
Probably = Girjhák *or* Jalálpur in Jhelam District .	II	14	. . .
Giryek (Giriyák), in Patna District, Bengal—			
Extensive Buddhist ruins at—	I	16	XIV,
	III	149	XLIV.
Position and structure of the '*Járasandh-ká-Baithak*' *stúpa* at—	I	16—19	XV,
Corresponds to Fa-Hian's 'Hill of the Isolated Rock', and Hwen Thsang's '*Indra Sila-Guha*' hill . .	,,	18	. . .
	III	150	. . .
84 lac seals with Buddhist creed found at— . . .	I	17	. . .
'Vultures' cave' at—	,,	18, 20	. . .
Gobari, in Mahiyár State, Baghelkhand—			
Imperfect inscription at—	XXI	76	. . .
Gohána Kherá, in Alígarh District, N.-W. P.—			
Remains at—	XII	3	. . .
Gokal, in Mathurá District, N.-W. P.—			
Identified by Mr. Growse with Klisobora of Arrian .	XX	44	. . .
Gold leaf—			
See **Gilding.**			
Gomal R.—			
Perhaps = Saparnus R. of Arrian	II	32	. . .
Gomitra of Bárán—			
Coins of—	XIV	147	XXXI.
Gonarda III., King of Káshmír—			
Restored serpent-worship	II	10	. . .

	Vol.	Page.	Plate.
Gond dynasty of Garhá Mandala—			
Account of—	XVII	46—54	. . .
Gond race—			
The name probably means 'inhabitants of Western Gauda' (Kosala)	IX	151	. . .
Perhaps = Kondali or Gondali of Ptolemy . .	,,	,,	. . .
	XVII	124	. . .
Temples in Lalitpur and Central Provinces wrongly ascribed to—	IX	152	. . .
	XVII	34	. . .
Traditions of origin of, closely resemble those of the Turks and Mughals	IX	158	. . .
Call themselves Koitur	,,	151	. . .
	XVII	124	. . .
Gonda, in Bándá District, N.-W. P.—			
Chandel temples at—	XXI	13	VI.
Gonda District, in Oudh—			
Supposed to be the same as Gauda (Gaura) . .	I	327	. . .
Gondali—			
See **Kondali of Ptolemy.**	. .	. . .	. . .
Gondophares, king—			
= Gundoferus of Christian legends of St. Thomas .	II	60	. . .
	V	,,	. . .
Contemporary with Artabanus III. of Parthia . .	,,	,,	. . .
Reigned subsequently to Arsakes and Sanabares .	II	61	. . .
Successors of—	,,	60	. . .
	V	62	. . .
Inscription of, from Takht Bahi dated 103 . .	,,	59	. . .
Coins of, found in Panjáb and at Kábul . . .	II	59, 60	. . .
	XIV	48, 116	. . .
Gondwá, in Singhbhúm District, Bengal—			
Short ancient inscriptions at—	VIII	193	. . .
Gondwána—			
Used by Muhammadan writers to designate the wild tracts between Kándés and Orissa	IX	150	. . .
Gopála, King of Bengal—			
Mentioned in Nálanda inscription	I	36	. . .
Gorakhpur District, N.-W. P.—			
Modern copper-plate grants from—	XXII	61	. . .
Some ancient sites in—	,,	64—72*	. . .

* Some of the places named are in the Bastí District.

	Vol.	Page.	Plate.
Gordian, Roman Emperor—			
Coins of, found in Singhbhúm District, Bengal . .	XIII	72	. . .
Gotamiputra Satakarni—			
Inscriptions of, and of his successors . . .	I	Intr. xxi, xxiii	. . .
Perhaps identical with Sáliváhan or Sátaváhan . .	V	20	. . .
Sánchí gateway erected in reign of—	"	189	. . .
Govinda Chandra Deva, Rájá of Kanauj—			
Inscription of reign of, dated 1207 Samvat at Hathiyá-Dih	I	96	. . .
Govindgarh—			
The fort of Bhatinda in Patiála State . . .	XXIII	2	. . .
Govisana of Hwen Thsang—			
=Ujjain in Tarái District	"	252	. . .
Gowror (Gauror) in Ráipur District, C.P.—			
Ancient temples and Chálukya inscription at— . .	VII	139—142	XVIII.
Greek art—			
Influenced sculpture and architecture in Northern India	I	243	. . .
	V	189	. . .
Characters of, in Panjáb	"	V	. . .
Age of, in Panjáb 80 B.C.—100 A.D.	"	VI, 185	. . .
Traces at Buddhá Gayá of—	III	97, 100	XXVII—XXIX.
Greeks—			
Encountered Agnimitra on the Indus	II	41	. . .
Advanced to Ganges under Menander	"	"	. . .
Gugá Chauhán—			
Legend of, widely diffused in Northern India . .	XIV	81	. . .
	XVII	159	. . .
Songs in honour of—	XIV	84	. . .
Also known as Gugá Pír and Záhir Pír . . .	"	81	. . .
Guhila—			
Coins bearing name of, found at Agra	IV	95	. . .
Guhila Pati—			
Coin of, found at Narwár	"	96	. . .

	Vol.	Page.	Plate.
Gújar race—			
About half as numerous as Játs in the Panjáb; but not numerous elsewhere	II	4, 71, 81	. . .
Not Rájpúts, and are probably descendants of Yuchi or Tochari	„	70, 72, „	. . .
May have captured Valabhi in A.D. 523 . . .	„	„	. . .
Gunamati monastery of Hwen Thsang—			
Perhaps = Dharáwat in Gayá District, Bengal . .	VIII	39	. . .
Gunariá in Gayá District, Bengal—			
Buddhist and Hindu ruins at—	„	63	. . .
Gupta—			
Coins with name of Bhadra or Chandra, of earlier date than the Sungas	XXII	4	. . .
Gupta alphabet—			
See **Alphabet.**			
Gupta dynasty, Early or Imperial—			
Preceded, not followed, by the five kings of Magadha mentioned by Hwen Thsang	I	Intr. XL	. . .
Succeeded by Valabhi dynasty in W. India . .	IX	20	. . .
Oudh traditions probably referring to— . . .	XI	99	. . .
Pátaliputra, probably capital of —	„	153	. . .
Approximate proposed chronology of— . . .	IX	21	. . .
See **Gupta era.**			
List of kings of—	X	111	. . .
Names of queens of—	I	Intr. XXXIV	. . .
Professed Brahman religion	III	4	. . .
	X	52, 54	. . .
Gold coins of, known as *dínárs*	III	56	. . .
	X	10	. . .
Silver coins of, described	IX	21—26	v
One coin of, found in Panjáb	XIV	65	. . .
List of principal inscriptions of—	X	112	. . .
See **Budha Gupta, Chandra Gupta, Ghatotkacha, Kumára Gupta, Samudra Gupta, Skanda Gupta, and Alphabet.**			
Obelisk of period of, at Pathári	VII	67	. . .
at Katká	XXI	120	. . .
Remains of period of at Sultánganj	XV	30	. . .
See **Gupta style of architecture.**			

	Vol.	Page.	Plate.
Gupta dynasty, Later, of Eastern Magadha—			
Notices of—	III	136	. . .
Aphsar inscription of—	I	40	. . .
	IX	27	. . .
	XV	11	. . .
	XVI	79	. . .
List of inscriptions of—	„	60, 78	. . .
Genealogy of—	III	137	. . .
	XVI	79	. . .
Chronology of—	XV	166	. . .
Used era of Harsha	XVI	79	. . .
Certainly preceded Sasángka Narendra Gupta, A.D. 600	IX	28	. . .
Antagonistic to Maukharí dynasty of W. Magadha	XVI	80	. . .
Titles of kings of, terminate in—*áditya*	„	81	. . .
Gold coins of—	I	40 *Note*	. . .
	III	137	. . .
	XVI	81	. . .
Gupta dynasty, Later, of Mahákosala—			
Mentioned in inscriptions from the C. P.	VII	vi	. . .
	XVII	17, 85, 87	. . .
Gupta dynasty, Later, of Orissa—			
Perhaps identical with last—	„	„ „ „	. . .
Gupta dynasty, Later, of W. Gauda—			
In 600 A.D., descended from early Gupta dynasty	IX	156	. . .
Gupta era—			
Data for fixing initial point of—	„	16	. . .
A.D. 195, proposed as initial point of—	„	19 and Pref.	. . .
Discussion of Abú Rihán's account of—	„	20	. . .
Inscriptions of Rájá Hastin, &c., dated in—	„	9	IV.
A.D. 167, proposed as initial point of—	X	Pref. & App.	. . .
Gupta style of architecture—			
Derived from Indo-Persian style	V	186—189	. . .
	IX	44	. . .
Seven characteristics of—	„	42	. . .
	X	60	. . .
Supplies earliest known specimen of structural temple	„	„	XVI., XX.
Principal examples of—	IX	45	. . .
Bell capitals of—	X	61	. . .
Later development of—	„	110	. . .

	Vol.	Page.	Plate.
Gupta style of architecture—*contd.*			
Specimens of, at Besnagar	X	41	. . .
Bhitarí	I	99, 100	. . .
Bilsar	XI	17	VI.
Eran	X	81	XXV—XXX.
Garhwá	„	11—15	VI, VII.
Jhelam	XIV	42	. . .
Náchná	XXI	96, v	XXVII.
Pálí	XVI	52	. . .
Párolí	XX	105	XXIII.
Pataini Deví (?)	IX	31	VI.
Sánchi	X	60	. . .
Tigowá	IX	42, 45	IX—XI.
Udayagiri	X	48	XVIII.
Gupta Hari—			
Inscription of, at Sárnáth	I	123	XXXIV.
Gupta Godávarí R.—			
A sacred stream at Chitrakúta	XXI	13	. . .
Gurgaon in Gurgaon District, Panjáb—			
Pillar with inscription, dated (?) S. 729 at—	XX	138	X.
Gúrgí-Masán in Rewá State—			
Inscriptions from—	XIII	13, *Note.*	. . .
Tradition of Rájá Karan Dahariya at—	XXI	149	. . .
Description of ruins at—	XIX	85	XX.
	XXI	150	XXXV.
Numerous sculptures at—	„	153	. . .
Gurjjara Kingdom—			
In time of Hwen Thsang	II	70	. . .
In 9th century A.D.	„	71	. . .
Gushán tribe—			
See **Kushán.**			
Gwáliár in Gwáliár State, C. I.—			
General description of—	II	330	LXXXVI.
Names of six gates of fortress of—	„	333	. . .
Inscription of Bhoja Deva, dated S. 933 = A.D. 876 at—	„	335, 355	. . .
State prisons at—	„	339, 369	. . .
British assaults on—	„	„	. . .
Muhammadan sieges of—	„	340, 379	. . .
Tanks at—	„	341	. . .

	Vol.	Page.	Plate.
Gwaliár in Gwáliár State, C. I.—*contd.*			
Six palaces at—	III	346	. . .
Palace of Rájá Mán Singh at—	„	347	LXXXVII.
Muhammadan palaces at—	„	351	LXXXVIII.
Eleven temples at—	„	453	. . .
Temple of Sun at, probably destroyed by Iltitmish	„	„	. . .
Telí mandir temple at—	„	356	XC.
Sás báhu temple at—	„	357	LXXXIX, XC.
Inscription, dated S. 1150 = A.D. 1093 at—	„	„	. . .
Pilgrims' records on great *Sás báhu* temple at—	„	361	. . .
Jain temple with inscription, dated S. 1165 = A.D. 1108 at—	„	363	XC.
Inscription, dated S. 1161 = A.D. 1104 at—	„	364	. . .
Jain rock sculptures with inscriptions at—	„	„	. . .
Tomb of Muhammad Ghaus, saint at—	„	369	XCI.
Tomb of Tánsen, musician at—	„	370	. . .
Jámi masjid at—	„	„	. . .
Native annals of—	„	„	. . .
Probably founded in A.D. 275	„	372	. . .
Originally named Gopagiri or Gopachala	„	„	. . .
Legend of Súraj Sen of—	„	373	. . .
Kachhwáha Rájás of—	„	374	. . .
Story of Tej Karan Dulhá Rai of—	„	376	. . .
Parihár Rájás of—	„	378	. . .
Tomar „ „	„	382	. . .
Reign of Rájá Mán Singh of—	„	387	. . .
Fall of Tomar dynasty of—	„	388	. . .
Death at Pánipat of Vikramáditya, last Tomar Rájá of—	„	389	. . .
Great diamond of Rájá of—	„	390	. . .
Capital of Islám Sháh, A.D. 1546	„	393	. . .
Recent history of—	„	395	. . .
List of inscriptions connected with—	„	„	. . .
Gyárispur in C. I.—			
Temples and *stúpas* at—	VII	90-93	. . .
	X	31—34	XI.
H			
Haihaya—			
A name of the **Kalachuri dynasty of Chedi**, *q. v.*	IX	77	. . .
Hairát—			
Said to be an old name of Gujarát in the Panjáb	II	71	. . .
Hájípur in Muzaffarpur District, Bengal—			
Mosque at—	XVI	5	. . .
Excavations in mound near—	„	84	. . .
Bronze images with inscriptions of reign of Mahípála Deva found in mound near—	„	88	. . .

	VOL.	PAGE.*	PLATE.
Haliyá in Mirzápur District, N.-W. P.—			
English and Hindi inscriptions at, recording capture of Bhopárí fort	XXI	121	XXXI.
Hamilton—			
See **Buchanan Hamilton, Dr.**			
Hánsí, in Hissár District, Panjáb—			
Probably a chief stronghold of Indo-Scythians . .	V	140	. . .
Shrine of Niámat-ullah at—	XXIII	13	VII.
Mosque at—	„	15	. . .
Muhammadan inscriptions at—	„	„	. . .
Tomb of Alam or Alí Mír Tijára at—	„	16	V.
family of Kutb Jamál-úd-dín at— . .	„	19	VI.
Hanswá (Haswá) in Fatehpur District, N.-W. P.—			
Legend of Hansadhwaja, Moradhwaja, and Sankara-dhwaja at—	XVII	98	. . .
Hantha—			
The Chinese name of Gándhára	II	63	. . .
Hara Singha, Rájá—			
Tradition of—	XVI	4	. . .
Hárahaura *or* **Hárahúna of Varáha Mihira—**			
= Country between Jhelam and Indus	V	79	. . .
See **Salt Range.**			
Harapá in Montgomery District, Panjáb—			
Extensive mounds at—	„	105	XXXII.
Seal and other relics from—	„	106, 108	XXXIII.
Perhaps destroyed by Muhammad Kásim . . .	„	107	. . .
? = Po-fa-to *or* Po-fa-to-lo of Hwen Thsang . .	„	„	. . .
Indo-Scythian and later coins at—	„	108	. . .
Hardaur Lála—			
Legend and worship of—	XVII	162	. . .
Traditional association of cholera with worship of— .	„	163	. . .
Hari Gupta—			
Inscription of, on bas-relief at Sárnáth	I	123	XXXIV.
Haridwár *or* **Gangádwára in Sahâranpur District, N.-W. P.—**			
Ancient town at, named Máyápura *or* Máyúra . .	II	232	. . .
Various remains near—	„	233—4	LXXII.
Bathing festival at—	„	235	. . .

	Vol.	Page.	Plate.
Harlájhurí near Baijnáth in Sháhábád District, Bengal—			
Inscription at—	VIII	145	. . .
Haro city—			
Old name of Hasan Abdál in Ráwal Pindí District, Panjáb	V	79	. . .
Haro R. in Panjáb—			
Undisturbed *stúpas* along	II	148	. . .
Harsha-charita of Bána—			
Extracts from—	IX	154	. . .
Harsha, era of—			
Initial year of, is A.D. 607	I	282	. . .
Used by later Guptas and in Nepál	XVI	79	. . .
Harsha Gupta of Kosala—			
Mentioned in Sirpur inscription	XVII	17	. . .
Harsha Gupta of the later Gupta dynasty of Magadha—			
Mentioned in Aphsar inscription	IX	27	. . .
	XV	11	. . .
Harsha Varddhana, King of Kanauj—			
Defeated by Vikramáditya Chálukya	I	281	. . .
Chronology of reign of—	"	"	. . .
Established era in 607 A.D.	"	282	. . .
Probably referred to in Rájávalí	"	"	. . .
Triumphal procession of, from Prayág to Sankisa	"	305	. . .
Wide extent of empire of—	I	280	. . .
Subjected country between Jumna and Narbadá	II	311	. . .
Bána's account of the war between the king of W. Gauda (Sasángka) and—	IX	154	. . .
Probable revival of Buddhism in reign of—	XI	98	. . .
Legend of search for Rájyasrí by—	XVII	128	. . .
Harshu Bábá—			
Legend of—	"	160	. . .
Hasan Abdál in Ráwal Pindí District, Panjab—			
Spring at, identified with Hwen Thsang's tank of the Nága Elápatra	II	135—138	. . .
Buddhist ruins at—	"	138	LX.
Anciently named Haro	"	139	. . .
	V	79	. . .
Hasan Khán Mewátí—			
Opposed Bábar	XX	12	. . .

	Vol.	Page.	Plate.
Hasanpur Káko—			
See **Káko in Gayá District, Bengal.**			
Hashka Gupta—			
A misreading for **Harsha Gupta,** *q.v.*	IX XV	27 *Note* 11	. . . . . .
Hashtnagar—			
See **Chársada** *or* **Hashtnagar.**			
Hasrá in Gayá District, Bengal—			
Buddhist remains at—	VIII	104	II.
Hastin, Rájá of Uchahara—			
Inscription of—	IX X	9 113	IV. . . .
Hastinapura—			
See **Delhi.**			
Hathgáon in Fatehpur District, N.-W. P.—			
Ancient temple converted into mosque at— . . .	XVII	96	XXIX.
Hathiyá Dih in Azamgarh District, N.-W. P.—			
Pillar with inscription of Govinda Chandra Deva at—	I	95, 96	. . .
Hátila, or Asokpur, in Gondá District, Oudh—			
Buddhist 'tooth-brush' legend at—	"	328	. . .
Traditions of conflict between Sálár Masaúd and Rájá Sohrí Dal at—	"	329	. . .
Ghorí and Khiljí coins, and *Varáha drammas* found at—	"	"	. . .
Hayamukha of Hwen Thsang—			
See **Ayumukha.**			
Hazrat Pandua—			
See **Pandua in Málda District**	XV	79	. . .
Heliocles, King of Bactria—			
Scythian imitations of copper coins of—	II	59	. . .
Hemád Panth—			
Central Provinces legends of—	VII IX	114 142	. . . . . .
Herakles (Hercules)—			
Sculptures of, at Mathurá	XVII	109	XXX.

	Vol.	Page.	Plate.
Hesidrus R. of Pliny—			
= Satlaj R.	II	12	. . .
Hesychius—			
Alludes to Maurya dynasty	I	Intr. x.	. . .
Hetunpur in Mirzápur District, N.-W. P.—			
Carved obelisks at—	XI	131	. . .
Hilsá in Patna District, Bengal—			
Mosque on site of temple at—	VIII	66	. . .
Legend of Hilsá Deo at—	XI	163	. . .
Tomb of Sher Sháh's reign at—	"	164	. . .
Hima Kadphises—			
See **Wema Kadphises, King.**			
Himatgarh near Gwáliár, C. I.—			
Captured by Sikandar Lodí	II	329	. . .
Hind—			
See **Ohind.**			
Hindoria in Damoh District, C. P.—			
Inscribed *satí* stones at—	XXI	167	. . .
Hiranyaváha—			
= Son R., *q.v.*	VI	24	. . .
Hiranyvátí R.—			
= Hirana *or* Chhotá Gandak R.	VIII	25	. . .
Hisár (Hissár) in Hisár District, Panjáb—			
Pillar with pilgrims' inscriptions at—	V	141	XLI.
Hiuen Tsiang—			
See **Hwen Thsang.**			
Hiungnu—			
A Scythian tribe, rivals of the Yuchi	II	62	. . .
Hodí Rájá—			
See **Hudi Rájá.**			
Hoerke—			
See **Huvishka, King.**			

	Vol.	Page.	Plate.
Holung—			
A Chinese name for the Ganges	VIII	xii	. . .
Hooemo—			
See **Wema Kadphises, King.**			
Hooorkes, King—			
See **Huvishka, King.**			
Horne, Mr. C.—			
Excavations at Bhitarí by—	I	100—103	. . .
Hudí Rájá—			
Succeeded Rasálu in Sálbáhanpur (Siálkot)	II	21	. . .
Perhaps an Indo-Scythian	„	„	. . .
Forts at Ránígat and opposite Attock attributed to—	„	96, 97	. . .
Legend of—	V	65	. . .
Humayún, Emperor—			
Inscription recording ascent of the Chaukandí mound at Sárnáth by—	I	117	. . .
Repaired Indarpat Fort at Delhi	„	221	. . .
Tomb of, at Delhi	„	223	. . .
Inscription and mosque of, at Fatehábád	XXIII	11, 12	III, IV.
Hún—			
A Rájput clan formerly in Mewár	VI	234	. . .
Hund—			
See **Ohind.**			
Huns, White—			
See **White Huns.**			
Husainpur Káko—			
See **Káko in Gayá District, Bengal.**			
Huvishka, King—			
Monastery of, at Mathurá	I	238	. . .
Mathurá inscriptions of—	III	32	. . .
Named Hushka in Káshmír history	II	67	. . .
Coins of, found in Mánikyála No. 1 Tope	„	159	. . .
Curious gold medal of, found at Buddha-Gayá	XVI	Pref. iv	. . .
Hwen Thsang—			
Travelled in India A.D. 629—642, and returned to China A.D. 645	I	4	I, II.
	II	84	. . .
Work of, invaluable to the archæologist	„	85	. . .
Route of, between Kanauj and Prayág	I	294	. . .

	Vol.	Page.	Plate.
Hwen Thsang—*contd.*			
Route of, between Kapilavástu and Gayá	XXII	1	. . .
Kosámbi and Sankisa	I	305	. . .
in Panjáb	II	84	LII.
in Magadha and Mithilá	VIII	13, 19	. . .
in Gházípur District	XXII	88	. . .
Hwui Seng—			
A Chinese pilgrim in Kábul and W. Panjáb, A.D. 502	II	84	. . .
Hypæthral Temples—			
Dedicated to 64 Joginís	IX	74	. . .
I			
Iatii of Pliny and Ptolemy—			
Perhaps = Ját tribe	II	55	. . .
Ibráhím Lodí, Emperor—			
Built so-called Jahángír's Palace at Agra	IV	XII	. . .
Iltitmish, Emperor—			
Made additions to Kutb Mosque at Delhi	I	187	. . .
Completed Kutb Mínár	„	203	. . .
Tomb of, at Delhi	„	204	. . .
Captured Gwáliár, A.D. 1232	II	253	. . .
Great Mosque at Ajmer built in reign of—	„	261	. . .
Was first Governor of Badáun	XI	1	. . .
Built *Idgáh* and *Jámi Masjid* at Badáun	„	3	II—IV.
Correct form of name of—	„	5 *Note*	. . .
Buildings of reign of, near Delhi	XX	142, 160	XXXII.
Indappe (Indpa) in Mongír District, Bengal—			
Fort and *stúpa* at—	III	162	. . .
	VIII	120	. . .
Indian Pálí alphabet—			
First partially deciphered by Lassen	I	Intr. XII	. . .
Further deciphered by J. Prinsep	„	„ VIII	. . .
Indo-Corinthian style of architecture—			
At Jamál-garhi	V	48	XLVIII—L.
In Kábul Valley	„	186, 190	. . .
Compared with pure Corinthian	„	192	XLVII.
Date of remains of—	„	194	. . .

	Vol.	Page.	Plate.
Indo-Doric style of architecture—			
In Káshmír and Salt Range continued in use till Muhammadan conquest	V	186, 196	. . .
Indo-Grecian style of architecture—			
Remains of—	III	3	. . .
In Kábul valley and W. Panjáb	V	App. A.	
Indo-Ionic style of architecture—			. . .
Known only from ruins of Taxila	,,	68, 69, 190	XVII, XVIII.
	XIV	9	VII.
Indo-Persian style of architecture—			
Characteristics of—	V	185	. . .
Two columns near Kábul are only specimens west of Indus of—	,,	186	XLV.
Examples of, in Yusufzai bas-reliefs compared with pure Persian style	,,	187	. . .
Examples of, at Bhárhut, Sánchi, and Buddha-Gayá .	,,	188	XLVI.
Modified by the Guptas	,,	186, 189	. . .
Indo-Sassanian coins—			
See **Coins, Indo-Sassanian.**			
Indo-Sassanian period—			
Remains of—	III	4	. . .
Indo-Scythia—			
According to Ptolemy, comprised Sindh and valley of Gomal river to west of Indus	II	46	. . .
According to author of Periplus = valley of Lower Indus under name of Scythia	,,	,,	. . .
Ruled by Parthians, according to author of Periplus .	,,	47	. . .
Indo-Scythian alphabet—			
See **Alphabet.**			
Indo-Scythian coins—			
See **Coins, Indo-Scythian.**			
Indo-Scythian dynasty—			
Took titles of Devaputra and Sháhí	III	42	. . .
Early adopted Hindu names	V	140	. . .
Speculations as to date of—	III	44	. . .
Dominion of, barely acknowledged by Hindu writers .	I	Intr. XLIII	. . .
Indo-Scythian period—			
Remains of—	III	3	. . .

	Vol.	Page.	Plate.
Indo-Scythians—			
Name first used by Ptolemy for nomad tribes who overthrew successors of Alexander	II	43	. . .
Detailed accounts of, in Chinese annals only	"	44	. . .
Comprised Su and Yuchi hordes according to Chinese	"	43	. . .
Sarancæ and Asiani of Trogus Pompeius	"	"	. . .
Asii, Pasiani, Tokhari, and Sakarauli, according to Strabo	"	"	. . .
Indor on border of Gurgáon District, Panjáb—			
A Mewátí stronghold	XX	133	. . .
Indor-Khera (Indrapura) in Bulandshahr District, N.-W.P.—			
Traditions of—	XII	37	. . .
Translation of copperplate inscription of Skanda Gupta, dated 146, found at—	"	38	. . .
Punch-marked coins at—	"	40	. . .
Early moulded coins, with Buddhist symbols at—	"	41	. . .
Unique inscribed coin at—	"	"	. . .
Coins of Buddhist Satraps at—	"	41—43	. . .
Indo-Scythian coins at—	"	"	. . .
Indo-Sassanian coins at—	"	44, 68	. . .
Seals, &c., found at—	"	45	. . .
Pottery and terra-cotta work found at—	"	47, 50	VII.
Stone sculptures found at—	"	51—53	. . .
Description of ancient city at—	"	56	I.
Labyrinthine building at—	"	58	. . .
Remains on Kundanpura *or* Great Temple mound at—	"	67—78	VI.
Skeletons in Ahírpura mound at—	"	79	. . .
Remains on Vaidyapura "	"	80	. . .
Indradyumna—			
Last Pála Rájá of Magadha	III	135, 159	. . .
Forts of, at Jaynagar and Indappe	"	159, 162	. . .
Indraprastha (Indarpat)—			
Distinct from old Delhi	I	134	. . .
Legendary history of—	"	136	. . .
Also known as Purán Kila, Shergarh, and Dínpanáh	"	136, 221	. . .
Indrasilaguha—			
= Giryek in Gayá District	III	150	. . .
Inkstand, inscribed—			
From Besárh	XVI	12	IV.
Inscriptions—			
Rarely dated in intercalary month	XXI	102	. . .

	Vol.	Page.	Plate.
Inscriptions, Muhammadan—			
List of, from E. Rájputána and Panjáb . . .	XX	. . .	VIII.
Intercalary month—			
Examples of inscriptions dated in—	XXI	102	. . .
Ionic architecture—			
See **Indo-Ionic style of architecture.**			
Irich in Jhánsí District, N.-W. P.—			
Muhammadan remains at—	VII	32	. . .
Iron—			
The sole material of the Iron Pillar at Delhi . .	I	170	. . .
Works at Narwár	II	325	. . .
Iron Pillar—			
See **Delhi.**			
Isána Varmma—			
One of the Maukharí dynasty of Magadha . .	XVI	79, 81	. . .
Dated silver coins of—	IX	27	V
Islám Sháh—			
Made Gwáliár his capital	II	393	. . .
Tomb of, at Sahsarám	XI	133	XXXVIII.
Islámábád—			
Name given to Mathurá by Aurangzeb . . .	XX	39	. . .
A name of Tahangarh in Karauli State . . .	„	91	. . .
Islámpur in Patna District, Bengal—			
Remains at—	VIII	47	. . .
Iswara Varmmá, Rájá—			
Inscription of, at Jaunpur	XI	104, 124	XXXVII.
J			
Jabalpur in Jabalpur District, C. P.—			
'*Madan Mahal*' at—	VII	54	. . .
Jádava, Jádon, *or* Jádovansí—			
See **Yáduvansi Race.**			
Jagannáth, temple of—			
Inscriptions of a Gupta dynasty at —	„	VI	. . .

	Vol.	Page.	Plate.
Jagdíspur in Patna District, Bengal—			
= Kulika, birth-place of Mogalána	I	29	. . .
Jagner in Agra District, N.-W. P.—			
History of —	VI	24	. .
Ruined temple at —	„	27	. . .
Jahánára Begum—			
Daughter of Sháhjahán, buried at Delhi . . .	I	230	. . .
Jahángír, Emperor—			
So-called palace of, at Agra	IV	xii, 124	xiii.
Throne and bath of, „	„	132, 135	. . .
Jahánpanáh at Delhi—			
Described—	I	218	. . .
Jáhngira in Bhágalpur District, Bengal—			
Legends of —	XV	21	. . .
Hindu, Buddhist, and Jain rock-sculptures at — .	„	22	viii, ix.
Short inscription in early Gupta characters at — .	„	23	xi.
Island temple at —	„	22	vii.
Sculptures and short inscriptions of Gupta age at Baiskaran near—	„	23	xi.
Great fairs held at —	„	24	. . .
Jaichand—			
See **Jaya Chandra, Rájá.**			
Jain Tírthánkaras—			
Stages in life of —	XI	171	. . .
Jainism—			
Relation of, to Buddhism	X	63	. . .
Flourished at Mathurá at beginning of Christian era .	III	45	. . .
Alluded to by Hwen Thsang	V	92	. . .
Flourished in Bundelkhand under Chandel dynasty .	II	445	. . .
Persecuted by Brahmans	XX	104	. . .
Present extent of—	„	„	. . .
Legendary origin of Swetámbara sect of— . . .	X	55	. . .
Jaitpur in Hamírpur District, N.-W. P.—			
Fort at—	VII	29	. . .
Jajáhutiya *or* **Jijhotiya Brahmans and Baniyas—**			
In Bundelkhand, the ancient *Jejákabhukti-désa* . .	X	99	. . .
	XXI	vi, 173	. . .

	Vol.	Page.	Plate.
Jajao in Agra District, N.-W. P.—			
Mosque and inscription at—	IV	213	. . .
Jajhoti—			
See **Jijhotí.**			
Jalál Khán—			
A famous Mewátí Chief	XX	18	. . .
Jalálpur in Jhelam District, Panjáb—			
Anciently named Girjhák	II	176	. . .
? = Girivraja of Rámáyana	,,	177	. . .
The site of Alexander's head-quarters	,,	183	LXVII.
? = Bukephala	,,	186	. . .
Jalál-ud-dín Khiljí—			
Murder of, at Karrá	XVII	89	. . .
Jalandhar, Chandel Rájá—			
Traditions of, in Lalitpur District	X	91	. . .
Jálandhar District in Panjáb—			
Puranic legends relating to—	V	145	. . .
Also called Trigartta *or* Traigartta-desa, and Báhika	,,	148	. . .
Rájás of, in early times	,,	149—152, 181	. . .
Chief places of note in—	,,	152	. . .
Tributary to Kanauj in Hwen Thsang's time	,,	150	. . .
Jamál-garhi in Yusufzai, Panjáb—			
Buddhist ruins at—	,,	46—53	XIII—XV.
Indo-Corinthian architecture at—	,,	48	. . .
Inscribed statue of king at—	,,	49	XVI.
Other inscriptions from—	,,	63	. . .
Masons' marks in Arian characters prove age of remains at—	,,	64	. . .
Numerous sculptures found at—	,,	197	. . .
Jamná R. in Bihár—			
Flowing from Barábár hills	VIII	127	. . .
See **Jumna R.**			
Jamui in Hoshangábád District, C. P.—			
Temples and sculptures at—	VII	239	. . .
Janakpur—			
Ancient capital of Mithila	XVI	34	. . .

	Vol.	Page.	Plate.
Janapada country ?—			
Coins of—	XIV	151	XXXI.
Janer (Jajner) in Fírozpur District, Panjáb—			
An ancient town	„	67	. . .
Analysis of 184 coins found at—	„	69	. . .
Legend of—	„	„	. . .
Janjgír (Jangír) in Biláspur District, C. P.—			
Vaishnava sculptures at—	VII	204, 205	. . .
Construction of tower of temple at—	„	207	. . .
Two imperfect inscriptions at—	„	„	. . .
Janjúhás—			
A tribe in the E. Salt Range	II	18	. . .
	V	81, 82	. . .
Jánkí Kot in Champáran District, Bengál—			
An ancient site	XXII	50	. . .
Jaolí in Ráwal Pindí District, Panjáb—			
Ruins with relics and coins at—	II	146	. . .
Jarásandha, King of Magadha—			
'Girivraja' = **Rájgír**, *q.v.*, was capital of— . . .	I	21	. . .
'*Baithak*' at Giryek of—	„	16—19	XV.
Jártika tribe—			
= **Madra tribe**, *q.v.*	II	195	. . .
Jaspur—			
Probably a corruption of Yasovarmmapura, a name of Bihár city	VIII	76	. . .
Jasso (Jaso) State in Bundelkhand—			
Short inscriptions in—	XXI	99	XXVII.
Jaswár Kahárs—			
In neighbourhood of Bihár city	VIII	76	. . .
Ját (*or* Jat) tribe—			
The most numerous race in Panjáb	II	3, 56	. . .
Conjectured to be = Zanthii of Strabo, = Iatii of Pliny and Ptolemy, = Zaths of Muhammadan writers .	„	55	. . .
Are mostly Musalmán in Panjáb and Sindh, but Hindu in Rájputána	„	56, 57	. . .
Hindus say they come from Kandahár . . .	„	54	. . .
Musalmáns say they come from Gajni . . .	„	55	. . .

	Vol.	Page.	Plate.
Ját (*or* Jat) tribe—*contd.*			
Not Rájputs	II	81	. . .
Now hold Bharatpur State	XX	68	. . .
Játakas—			
Panjáb sculptures illustrating the—	V	197, 199	. . .
Jatkarí near Khajuráho in Chhatarpur State, Bundelkhand—			
Temple of Vishnu at—	X	20	IX.
Jaugada in Ganjam District, Madras—			
Asoka's edict inscription at—	XIII	113	. . .
Indo-Scythian coins found at—	"	115	. . .
Jaunpur in Jaunpur District, N.-W. P.—			
Capital of the Sharkí kings in 15th century A.D.	XI	102	. . .
Speculations as to original name of—	"	103	. . .
Mosques on sites of temples built by Rájás Jaya Chandra and Vijaya Chandra Ráthor	"	104	. . .
The fort mosque is oldest building at—	"	105	XXXI.
Inscription of Fírúz Sháh's brother at—	"	106	. . .
The great Atála Mosque at—	"	107	XXXII, XXXV—XXXVII.
Hindu masons' inscriptions dated S. 1464 = A.D. 1407 on Atála Mosque	"	110	XXXVII.
Khális-mukhlis and *Zanzírí* mosques at—	"	112	XXXI.
Jámi-ush-shark mosque at—	"	113	XXXIII.
Bíbí Rájí or *Lál Darwáza* mosque at—	"	116	XXXIV.
Inscription of Vijaya Chandra Deva of Kanauj, dated S. 1225 = A.D. 1168 at—	"	117, 125	XXXVII.
Inscription, dated S. 1353 = A.D. 1296 at—	"	118, "	"
Old tombs at—	"	119	. . .
Fort and bridge at—	"	120	. . .
Inscription of Rájá Iswara Varmma at—	"	104, 124	XXXVII.
Burial-ground of Sharkí kings at—	"	116	. . .
Destruction wrought by Sikandar Lodí at—	"	115, 117	. . .
Jaunpurí-Pathán architecture—			
Described	III	11	. . .
Jaya Chandra, Rájá of Kanauj—			
Defeated by Muhammad Ghorí at Benares	I	283	. . .
Built temple at Jaunpur	XI	104	. . .
Jaya (Gupta)—			
Gold coins of—	I	40, *Note*	. . .

	Vol.	Page.	Plate.
Jayanáth, Rájá of Kárí-Talái—			
Inscription of—	IX	7	IV.
Jayapura-dúrgga—			
Ancient name of **Ajaygarh,** *q.v.*	XXI	46	. . .
Jayendra, King of Káshmír—			
Not contemporary with Hwen Thsang	I	Intr. xxxiv.	. . .
Jaynagar in Mongír District, Bengal—			
Stronghold of Indradyumna, last Rájá of Magadha .	III	159	. . .
Jaypál, Rájá of Kanauj—			
Date of death of—	I	~~101~~	. . .
Jaypur city in Jaypur State, Rájputána—			
Founded by Jay Singh early in 18th century . .	II	251	. . .
Jaypur State—			
Anciently called Dhundhár	„	„	. . .
Jejákabhukti—			
Old name of Bundelkhand	X XXI	23, 99 VI, 57, 173	. . . . . .
Jejákasukti—			
A misreading for **Jejákabhukti,** *q.v.*			
Jesalmer (Jáisalmír) in Jesalmer State, Rájputána—			
Head quarters of Hindu section of Bhatí tribe at— .	II	22	. . .
Jesalmer annals—			
On the history of Sálivahan	„	21, 22	. . .
Jetavana monastery of Srávastí—			
Further excavations of— . . . . *See* **Srávastí.**	XI	82	XXIV.
Jethian in Gayá District—			
= Ancient Jashtivana	III	140	. . .
Jethur in Bhágalpur District, Bengal—			
Inscription, dated 1053 S. at—	VIII	130	. . .
Jhaloni in (?) Lalitpur District, N.-W. P.—			
Inscribed slab at—	XXI	176	. . .

	Vol.	Page.	Plate
Jhálra Pátan in Jhalláwár State, Rájputána—			
= Ancient Chandrávatí	II	264, 270	. . .
Temples at—	XXIII	126	XXVI.
Major Abbott's account of—	„	130	. . .
Jhárkhand—			
Ancient name of a tract along the Damúdá river, in Mánbhúm District, Bengal	VIII	50, 157	. . .
Jharkon in Central India—			
Capital of the Khichí Rájás	II	295	. . .
Jhelam city, in Jhelam District, Panjáb—			
Iron tripods and brass bowls found at—	XIV	42	. . .
Remains of temple in late Gupta style at— . . .	„	„	. . .
Ancient coins abundant at—	II	174	. . .
Jhelam River—			
Formerly joined Chenáb about 50 miles above present junction	„	38	. . .
Jhirká—			
See **Fírozpur-Jhirká in Gurgaon District.**			
Jhirná in Rewá State—			
See **Piáwan.**			
Jihonia (Zeionises) Satrap—			
Coins of, found at Maníkyala	„ XIV	152, 167-8 6	LXV. . . .
Jijhoti—			
Ancient name of Bundelkhand	II	413	. . .
Jijhotiya Brahmans—			
Named from Jijhoti	„	414	. . .
Jivita Gupta, Rájá—			
Inscription of, at Deo-Barnárak	XVI	68, 73	XXIV—XXVI
Jobnáth, Rájá—			
Legend of—	V	96	. . .
See **Chobnáth, Rájá.**			
Jodh Bái, Akbar's queen—			
Mausoleum at Agra of—	IV	121	. . .

	Vol.	Page.	Plate.
Jodhpur in Jodhpur State, Rájputána—			
Modern temples at —	XXIII	85	. . .
Jogí-guphá in Dinájpur District, Bengal—			
Hindu remains at—	XV	120	. . .
Jogínís, 64—			
Five temples known to be dedicated to—	IX	74	
Detailed description of Bherá Ghât temple of— . .	"	61—74	XII—XVI.
Ditto of Khajuráho ditto . .	II	416	. . .
	XXI	57	. . .
Johlyas of Baháwalpur—			
= Yaudheya tribe	XIV	140	. . .
Jones, Sir William—			
Contributions of, to oriental learning	I	Intr. I	. . .
Júd, Mount—			
The Muhammadan name of the Salt Range . .	V	79	. . .
Julien, M. Stanislas—			
Translated Life and Travels of Hwen Thsang . .	II	85	. . .
Jumná R.—			
Symbolised by tortoise	X	49	. . .
Statue of, characteristic of Gupta style of architecture .	IX	43, 70	. . .
Júná Kherá in Jodhpur State, Rájputána—			
Ruined temples at—	XXIII	97	. . .
Jupiter, 12-year cycle of—			
Preliminary discussion of—	IX	18	. . .
Method of calculating—	X	Pref. and App.	. . .
Used in the Dakhin and Burma	"	127	. . .
Jupiter, 60-year cycle of—			
Used in dates of Satí inscriptions at Boram Deo, C. P. .	XVII	41	. . .
Jushka—			
A brother of Kanishka, according to Káshmír history .	II	64	. . .
Jwála Mukhí in Kángra District, Panjáb—			
Famous temple at—	V	169	. . .
Natural flames at—	"	170	. . .
Alleged visit of Fíroz Tughlak to—	"	117—175	. . .

	Vol.	Page.	Plate.
Jyestha datta—			
Coin of, from Bairánt in Benares District . . .	XXII	115	. . .

K

	Vol.	Page.	Plate.
Kábar *or* **Shergarh in Barelí District, N.-W. P.—**			
An ancient city	I	358	. . .
Kabír, reformer—			
Died at Maghar in Bastí District	XII	72 *	. . .
Kabír-ud dín Auliyá—			
Tomb of, near Delhi	XX	147	. . .
Kábul—			
Divided between Parthians, Indians, and Su Kings of Kipin in 126 B.C.	II	45	. . .
Occupied by Great Yuchi	"	73	. . .
Sarhind most easterly possession of Hindu kings of— .	"	206	. . .
Names of Hindu kings of—	"	74	. . .
	V	82	. . .
Silver coinage of, current in Panjáb in Mahmúd's time .	"	156	. . .
Surkh Mínár and *Mínár Chakrí* at— . . .	"	186	XLV.
Kachchh—			
= Pliny's country of the Odonbeores, = Audumbara .	"	155	. . .
	XIV	136	. . .
Kachhwáhá clan—			
Etymology of name of—	II	379	. . .
Kachhwáhá Rájás of Gwáliár—			
List of—	"	374	. . .
Kadaphes—			
Perhaps the same title as Kadphises, *q.v.* . .			
Kádasa (Kádra)—			
Snake coins bearing name of—	"	10	. . .
	VI	167	. . .
Kadphises—			
See **Kujula Kara Kadphises,** *and* **Wema Kadphises, King—**			
Kadwai in Gwáliár State, C. I.—			
Old Hindu temple at—	XX	105	. . .

* The text erroneously states that Kabír was born at Maghar.

	Vol.	Page.	Plate.
Káfir-kot in Derá Ismáil Khán District, Panjáb—			
Fort and temples at—	XIV	27	XI—XIII.
Kagol in Mongír District, Bengal—			
Dargáh of Pír Makhdúm Maulána Núr at— . .	III	153	. . .
Kahalgaon in Bhágalpur District, Bengal			
Temples at—	XV	35	XII.
Formerly a haunt of Thugs	"	"	. . .
Kaháon in Gorákhpur District, N.-W. P.—			
Temples and other ruins at—	I	91—95	XXVIII.
Pillar with inscription of Skanda Gupta's reign at— .	"	92	XXX.
	XVI	. . .	XXIX.
Kahror in Multán District, Panjáb—			
Alleged battle at, between Sáliváhan and the Sakas .	II	21	. . .
Kaikeya—			
Ancient name of part of Panjáb along (?) the Jhelam .	"	14	. . .
Kailakila Yavanas of the Puránas—			
Probably = the Sena Rájás of Vakátaka . . .	XVII	84, 86	. . .
Kaisobora—			
See **Klisobora—**			
Kakarári in Rewá State—			
Ruins at—	X	15	. . .
Kakarsihá in Rewá State—			
Ruined temples at—	XIII	19	. . .
Káker (Kákair) in Nágpur District, C. P.—			
Temples at—	VII	147	. . .
Two inscriptions at—	"	148	. . .
Káko (Husainpur-Káko) in Gayá District, Bengal—			
An ancient town	XVI	36	. . .
Muhammadan inscriptions at—	VIII	64	. . .
	XVI	37	X.
Legends of Bíbí Kamálo at—	"	38	. . .
Kákúpur in Cawnpore District, N.-W. P.—			
Perhaps = Hwen Thsang's A-yu-to . . .	I	295	. . .
Kálá-ká Sarai in Ráwal Píndí District, Panjáb—			
A halting-place of the Mughal emperors . . .	II	111	. . .

	Vol.	Page.	Plate.
Kalachuri dynasty of Chedi—			
Said to have come from the south	XXI	153	. . .
Occupied Kálanjar early, perhaps in A.D. 249	„	22, 153	. . .
Also called Haihaya	IX	77	. . .
Defeated by Chálukyas in 6th & 7th centuries A.D.	„	„	. . .
	XVII	83	. . .
Intermarried with Ráshtrakuta dynasty of south	IX	80	. . .
Came in contact with Chandel dynasty of Mahoba	„	86	. . .
Bhárhut included in dominions of—	„	94	. . .
Held Rewá in 11th and 12th centuries A.D., and earlier	XXI	103, 153	. . .
History, chronology, and inscriptions of—	IX	77,—112	. . .
Coins of—	X	25	X.
Kalachuri era—			
A.D. 250 is probably initial year of—	VII	vi	. . .
Probably dates from capture of Kálanjar by Kalachuri dynasty	XVII	84	. . .
	XXI	154	. . .
Data for determination of—	IX	86, 111	. . .
Kálanjar Fort in Bándá District, N.-W. P.—			
Sieges of—	XXI	20, 24, 26	. . .
Description of—	„	21	VIII.
Occupied by Kalachuri kings in (?) A.D. 249	XVII	84	. . .
	XXI	22, 153	. . .
Defeat by Mahmúd of Ghazní of Ganda, king of, A.D. 1019	„	23	. . .
Taken by Mahmúd of Ghazní and Kutb-ud-dín Aibak	„	24, 87	. . .
Later history of—	„	25	. . .
Gates of—	„	28	. . .
Reservoirs, &c., in—	„	32	. . .
List of inscriptions at—	„	33—45	IX, X.
Perhaps = Tamasis of Ptolemy	„	58, 91	. . .
Kálásoka, King of Magadha—			
Succeeded Susinága	VIII	3	. . .
Kallar, King of Gándhára—			
= Syálapati Deva of coins	V	83	. . .
Kálpí in Jálaun District, N.-W. P.—			
History of—	XXI	131	. . .
Muhammadan tombs at—		132	XXXIII.
Kálsí—			
See **Khálsí.**			

	Vol.	Page.	Plate.
Kamál Khán Gakkar—			
Jágírdár of Karrá, 1564 A.D.	XVII	93	. . .
Kamálo, Bíbí—			
Legends of—	XVI	38	. . .
Káman in Bharatpur State, Rájputána—			
A place of pilgrimage	XX	54	. . .
Chaunsat Khamba mosque at—	,,	55	XI.
Inscription of Iltitmish at—	,,	56	. . .
Long Sanskrit inscription probably of 8th century at—	,,	57	XII.
Inscription dated 754 A.H. = 1353 A.D. at— . .	,,	,,	. . .
Genealogy of Surasena chiefs of—	,,	59	. . .
Kamantipuri—			
Ancient name of Dongargarh in Ráipur District, C. P.	XVII	2	. . .
Kambistholi of Arrian—			
= Kapisthalas in Panjáb hills	XIV	116	. . .
Kambojas—			
Mentioned in Sháhbázgarhi inscription . . .	V	20	. . .
Kamlu (Kamlua), King of Gándhára—			
Coins doubtfully ascribed to—	,,	83	. . .
Kampil (Kampilya) in Farrukhábád District, N.-W. P.—			
Capital of S. Pancháála	XI	11	. . .
Scene of *Swayamvara* of Draupadí	,,	12	. . .
Kámrúp (Assám)—			
Was subject to Harsha Vardhana of Kanauj . .	XV	112	. . .
Kanaka Muni, a Buddha—			
Birth-place of, near Kapilavástu	XII	IV, 184	. . .
Kanauj in Farrukhábád District, N.-W. P.—			
Tomar capital moved to Bárí from, in 1022 A.D. .	I	150, 283	. . .
Captured by Chandra Deva Ráthor about A.D. 1050	,,	151	. . .
Early accounts of—	,,	279	. . .
Capital of Rájá Harsha Vardhana	,,	280	. . .
Description of—	,,	284	XLVII.
Hindu temples utilised by Muhammadans at— . .	,,	286	. . .
Discovery of gold ingots at—	,,	287	. . .
Tomb of Makhdúm Jaháníya at—	,,	289	. . .
Hindu sculptures at—	,,	290	. . .
Site of Asoka's great *stúpa* not traceable at— . .	,,	291	. . .

	Vol.	Page.	Plate.
Kanauj in Farrukhábád District, N.-W. P,—*contd.*			
Inscription dated S. 1193 = A. D. 1136 at—	I	290, 293	. . .
Formerly on bank of Ganges	,,	279, 284	. . .
Jálandhar tributary to, in time of Hwen Thsang	V	150	. . .
Kandahár—			
Traditionally the original seat of Játs of Bayána and Bharatpur	II	54	. . .
Alms-bowl of Buddha near—	,,	88	. . .
	XVI	10	. . .
Kanerkes, King—			
See **Kanishka, Indo-Scythian King.**			
Kángra town and fort in Kángra District, Panjáb—			
Also known as Nagarkot and Bhímnagar	V	155, 156	. . .
Sacked by Mahmúd of Ghazní	,,	,,	. . .
Captured by Hindus in 1043 A.D.	,,	157	. . .
Subsequent sieges of—	,,	157—162	. . .
Description of—	,,	163	. . .
Temples and sundry inscriptions at—	,,	163—167	. . .
Repair of noses practised at—	,,	168	. . .
Rájás of—	,,	150	. . .
Coins of Rájás of—	,,	152	. . .
Kángra Valley—			
Buddhism traceable at Chári only in—	,,	178	. . .
Kánhari caves in Salset, Bombay—			
Described by Salt in Bombay Transactions, 1819	I	Intr. vi	. . .
Date of, proved by inscriptions	,,	,, xxi	
		xxiii	. . .
Kanhiárá in Kángra District, Panjáb—			
Short Ario-Pálí and Indo-Pálí rock inscriptions at—	V	175	XLII.
Kanishka, Indo-Scythian King—			
A member of the Kushán tribe	,,	62	. . .
Abolished serpent worship in Káshmír	II	10	. . .
Events of reign of—	,,	67	. . .
Erected great buildings at Pesháwar	,,	88	. . .
Perhaps founded Vikrama era	,,	68 *Note*	. . .
Kept Chinese hostages	XIV	53	. . .
Inscriptions of, from Mathurá	III	30	XIII.
,, ,, ,, Zeda in Yusufzai	V	57	. . .
Coins of, found in Topes No. 1 and 2 at Mánikyála	II	159, 162	. . .
Kankáli in Kamarda State, C. P.—			
Inscriptions of Jasa Rájá and Magaradhwaja Jogí at—	XVII	44	XXII.

	Vol.	Page.	Plate.
Kánkjol (Kákjol) Province—			
Comprised parts of Purania, Máldah and Bhágalpur Districts, and was also known as Rárh or Rádha, and Audumbara	XV	37, 38	. . .
Kántára, Mahá, of Samudra Gupta—			
Probably the same as the province of **Varendra,** *q.v.* .	„	112	. . .
Kántípuri—			
= Modern Kotwál or Kutwár near Gwáliár . .	II	308, 398	. . .
Kanwa dynasty of Puránas—			
Perhaps identical with that of Vásudeva, Indo-Scythian	III	42	. . .
	V	140	. . .
Kanyá Kubja—			
The Sanskrit name of Kanauj	I	280	. . .
Kapál mochan—			
A holy tank east of Ambála	XIV	75	XXIV.
Broken inscriptions of Gupta age at—	„	77	XXV.
Kapilavástu—			
= **Bhuilá Dih in Basti District N.-W.P.,** *q.v.* . .	XII	IV, 142	. . .
Identification of sites surrounding	„	112, 157	
		172	. . .
Kapisa, near Kábul—			
Gold, silver, and small copper coins of, in time of Hwen Thsang	II	79	. . .
Kapisthala people—			
In Panjáb hills, = Kambistholi of Arrian	XIV	116	. . .
Kapurdi-garhi—			
See **Sháhbázgarhi**	V	8	. . .
Karachuri—			
See **Kalachuri dynasty of Chedi.**			
Káramár hill at Sháhbázgarhi—			
= Mount Dantalok of Hwen Thsang	II	106	. . .
	V	17	. . .
Karanbel—			
Name of the ruins near **Tewar in Jabalpur District** (*q.v.*)	IX	58	. . .
Karath in Sháhábád District, Bengal—			
Remains of (?) *stúpa* at—	XVI	61	. . .

	Vol.	Plate.	Page.
Kárátoya river—			
Formerly boundary between Bengal and Kámrúp (Assam)	XV	114	. . .
Karanli—			
Jádon (Yáduvansi) Rájás of—	XX	7	. . .
Kári Tálai or Karnapura in Nágaudh State, Baghelkhand—			
Inscriptions of Mohárájá Jayanáth and of the Kala-churi Dynasty at—	IX	8	II.
Karkota—			
Name of a range of hills in Rájputána	VI	166	. . .
A synonym for Nága or Takshaka	„	167	. . .
Karkota Nagar—			
See **Nagar (Karkota).**			
Kárle caves in Púná District, Bombay—			
Objecions to Fergusson's late date for— . .	I	Intr. XXI	. . .
Karluki family in Panjáb—			
Coins of, in 13th century A.D.	II	19	. . .
Karmanasa R.—			
The boundary between the Aryans and Medo-Scythians	IX	160	. . .
Karna Deva, King of Chedi—			
Founded Bilhari and Karnávatí (Karanpur) . .	„	107	. . .
Defeated by Kírtti Varmma Chandel	II IX	453 108	. . . . . .
Remembered in Rewá as a Bhar	XXI	149	. . .
Apparently referred to in tradition of Amarkantak in Central Provinces	VII	227	. . .
Karna, Rájá—			
Mentioned in legends of Mongír and Champánagar, near Bhágalpur	XV	31	. . .
Karrá in Alláhábád District, N. W. P.—			
An ancient place of Hindu pilgrimage	XVII	88	. . .
Tomb of Khwája Karrak at—	„	„	. . .
Murder of Jalál-ud-dín Fíroz Khiljí at, in 1296 A.D.	„	„	. . .
Replaced Kosam as seat of government about 1200 A.D.	„	91, 94	. . .
Superseded by Alláhábád, 1575 A.D.	„	94	. . .
Sundry historical events at—	„	92	. . .
Tomb of Kamál Khán at—	„	93	. . .
Extensive ruins at—	„	94	. . .
Inscription of Yasa Pála, dated S. 1092 = A.D. 1035 from—	„	89, 95	. . .
Copperplate inscription of Rájá Rámachandra of Rewá, dated A.H. 966 = A.D. 1557-58 at—	„	88, 95	. . .

	Vol.	Plate.	Page.
Kárusha Desa—			
Ancient name of Sháhábád District, Bengal	III	70	. . .
	XV	155	. . .
Kasaundhi Garhi *or* **Báwan Garhi in Agra District, N.-W. Provinces—**			
An ancient site	IV	208	. . .
Káshípur (Kasipur) in Tarai District, N.-W. P.—			
Ancient fort at Ujjain near, probably = Govisana of Hwen Thsang	I	252	XLII.
Káshmír—			
Essay by H. H. Wilson on history of—	,,	Intr. V	. . .
Ruled by Kanishka and his brothers	II	67	. . .
Conquest of Gándhára by—	V	83	. . .
Lok-kál reckoning of—	,,	181	. . .
Takári alphabet used in—	II	9	. . .
Káshmír style of árchitecture—			
Characteristics of—	,,	189	. . .
Salt Range temples in—	V	186, 196	. . .
	,,	84	. . .
	XIV	33	XV.
Kasiá in Gorakhpur District, N.-W. P.—			
= Ancient **Kusinagara**, *q.v.*	I	76—85	XXVI.
Sepulchral barrows near—	XVIII	55	. . .
	I	76, *Note* 79	. . .
Old river channels ,,	XVIII	94	. . .
Terra-cotta statuette of Buddha at—	,,	97	. . .
Dedicatory inscription in Kutila characters at—	,,	67, 100	. . .
Colossal recumbent statue of Buddha at—	,,	56	. . .
	I	79	. . .
Inscription of Haribala at—	XVIII	57, 99	V, VI
Restorations by Mr. Carlleyle at—	,,	60	. . .
	,,	61	. . .
Traces of action of fire in ruins at—	XXII	16—29, 58	III, IV
Great *stúpa* of the Nirvána at—	XVIII	62	. . .
Small *stúpas* at—	,,	63, 73	V, VI,
Inscription mentioning Sáriputra at—	,,	67	. . .
Buddhist creed inscription in Kutila characters at—	,,	68	. . .
on copperplate in characters of 5th century at—	,,	69	. . .
on seals at—	,,	70	. . .
Missing Nirvána inscription at—	,,	,,	. . .
Rámábhár *stúpa* at—	,,	72	. . .
Gradual destruction of remains at—	,,	75	. . .
	,,	87	. . .
Name of, perhaps connected with that of Mahá Kásyapa, chief disciple of Buddha	,,	93	. . .

	Vol.	Plate.	Page.
Kaspapuros of Hekatæus, Kaspaturos of Herodotus, and Kaspeira of Ptolemy—			
Probably = Multán	II	69	. . .
	V	129	. . .
Kaspeiræoi of Ptolemy—			
Probably = Great Yuchi	II	67, 69	. . .
Kasturia in Champáran District, Bengal—			
Supposed palace of Cherú Rájá at—	XVI	26	. . .
Kásyapa Buddha—			
Born and interred at Tandwa in Bahraich District, Oudh	I	349	. . .
	XI	71, 77	. . .
Kásyapapura—			
Ancient name of Multán	II	69	. . .
	V	129	. . .
Katahriya clan—			
Lakhnor, capital of—	I	257	. . .
Settled in Katehar (Eastern Rohilkhand) in S. 1231 = A.D. 1174.	"	356	. . .
Katár tribe—			
Probably = Cidaritæ, &c., = Yuchi	II	79	. . .
Not Rájpúts	"	80	. . .
Katás (Kataksha) in Jhelam District, Panjáb—			
A place of pilgrimage	"	188	LXVII.
'Sat-ghara' temples in Káshmír style at— . .	"	189—191	. . .
Site of holy fountain of Hwen Thsang	V	90	. . .
Katehar—			
Old name of Eastern Rohilkhand	I	352, 356	. . .
	XI	1	. . .
Kathæa—			
The territory of the Kathæoi (Káthi) in Central Panjáb	II	36, 37	. . .
Káthi—			
A numerous tribe in Central Panjab, = Kathaoi of Sangala, who opposed Alexander	"	33	. . .
Found also in Kathiáwár	"	"	. . .
Resemble the Gákars in physique and habits . .	"	"	. . .
Claim descent from the Bálas, and pay special adoration to the sun	"	34	. . .

	Vol.	Page.	Plate.
Káthi—*contd.*			
Greek accounts of—	II	35	. . .
Peculiar marriage customs of—	"	36	. . .
Boundaries of territory of—	"	37	. . .
Probably represent the subjects of **Sopeithes (Sophites)** *q.v.*	"	35	. . .
Katká in Alláhábád District, N.-W. P.—			
Sculptured obelisk of Gupta period at—	XXI	120	. . .
Katra *or* **Akbarpur in Darbhangá District, Bengal**—			
Ancient fort at—	XVI	35	. . .
Katrás in Mánbhúm District, Bengal—			
Small ancient temple at—	VIII	156	XV, XVI.
Surrounding district called Jhárkhand in Muhammadan history	"	157	. . .
Kauwá-Dol hill, in Gayá District, Bengal—			
Site of the Sílbhadra monastery	I	40	. . .
	VIII	40	. . .
	XVI	47	XIV.
Brahmanical and Buddhist sculptures at—	"	48	XV.
Kavi-Siva, Satrap—			
Inscription of, in Mánikyála No. 1 Tope	II	161	LXIII.
Kawardá (Kamardá) in Kawardá State, Biláspur District, Central Provinces—			
Worn inscription at—	XVII	34	. . .
Keljhar in Wardhá District, C. P.—			
Dolmens, or cromlechs, used as temples at—	IX	140	XXV.
Ken R.—			
Course and tributaries of—	XXI	157	. . .
Kesariyá in Champáran District, Bengal—			
Ruins at—	I	64	XXIII.
Stúpa at—	"	64—66	XXIV.
The place of parting between Buddha and the Lichchhavis	XVI	16	. . .
Kesopura muhalla of Mathurá—			
Probably = Klisobora of Arrian	XX	31, 45	. . .
Ketás in Salt Range, Panjáb—			
See **Katás (Kataksha) in Jhelam District, Panjáb**—			

	Vol.	Page	Plate.
Kevatí Kund in Rewá State—			
Pálí inscription of about 200 B.C., and four *satí* inscriptions at—	XXI	116, 142	XXIX.
Khairá Dih in Balliá District, N.-W. P.—			
Large quantities of Indo-Scythian coins found at—	XXII	108	XII.
Khairábád in Yusufzai, Panjáb—			
Great fort of—	V	64	. . .
Perhaps mentioned by Sung-Yun	"	66	. . .
Khairpur near Delhi—			
Jámi-Masjid of reign of Sikandar Lodí at—	XX	155	XXXVI.
Tombs at—	"	158	XXXVIII.
Old bridge at—	"	159	. . .
Khajuráho in Chhatarpur State, Bundelkhand—			
Mentioned by Hwen Thsang, Abú Rihán, and Ibn Batuta	II	412	. . .
A capital of Jijhoti *or* Bundelkhand	"	413	. . .
Extensive ruins at—	"	415	XCV.
Temple of Chaonsat Joginís at—	"	416	XCVI.
	XXI	57	. . .
Great temples at—	II	419	XCVII. XCVIII.
	VII	5	XII.
	X	18, 21	VIII.
Obscene sculptures at—	II	420	. . .
Temple of sun at—	"	422	. . .
Colossal statue of boar at—	"	427	. . .
Remains of Buddhist monasteries at—	"	428, 435	. . .
Jain remains at—	"	431	. . .
Ghantái temple at—	"	414, 431	. . .
	X	16	VIII.
Temples at Kurar Nála and Jatkarí, near—	II	436	. . .
Inscribed statue of Hanumán at—	"	437	. . .
	X	20	IX.
	XXI	64	XVI.
History of—	II	438	. . .
Early inscription mentioning Harsha Deva at—	XXI	56	. . .
Temple of Brahmá at—	"	"	. . .
Perhaps = Kuraporina of Ptolemy	"	58, 91	. . .
Minor inscriptions, masons' marks, &c., at—	II	433—435	. . .
	XXI	59	XX.
Longer inscriptions at—	II	423, 426	. . .
	XXI	63—69	XVI—XIX.

	Vol.	Page.	Plate.
Khalari in Ráipur District, C. P.—			
Temples at—	VII	156	XVII.
Inscription dated Samvat 1470 and Saka 1334 at— .	"	157	. . .
Khalpáni R.—			
See **Chalpáni R.**			
Khálsí (Kálsí) in Dehrá Dún District, N.-W. P.—			
Rock inscribed with edicts of Asoka at— . . .	I	245	XLI.
Khandagiri in Katák District, Orissa—			
Notes on caves and inscriptions at— . . .	XIII	79—91	. . .
Khandwá in Nímár District, C. P.—			
Probably = Kognabanda of Ptolemy . . .	IX	113, 121	. . .
Inscriptions dated S. 1189 = A. D. 1132 at— . .	"	114	. . .
Khánwa (Kanua) in Bharatpur State, Rájputána—			
Site of great battle between Bábar and Rájá Sanga A.D. 1527	XX	93	. . .
Bábar's *báoli* near—	"	94	. . .
Legends of battle-field at—	"	96	. . .
Correct date of Babar's battle at—	"	97	. . .
Khánzádas of Mewát—			
Claim descent from the Jádon Rájá Tahan Pála . .	"	11	. . .
Ancestors of, converted to Islám in reign of Fíroz Tughlak	"	"	. . .
Struggles of, with the emperors of Delhi . . .	"	13—22	. . .
Genealogy of Hindu ancestors of—	"	13	. . .
Bahádur Náhar, founder of ruling family of— . .	"	15—17	. . .
Jalál Khán, a famous chief of—	"	18	. . .
Hasan Khán, chief of, in Bábar's reign . . .	"	19	. . .
Decline of power of, from Akbar's reign . . .	"	22	. . .
Hindu usages of—	"	23	. . .
Kharkai in Yusufzai, Panjáb—			
Ruins at, not fully examined	V	53	. . .
Inscribed relic-receptacle at—	"	54	XII.
Masons' marks at—	"	55	. . .
Khárod in Biláspur District, C. P.—			
Inscription dated 933 Chedi Samvat at—	VII	201	. . .
Temple at	"	202	. . .
Other remains at—	"	203	. . .

	Vol.	Page.	Plate.
Khatkar-Bhimgaj in Rájputána—			
Sundry temples at—	XXIII	135	. . .
Kherá in Agra District, N.-W. P.—			
Sepulchral cairns at—	VI	13	II
Kherá Bajerá, near Koel in Alígarh District, N.-W. P.—			
Mounds at—	XII	7	. . .
Kherhi in Bhágalpur District, Bengal—			
Mounds and fort at—	VIII	128	. . .
22 inscriptions in shell characters at—	"	129	. . .
Mediæval inscription at—	"	"	. . .
Khetlál in Bagraha (Bogra) District, Bengal—			
Included in Kasba Kismat	XV	100	. . .
Hindu and Buddhist remains at—	"	100—102	. . .
Khichi Chauhán clan—			
History of—	II	295	. . .
Khichiwára territory—			
Extent of—	"	299	. . .
Khieu-tsieu-ki—			
Of the Kuei-shwang tribe, King of the Yuchi	"	63	. . .
Conquered Ariana, Kábul, and Gándhára	"	63, 65	. . .
= Kozoulo (or Kujula) Kadphises	"	66	. . .
Khiljí-Pathán architecture—			
Described	III	8	. . .
Kho (Khoh) in Nágaudh State, Baghelkhand—			
Ruins of Vaishnava temple at—	IX	6	III
Capital of the Teliyá Ráj	"	7	. . .
Copperplate inscriptions dated in Gupta era found at—	"	"	. . .
Kholví in Central India—			
Buddhist caves, rock-cut temples, and *stúpas* at—	II	280—288	LXXXIII, LXXXIV
Khond races—			
Traditions of—	XIII	110	. . .
Khúbrí Shekh—			
See **Kutb-ud-dín Chishti—**			

	Vol.	Page.	Plate.
Khukhundo in Gorakhpur District, N.-W. P.—			
An ancient site known to the Jains as Kishkindapura	I	86	XXVIII.
Sculptures at—	"	87—90	. . .
Would well repay excavation	"	91	. . .
Khurdá (Khurdhá) in Purí District, Orissa—			
Small early inscriptions at—	XIII	99	. . .
Khusrú Parvez of Persia—			
Invasion of Sindh by—	V	123	. . .
Khwája Karrak, Saint—			
Tomb of, at Karrá	XVII	89	. . .
Khichang, south of Chaibása in Singhbhúm District, Bengal—			
Ruins at—	XIII	74	. . .
Kilakila Yavanas—			
Probably either Indo-Scythians or Parthians . .	I	Intr. xxxv, *Note.*	. . .
Kipin, kingdom of—			
Nearly corresponded with Ariana, and was called Kophene by Greeks	II	45	. . .
Included Sakastene of Isidorus	"	"	. . .
Ruled by kings of Su horde shortly after 126 B.C. .	"	"	. . .
Kíragráma *or* Kirgraon in Kángra District, Panjáb—			
Temples of Baijnáth (Vaidyanáth) and Siddhnáth at—	V	178—179	. . .
Great inscriptions of Baijnáth temple at—	"	180	XLII.
Minor inscriptions at—	"	181—183	. . .
Tákarí cursive character used at—	"	182	. . .
Kirna Suvarna, the kingdom of Sasángka—			
(?) = Sápharan on Subanrikha R.	VIII	189, 191	. . .
Kírtti Varmma, Chandel Rájá—			
Inscription of, dated Samvat 1154 at Deogarh . .	X	102	XXXIII.
Defeated Karna Deva, King of Chedi . . .	II	453	. . .
	IX	108	. . .
Kispá in Gayá District, Bengal—			
Inscribed Buddhist statues at— .	VIII	53	. . .
Kitolo—			
Yuchi king of Gándhára early in 5th century A.D. .	II	63	. . .

	Vol.	Page.	Plate.
Kittoe, Major M.—			
Archæological work of—	I	Intr. XXIV —XXVII, 116, 124	. . .
	VIII	63	. . .
Kiyul in Mongír District, Bengal—			
Perhaps = Lo-in-ni-lo of Hwen Thsang . . .	III	156	. . .
Birdában *stupa* of late date near—	"	157	XLVI.
Lac seals found near—	"	158	"
Klisobora *or* **(Kaisobora) of Arrian—**			
Identified by Mr. Growse with Gokal . . .	XX	44	. . .
Probably the Kesopura Mohulla of Mathurá . .	"	31, 45	. . .
Koel (Koil) in Alígarh District, N.-W. P.—			
Mínár at, erected by Kutlugh Khán in A. H. 652 = A.D. 1254	I	191	. . .
Kognabanda of Ptolemy—			
Probably = Khandwá	IX	113, 121	. . .
Kohinúr diamond—			
Probably once belonged to Rájá of Gwáliár . .	II	390	. . .
Koitur—			
The name by which the Gonds call themselves . .	IX	151	. . .
	XVII	124	. . .
Kokalla I. and II.—			
Of Kalachuri dynasty of Chedi	IX	80, 102	. . .
		105	. . .
Kokila, Queen of Rasálu—			
Legend of—	V	65	. . .
Kolahala, *or* **Kanwa Hills of the Puránas—**			
= Kauwá-kol hills in Gayá District, Bengal . .	VIII	123—125	. . .
Koli, *alias* **Vyághrapura—**			
See **Vyághrapura.**			
Kols—			
Temples at Konch in Gayá District, ascribed to— .	"	61	. . .
Rude stone circles near Buddha Gaya ascribed to— .	"	66	. . .
Mentioned in legend of Barágaon in Patna District	"	81	. . .

	Vol.	Page.	Plate.
Konch in Gayá District, Bengal—			
Brick temple at—	VIII	54	VI.
	XVI	50	XVI—XVIII.
Arched vault, an integral part of temple at— . .	VIII	55	. . .
	XVI	„	. . .
Temple at, compared with temples at Nálanda and Buddha Gayá	VIII	57	. . .
	XVI	55	. . .
Temple at, Saiva, not Buddhist	„	56	. . .
Remarkable Das Avatár group at—	VIII	60	. . .
	XVI	57	. . .
Temple at, perhaps of 8th century, A.D.	„	58	. . .
Kondali (Gondali) of Ptolemy—			
Perhaps = Gonds	IX	151	. . .
	XVII	124	. . .
Kophene—			
= Arachosia	II	45	. . .
Koron-dih (Koraun) in Bastí District, N.-W. P.—			
Great mounds of ruins at—	XI	101	. . .
Perhaps site of Rámagráma	XII	216	XIV.
Kosala, Dakshina—			
= Mahá Kosala = Chhattísgarh	XVII	68	. . .
Kosala, Mahá, kingdom of—			
Manipur, capital of—	IX	55	. . .
= Chhattísgarh, distinguished from Uttara Kosala in Oudh, and also known as Dakshina Kosala . .	XVII	68	. . .
Extent of, at various times	„	„	. . .
= Ptolemy's country of the Adisathri	„	69	. . .
	XXI	93	. . .
Included in kingdom of Chedí in 12th century A.D. .	XVII	71	. . .
Ruled by a Buddhist king in A.D. 639	„	86	. . .
List of kings of, compared with those of Vákátaka and Orissa	„	87	. . .
Kosala, Uttara—			
= Oudh, north of the Ghágrá R.	I	327	. . .
	XVII	68	. . .
Kosala, Western—			
= Gauda (Western), or the Gond country . .	IX	150	. . .
Kosámbí (Kosam) in Alláhábád District, N.-W. P.—			
The city of King Udáyana, contemporary of Buddha .	I	301	. . .
Early notices of—	„	302	. . .

	Vol.	Page.	Plate.
Kosámbi (Kosam) in Alláhábád District, N.-W. P.—*contd.*			
Also named *Vatsa-pattana*	I	302	. . .
Legend of Bakkula connected with—	,,	303	. . .
Hwen Thsang's route to—	,,	305	. . .
Description of ruins at—	,,	306	XLVIII.
Site of sandal wood statue of Buddha at— . . .	,,	308	. . .
Great monolith at—	,,	309	. . .
Various ancient sites near—	,,	311	. . .
A resort of Jain pilgrims	,,	303	. . .
Jain and Buddhist sculptures at—	X	1, 2	. . .
Inscription of Mahárája Sri Bhima Varmma dated 136 at—	,,	3	. . .
Brass seal ring with Gupta characters found at— .	,,	4	. . .
Coins found at—	,,	4, 5	II.
Superseded by Karrá as seat of Government about 1200 A.D.	XVII	91, 94	. . .
Perhaps stronghold of Dalaki-wa-Malaki . . .	,,	91	. . .
Inscription of Yasa Pála Rájá of, dated S. 1092 = A.D. 1035, from Karrá	,,	89, 95	. . .
Further identification of Buddhist sites at— . .	XXI	1	II.
Kosgain State, C. P.—			
Fort and sculptures in—	XIII	153—157	. . .
Kot in Gonda District, Oudh—			
An ancient site	XII	155	. . .
Kotá in Mathurá District, N.-W. P.—			
Buddhist sculptures at—	XX	49—52	III.
Kotgarh in Biláspur District, C. P.—			
Temples and inscription at, preserved at Muhammadpur	VII	212	. . .
Kotila in Alwar State, Rájputána—			
The capital of Bahádur Khán Náhar	XX	129	. . .
Fine mosque at—	,,	130	. . .
Kotila (Mubárakpur), near Delhi—			
See **Mubárakpur.**			
Kowaya in Mongír District, Bengal—			
Ruins at—	III	156	. . .
Kozoulo Kadphises—			
= Khieu-tsiu-ki of Chinese	II	65, 66	. . .
See **Kujula** Kara **Kadphises.**			

	Vol.	Page.	Plate.
Krakuchanda, the fourth Buddha—			
Birth-place of, near Kapilavástu	XII	IV, 177	XIII.
Krelulendra—			
A name found in an inscription from Gházípur District, and perhaps on a Gupta coin	XXII	97	X.
Krimila Desa—			
Mentioned in Mongír inscription	VIII	145	. . .
Krishna, god—			
First mentioned in the Sútras of Pánini	XX	45	. . .
Kríshna Gupta—			
Inscription of, at cave in Yusufzai	XIX	115	. . .
Krishna Rájá Ráshtrakúta—			
Silver coins of—	IX	29	V.
Kúcherá in Rájputána—			
Stone circles at, constructed for game of *táhar* or *ewáro*	XXIII	49	. . .
Kúdawa Nála in Bastí District, N.-W. P.—			
= Anoma R. of Buddhist tradition	XII	224	. . .
	XVIII	13	. . .
Kuei-Shwang tribe—	XXII	3, 111	. . .
= **Kushán**, *q.v.*			
Kujula Kara Kadphises, King—			
= Khieu-tsiu-ki of Chinese	II	65, 66	. . .
Coins of, found at Mánikyála	,,	168*	LXV.
Kulachuri—			
See **Kalachuri dynasty.**			
Kulháras in C. I.—			
Inscribed *Sati* pillars at—	,,	302	. . .
Kulika—			
= Jagdíspur near Nálanda	I	29	. . .
Kulindrine of Ptolemy—			
= Kuninda (Kulinda) country, *i.e.*, Kulu, &c. . .	XIV	138	. . .
Kumára Gupta (Early or Imperial Gupta dynasty)—			
Inscription of, at Bihár	I	37	. . .
on bricks at Bhitarí	,,	97	XXX.

* In pp. 65, 66, Kujula, or Kujulaka Kadphises, is identified with Khieu-tsiu-ki and Kozoulo Kadphises, but at p. 168 Kujula Kara Kadphises is described as the successor of Kozola Kadaphes.

	Vol.	Page.	Plate.
Kumára (Gupta Early or Imperial Gupta dynasty)—*contd.*			
Inscription of, at Garhwá	III	55	XX.
	X	9, 10	V.
near Bithá	"	7	IV.
at Bilsar	XI	18	VIII.
Perhaps referred to by Chinese author in A.D. 222-280	"	153	. . .
Gold coins of—	I	40, *Note*	. . .
	XV	116, 117	. . .
Silver ditto	IX	24	V.
Kumára Gupta (Later Gupta dynasty of Magadha)—			
Took title of Kramáditya	XVI	81	. . .
Coins of—	III	137	. . .
Defeated Isána Varmma	IX	28	. . .
Kumáril Bhatta, Mimánsaka philosopher—			
Instigated persecution of Buddhism in (?) 6th or 7th century A.D.	XX	103	. . .
Kunála, eldest son of Asoka—			
Stúpa in memory of, at Kurmál, S.-E. of Sháhdheri (Taxila)	II	149	. . .
Kundalpur in Damoh District, C. P.—			
50 Jain and two Brahmanical temples at— . .	XXI	166, 167	XLII.
Inscription of Chhatarsál at—	VII	58	. . .
	XXI	166	. . .
Kundilpur—			
Ancient name of Ahár in Bulandshahr District, N.-W. Provinces	XII	27	. . .
Kunet race of Punjáb Hills—			
Connected with the Khasias and Kols	XIV	125, 133	. . .
Distribution of—	"	126	. . .
Also called Mowa, or Mon, or Motan . . .	"	127	. . .
= Kulindas or Kunindas of early Hindu history . .	"	129	. . .
Three tribes of—	"	130	. . .
Origin of—	"	"	. . .
Language of—	"	131	. . .
Kuninda (Kulinda) country—			
= Hwen Thsang's kingdom of Srughna	"	134	. . .
Mentioned in the Mahábhárata	"	135	. . .
= Kulindrine of Ptolemy	"	131	. . .
Identified with Kulu and other territories now occupied by Kunets	"	138	. . .
	"	129	. . .
Coins of Amogha Bhúti, King of—	"	65, 134, 138	XXXI.

	Vol.	Page.	Plate.
Kunwára in Ráipur District, C. P.—			
Jain and Brahmanical temples at—	XVI	32	. . .
Kuraporina of Ptolemy—			
Perhaps = Khajuráho	XXI	58, 91	. . .
Kurkihár in Gayá District, Bengal—			
Topes, &c., at—	I	14	XXI.
Inscriptions of *circa* A.D. 800-1000 found at— . .	"	15	XIII.
Suggested derivation of name of—	XV	6	. . .
Buddhist legends of—	I	15	. . .
	XV	4	. . .
Kurmál, near Sháhdheri (Taxila) in Ráwalpindi District, Panjáb—			
Chief *stúpa* at, = that built in memory of Kunála, elder son of Asoka	II	149	. . .
Other Buddhist remains at—	"	150	. . .
Kuru-kshetra battle-field, near Thánesar in Umballa (Ambála) District, Panjáb—			
Position and limits of—	"	213	. . .
	XIV	87	XXVI.
Holy sites in—	"	90, 97	. . .
Mediæval history of—	"	95	. . .
Terra-cotta figures from—	"	98, 102	XXVII.
Kuságarapura—			
A name of Rájagriha	III	140	. . .
Kusapura (Kasapura) of Hwen Thsang—			
= Sultánpur, in Oudh	I	313	. . .
Kushan, *or* Khushan tribe—			
= Kuei-Shwang of Chinese authors, and also known as Gushán, Korsou, Korsea, Khoransu, Korano, and probably = Asiani of Trogus.	II	43, 64	. . .
	V	62	. . .
Kanishka, &c., belonged to—	"	"	. . .
Kusinagara—			
= Modern Kasiá, 35 miles east of Gorakhpur . .	I	76-85	XXVI.
	XVII	55	. . .
Position of, according to Fa-Hian and Hwen Thsang	I	80	. . .
Almost deserted in time of Hwen Thsang . . .	"	81	. . .
Ceylonese account of Buddha's obsequies at— . .	"	83	. . .

	Vol.	Page.	Plate.
Kusinagara—*contd.*			
Prominent share of Aniruddha in the obsequies at—	I	82, 84	. . .
Stûpas built by Asoka at—	"	" 85	. . .
Pillar recording history of *nirvána* formerly existed at-	"	"	. . .
Occupied by the Mallian kings	"	"	. . .
Ajátasatru removed relics of Buddha from—	XVIII	75	. . .
Hwen Thsang's list of sacred sites at—	"	88	. . .
Discussion as to site of Coronation hall and palace of Mallian kings at—	"	91	. . .
Secular and religious cities of—	"	94	. . .
Kusumapura—			
A name of Patna (Pátaliputra)	VIII	1	. . .
Kutb Mínár at Delhi—			
Controversy as to Hindu or Muhammadan origin of—	I	189	. . .
Is a purely Muhammadan building with Hindu details.	IV	x, xv	. . .
Dimensions of—	I	195	. . .
English repairs to—	"	199	. . .
Inscriptions on—	"	200	. . .
Builder of—	"	203	. . .
Kutb Mosque at Delhi—			
Cost of—	"	175	. . .
Hindu pillars in—	"	176	XXXVII
Date of—	"	185	. . .
Description of—	"	186	. . .
Additions to, by Iltitmish and Alá-ud-dín Khiljí	"	187, 188	. . .
Built under Muhammadan supervision out of materials of 27 temples	IV	v	. . .
Kutb-ud-dín Aibeg—			
Built Kutb Mosque and *Mínár* at Delhi	I	185, 202	. . .
Kutb-ud-din Chishti—			
Governor of Bihár under Jahangír	XI	2	. . .
Kútharâ—			
See **Náchná.**			
Kutwár, north of Gwáliár, C. I,			
Also named Kuntalpuri and Kamantalpuri	II	398	. . .
	XX	112	. . .
Most ancient capital of Gwáliár	II	398	. . .
Probably = Kántipurí of the Puránas	"	308	. . .
Inscription of the Tomara Rájá Kírtti Sinha Deva, dated A.D. 1465, at—	XX	112	. . .

	Vol.	Page.	Plate.
L			
Labokla of Ptolemy—			
= Lahore	II	205, *Note*	. . .
Labyrinth—			
At Indor Kherá	XII	58	. . .
Lahore (Láhor), capital of the Panjáb—			
= Labokla of Ptolemy	II	205, *Note*	. . .
Named Mahmúdpur by Mahmúd of Ghazní	XIV	67	. . .
Museum at—	V	55, *Note*	. . .
Láhor, near Ohind in Peshâwar District, Panjáb—			
= Ancient **Sálátura (So-lu-to-lo)**, *q.v.*	II	95	. . .
Lákhanú in Alígarh District, N.-W. P.—			
Buddhist remains at—	XII	1	. . .
Lakhísarai in Mongír District, Bengal—			
Ancient sites near—	III	153	. . .
Inscribed statue of Ganesa at—	VIII	118	. . .
Lakhnantí—			
A name of **Gaur (Gauda) city**, *q.v.*	XV	43	. . .
Lakhnor in Bengal—			
Perhaps=**Kánkjol**, *q.v.*	„	44	. . .
Lakhnor (Sháhábád), in Rámpur State, Rohilkhand—			
The capital of the Katahriya clan	I	257	. . .
Lakhuria—			
See **Náchná.**			
Lakshmana Sena, King of Bengal—			
Died in A.D. 1106	XV	167	. . .
Lakshmana era—			
Began in 1107 A.D.	„	160	. . .
Lalitpur in Lalitpur District, N.-W. P.—			
Legend of—	XXI	175	. . .
Old mosque at—	„	176	. . .
Lalitpur District—			
Temples of, wrongly ascribed to Gonds	IX	152	. . .

	Vol.	Page.	Plate.
Lálkot at Delhi—			
Identification and description of—	I	180	...
Lameta Ghát, near Jabalpur, C. P.—			
Perhaps = Malaita of Ptolemy	IX	57	...
Láphá in Bilášpur District, C. P.—			
Great fort at—	VII	219	...
Temple at—	,,	223	XX, XXI
Lapis Lazuli—			
Found at site of Taxila and at Baoti Pind	II	117, 141	...
Lassen, Professor—		Intr. xii	
Archæological work of—	II	85	...
Lát in Patna District, Bengal—			
Monolith at—	VIII	47	...
Latyá in Ghâzípur District, N.-W. P.—			
Monolith of Gupta period at—	III	61	...
Lauri—			
See **Lokhrí in Bándá District, N.-W. P.**			
Lauriyá-Araráj in Champáran District, Bengal—			
Edict pillar of Asoka at—	I	67	...
Lauriyá-Navandgarh in Champáran District, Bengal—			
Fort at—	,,	68	...
	XXII	46	...
Ruins at, extensive and peculiar	I	69	XXIV
Not visited by Fa-Hian, or Hwen Thsang	,,	71	...
Three rows of sepulchral earthen tumuli or barrows at—	,,	69-72	...
	XVI	104, 108	...
	XXII	42, 48	...
Tumuli at, are the *chetiyas* of the Vrijis	,,	49	...
Earthen *stúpa* cased with brick at—	,,	37	...
Seal of black earthenware with Gupta characters found in one tumulus at—	I	71	...
Inscribed lamp found near—	XVI	106	XXVIII
Lion-pillar at, inscribed with Asoka's edicts and minor inscriptions	I	73	...
	XVI	...	XVII
Liako Kusuluko, Satrap—			
Inscription of, at Sháhdherí (Taxila)	II	132-134	LIX
	V	67	...

	Vol.	Page.	Plate.
Lichchhavi family—			
Vaisáli, the capital of—	I	63	. . .
Took leave of Buddha at Kesariyá	XVI	16	. . .
Little Yuchi—			
See **Yuchi, Little.**			
Lodí dynasty—			
Made Agra their capital	IV	98	. . .
Lohában, near Mathurá—			
Statue at—	XX	46	. . .
Lohárú in Panjáb—			
Worship of a dog at—	XXIII	26	. . .
Lo-in-ni-lo of Hwen Thsang—			
Either Rajaona (Kiyul), or Nongarh in Mongír District	III	153, 155, 160	. . .
	XV	15	. . .
Lokhrí (Lukhrí *or* Laurí), in Bándá District, N.-W. P.—			
Sculptures at—	X	15	. . .
Lok-kál era—			
Used in Káshmír	V	181	. . .
Luckeesarai—			
See **Lakhí sarái.**			
Lumbiní garden, near Kapilavástu—			
Identified	XII	208	. . .
Lunde—			
A name of the Tákarí character	II	9	. . .

M

	Vol.	Page.	Plate.
Macedonian months—			
Mentioned in Ariano-Pálí inscriptions . . .	I	Intr. x	. . .
Máchárí in Alwar State, Rájputána—			
Anciently named Sánchárí	VI	77	. . .
Inscription dated Samvat 1439, Saka 1304 = A.D. 1382, at— . .	„	79	XI.
1515 = A.D. 1458 at— .	„	81	. . .
Traditions of Rájá Vena (Ben) Chakravartí at— .	„	85	. . .
Ancient temple at—	„	„	IX, X.
Ruined palace at—	„	87	. . .
Aboriginal tomb near—	„	88	. . .

	Vol.	Page.	Plate.
Machchhakanda, Rájá—			
Traditional founder of Nágar in Jaypur State . .	VI	162	. . .
Mackenzie, Col. Colin—			
Collection of MSS., inscriptions, &c., of S. India made by—	I	Intr. vi, xxix	. . .
'Madan Mahal'—			
At Jabalpur, C. P.	VII	54	. . .
Madan-Banáras—			
Old name of Zamánia in Gházípur District . .	III	63	. . .
Madana Pála Deva—			
Inscription of, at Baijnáth	XIX	30	XI.
Madana Varmma Deva, Chandel King—			
A powerful monarch	II	454	. . .
Kálanjar inscriptions of—	XXI	34	. . .
Madanpur in Lalitpur District, N.-W. P.—			
Temples and inscriptions at—	X	98, 100	XXXII.
	XXI	172	. . .
Inscriptions of Prithí Ráj Chauhán at—	X	98	XXXII.
	XXI	193	. . .
Madár, Sháh—			
Shrine at Makanpur of—	XVII	102	. . .
Madáwar (Mandáwar) in Bijnor District, N.-W. P.—			
= Madipur (Mo-ti-pu-lo) of Hwen Thsang . .	I	24	. . .
	II	231	. . .
Ruins and traditions of—	I	249	XLII.
Probably the country of the Mathæ of Megasthenes .	"	251	. . .
Site of Sanghabhadra's monastery at—	"	250	. . .
Mádhava Gupta—			
Seems to be mentioned in inscription at Eran . .	X	89	. . .
Madhuban-Bindrában in Champáran District, Bengal—			
Ruins at—	XXII	57	. . .
Madhyamikáya coins—			
Described	VI	201, 203	. . .
	XIV	146	XXXI.
Madipur (Mo-ti-pu-lo) of Hwen Thsang—			
Madáwar in Bijnor District, *q.v.*	I	248	. . .

	Vol.	Page.	Plate.
Madra, tribe—			
Occupied 'Madra-desa,' situated between Biás and Jhelam, or Biás and Chenáb, or Jhelam and Rávi .	II	14, 196	. . .
Also called Jártika and Báhika	,,	195	. . .
Magadha—			
Also known as Udandapura-desa = modern Bihár .	XI	185	. . .
Outline of history of, from 500 B.C. to 1200 A.D. .	III	138	. . .
Five kings of, mentioned by Hwen Thsang preceded the Guptas	I	Intr. XL	. . .
	III	95	. . .
Buddhism survived in, up to Muhammadan conquest .	,,	119	. . .
Magadha, Eastern—			
Later Gupta dynasty of—	,,	136	. . .
	XV	166	. . .
Magadha, Western—			
Varmma or Maukharí dynasty of—	III	135	. . .
	XV	78, 165	. . .
Magardhwaja Jogí—			
Inscriptions of, in eight places	XIII	8, *Note*, 99	. . .
in Central Provinces	IX	146	. . .
	XVII	36, 44,	XXII.
at Baijnáth	XIX	31	X.
Maghar in Bastí District, N.-W. P.—			
Birth-place (*sic*) of Kabír	XXII	72*	. . .
Mahában in Mathurá District, N.-W. P.—			
Inscription of Ajaya Pála Deva Yáduvansí, dated 1207 A.D. at—	XX	42, 46	X.
Assi Khambá mosque at—	,,	42—44	VII—IX.
Tomb of Sayyid Yahiá at—	,,	44	. . .
Mahában hill in Yusafzai, Panjáb—			
Visited by Hwen Thsang	II	98	. . .
Probably not = Aornos	,,	111, *Note*	. . .
Mahábhárata, war of—			
Abstract of story of—	XIV	91	. . .
Mahádeopur in Sháhábád District, Bengal—			
Curious brick temple at—	XVI	62	XX.
	XIX	14	III.
Mahá Kántára—			
See **Kántára, Mahá, of Samudra Gupta.**			
Mahá Kosala—			
See **Kosala, Mahá.**			

* Kabír died at Mahar, but was not born there. In the text Maghar is wrongly described as situated in the Gorakhpur District.

	Vol.	Page.	Plate.
Máhánadí R.—			
= Suktimatí R. of Mahábhárata	XVII	69	. . .
Also named Chitra Palavatí	„	70	. . .
Mahásamand in Ráipur District, C. P.—			
Mediæval temples at—	VII	159	. . .
Mahására—			
= Masár in Sháhábád District, Bengal . . .	III	66	. . .
Mahásthán in Bastí District, N.-W. P.—			
Site of *stúpa* of Chandaka at—	XXII	111, 5	. . .
Mahásthán in Bogra District, Bengal—			
Description of ruins and sculptures at—	XV	104—109	XXIX—XXXI.
Identified with **Paundra Varddhana**, *q.v.*	„	102, 110	. . .
Nothing Buddhist found at—	„	109	. . .
According to tradition capital of **Varendra**, *q.v.* . .	„	111	. . .
Identified with *Tagma Metropolis* of Ptolemy . .	„	114	. . .
Coins of Chandra Gupta II. and Kumára Gupta found near—	„	116	. . .
Coins of kings of Bengal found at—	„	117	. . .
Mahávíra, last Jáin hierarch—			
Buried at Pawá; was named Nirgrantha Jnáti-putra .	XI	170	. . .
Died in 527 B.C.	„	171	. . .
Mahendra Pála Deva, Rájá—			
Son of Bhoja Deva	X	102	. . .
Mahendra Pála Deva, King of Bengal—			
Two inscriptions of—	I	4	. . .
	XV	154	. . .
Mahendragiri of Samudra Gupta—			
Perhaps = Mahiyar (Máihar) in Baghelkhand . .	IX	10	. . .
Mahípála, King of Bengal and Magadha—			
Extent of dominions of—	XV	162	. . .
Coins of—	XI	177	XLIII.
Date of—	„	181	. . .
Inscription of, dated S. 1083 = 1026 A.D. . . .	I	114	. . .
	XI	181	. . .
Mahípála Deva Tomar, Rájá of Delhi and Kanauj—			
Built temple at Badaon	„	1	. . .
Inscription of, at Ahár	XII	36	. . .

	Vol.	Page.	Plate.
Mahípálpur, near Delhi—			
Tombs of reign of Iltútmish at—	XX	142—146	XXXII.
Mahirkul—			
See **Mihirkul.**			
Mahiyar (Máihar) in Baghelkhand—			
Perhaps = Mahendragiri of Samudra Gupta . .	IX	10	. . .
Temple of Sáraswatí (Sárddá Deví) at— . . .	VII	51	. . .
	IX	33	. . .
Inscribed *satí* pillar near—	"	34	. . .
Mahmúd of Ghazní—			
Conquest of Gándhára by—	V	84	. . .
Found great treasure at Kángra	"	155	. . .
Mahmúdpur—			
Name given to Lahore by Mahmúd of Ghazní . .	XIV	67	. . .
Mahoba in Hamírpur District, N.-W. P.—			
Extent of town	II	439	XCIX.
Palace of Parmál at—	"	440, 443	. .
Temple at Ráhilya near—	"	441	. . .
	VII	26	III.
Kakra temple at—	II	441	. . .
Madárí " "	"	442	. . .
Inscribed Jain statues at—	"	446	. . .
Buddhism at—	"	"	. . .
Perhaps = Empalathra of Ptolemy	X	99	. . .
	XXI	58, 92	. . .
Legends of—	II	445	. . .
	VII	13	. . .
	XXI	70	. . .
Inscriptions of Chandel period at—	II	448	. . .
	XXI	71	XXI-XX.
Mahodha in Nágpur District, C. P.—			
Curious *satí* monument at—	XVII	1	. . .
Mahwan in Mathurá District, N.-W. P.—			
Buddhist sculpture at—	XX	41	V.
Máihar—			
See **Mahiyar in Baghelkhand.**			
Maira in Salt Range, Panjáb—			
Arian inscription in well at— . . , ...	V	93	XXVIII.

	Vol.	Page.	Plate.
Majholí in Jabalpur District, C. P.—			
Varáha statue at—	IX	48	. . .
Makanpur in Farrukhábád District, N.-W. P.—			
Shrine of Sháh Madár at—	XVII	102	. . .
Visit of Aurangzeb to—	"	105	. . .
Makarbái in Hamírpur District, N.-W. P.—			
Temple at—	VII	26	. .
Makhdúm Jahániya, Saint—			
Tomb of, dated A.H. 881 = A.D. 1476 at Kanauj	I	289	. . .
Makundpur in Rewá State, Bághelkhand—			
Sculptures at—	XIII	4	. . .
Inscription, dated S. 772 from—	"	5, *Note*	. . .
Malaita of Ptolemy—			
Perhaps = Lameta Ghât near Jabalpur	IX	57	. . .
= Multai, N.-E. of Jabalpur	XXI	93	. . .
Malamantos R. of Arrian—			
= Chalpání R.	V	3	. . .
Málava country—			
Extent of—	XIV	151	. . .
Coins of, inscribed Jaya Málavána	VI	165, 173—183	. . .
	XIV	150	XXXI. .
Máldah in Máldah District, Bengal—			
Mosque and inscriptions at—	XV	77	. . .
Curious *minár* at—	"	78	. . .
Málhar in Bilászpur District, C. P.—			
Inscription from, removed to Bilászpur	VII	204	. . .
Malla country in Bengal—			
Rájás of—	VIII	12, 146	. . .
Malla, era in Bengal—			
Initial point of, is Saka plus 612	"	204	. . .
Malli, tribe—			
Perhaps represented by the existing Bála tribe	II	35	. . .
Capital city of, is now Múltan	V	129	. . .
Mallian kings of Kusinagara—			
Palace of—	I	82	. . .
	XVIII	91	. . .

	Vol.	Page.	Plate.
Mallot (Malot) in Salt Range, Jhelam District, Panjáb—			
Ruins at—	V	86—90	XXV—XXVII.
= Singhapura (Seng-ho-pu-lo) of Hwen Thsang	II	192	. . .
	V	85	. . .
Mán Singh, Rájá of Gwáliár—			
Glorious reign of—	II	387	. . .
Mand ***or*** **Mind—**			
An *alias* of the **Medi** ***or*** **Mer tribe,** *q.v.*	„	53	. . .
Mandár hill in Bhágalpur District, Bengal—			
Antiquities at, described by several writers	VIII	130	. . .
Temples, &c., at—	„	131	. . .
Remarkable rock-sculpture at—	„	132	. . .
Two rude rock-inscriptions at—	„	133	. . .
Gigantic sculptured head at—	„	134	. . .
Short ancient inscription at—	„	136	. . .
Sketch of—	„	„	II.
Two inscriptions of Áditya Sena Deva at—	„	134	. . .
	XVI	60, 79	. . .
Mandháta, Rájá—			
Central India and Rájputána traditions of—	VI	162	. . .
Mandi State in Panjáb—			
Inscription of doubtful date in temple at Nirmand in—	XIV	120	. . .
Satí pillars of Rájás of—	„	123	XXIX, XXX.
Mandlá in Mandlá District, C. P.—			
Fort at—	VII	103	. . .
Mandol in Mewár State—			
An old Mína village	VI	253	. . .
Mandor in Jodhpur State, Rájputána—			
Numerous gardens at—	XXIII	73	. . .
Cenotaphs at—	„	74	XV.
„ of Rao Gangá at—	„	75	XVI, XVII.
Mosques at—	„	77	. . .
Ceremony of building a cenotaph at—	„	83	. . .
Masons' marks in Júnágarh fort near—	„	84	. . .
Colossal late rock-sculptures at—	„	85	. . .
Maner—			
A town and pargana at junction of Son and Ganges	VIII	22	. . .

	Vol.	Page.	Plate.
Maneya of Buddhist legend—			
Identified with ruins near Táma (Tameswar Náth) in Bastí District	XII	223	. . .
	XVIII	12, 22	. . .
	XXII	2	. . .
Manigal, Satrap—			
Father of Zeionises (Jihonia)	II	152, 167	. . .
Perhaps founder of Mánikyála	XIV	5	. . .
Mánikyálá (Mánikiálá) in Ráwal Pindí District, Panjáb—			
Also known as Mánikpur or Mániknagar	II	152	. . .
Maps of ruins at—	„	. . .	LXII.
	XIV	. . .	II.
Excavations at—	V	75—79	XXI—XXIV.
	XIV	3	III.
Legend of Rasálu connected with—	II	153	. . .
Scene of Buddha's 'body-offering' to the seven hungry tiger-cubs	„	154	. . .
Numerous religious buildings but no large city at—	„	157	. . .
Destroyed by fire at time unknown	„	158, 164	. . .
Described by Hwen Thsang	„	„	. . .
Great Tope at, described	„	159	. . .
	V	76—78	. . .
Two Ario-Pálí inscriptions from Great Tope	II	160	LXIII.
No. 2, or General Court's Tope, = *stúpa* of Buddha's 'body-offering'	„	162	. . .
Monastery, &c., at—	„	164	. . .
Topes Nos. 3-14 at—	„	165—166	. . .
Sonála Pind mound at—	„	166	LXIV, LXV.
Parí-kí-dheri „ „	„	168	LXIV.
Mounds Nos. 17, 19, 20 at—	„	169	. . .
18, 21, and 22 at—	„	170	. . .
Remains of gilding on buildings at—	„	157, 171	. . .
Bronze statuettes from mound No. 22 at—	„	171	. . .
At least 15 topes and as many monasteries known to have existed at—	„	172	. . .
Probably first occupied in time of Satrap Manigal	XIV	5	. . .
Coins of Satrap Jihonia, Kuzula Kara Kadphises, and Kanishka found at—	II	152, 167	. . .
	XIV	6	. . .
Minor antiquities from—	„	„	IV.
Manipur in Biláspur District, C. P.—			
Formerly capital of Mahá Kosala	IX	55	. . .
Maniyágarh in Chhatarpur State, Bundelkhand—			
An ancient Chandel fort	XXI	69	. . .

	Vol.	Page.	Plate.
Mankuár—			
See **Bithá and Deoriyá in Alláhábád District, N.-W. P.**			
Manorhita, Buddhist Saint—			
Author of Vibhàshá Sástra	I	332	. . .
Taught at Peshawar *circa* A.D.	II	89	. . .
Mantras—			
See **Charms.**			
Márá in Rewá State, Baghelkhand—			
Saiva cave temples at—	XIII	20—31	V—IX.
Márkanda in Chándá District, C. P.—			
Group of temples at—	IX	143	XXVI.
Satí pillars at—	,,	144	. . .
Temple of Yama at—	,,	148	. . .
Das Avatár temple at—	,,	,,	XXVIII.
Inscribed monoliths at—	,,	149	XXX.
Márphá in Bándá District, N.-W. P.—			
A great fortress	XXI		. . .
Late inscriptions at—	,,	19	XVIII.
Was first settlement of the Baghels	,,	103	. . .
Martin, Montgomery—			
See **Buchanan-Hamilton, Dr.**			
Márttand in Káshmír—			
Earliest example of Indo-Doric architecture at— .	V	196	. . .
Masaon Dih near Saidpur-Bhitarí in Gházípur District, N.-W. P.—			
Inscription with name Krelulendra found near— .	XXII	97	IX, X.
Also named Dhanáwar	,,	98	. . .
Coins with name of (?) Dhana Deva in Asoka alphabet found at—	,,	99	. . .
Stone implements found in excavation near— . .	,,	100	. . .
List of ancient coins obtained at—	,,	103	. . .
Masár in Sháhábád District, Bengal—			
= Ancient Mahására	III	66	. . .
Changes in course of Ganges near—	,,	67	. . .
Hindu remains at—	,,	68	XXIII.
Jain inscriptions dated S. 1443 = A.D. 1386 at— .	,,	,,	XXIV.
Modern Jain inscription mentioning English rule at—	,,	70	,,
Find of 200 gold coins at—	,,	71	. . .

	Vol.	Page.	Plate.
Masons' marks—			
Are trustworthy proofs of age	V	72	. . .
At Nálanda	I	30	. . .
At Bairánt	III	101	. . .
In Arian characters at Jamálgarhi	XXII	118	. . .
	V	64*	. . .
Masúdí, geographer—			
Found four great kings in India in 915 A.D. . .	I	146	. . .
Máthá Kuar, fort of—			
At **Kasiá (Kusinágara)**, *q.v.*	,,	78, 82	. . .
Mathae of Megasthenes—			
Probably inhabitants of Madáwar in Bijnor District, N.-W. Provinces	,,	251	. . .
Mathiahpillar—			
See **Lauriyá-Navandgarh in Champáran District, Bengal.**			
Mathurá in Mathurá District, N.-W. P.—			
A great Buddhist centre in time of Chinese pilgrims, A.D. 400 and 634	,,	232	. . .
Site of Upagupta's monastery at—	,,	233	XXXIX.
	XX	32	. . .
Kesava Rai's great temple at, destroyed by Aurangzeb, in A.D. 1669	I	235	,,
	XX	39	. . .
Plundered by Mahmúd of Ghazní A.D. 1017 . .	I	236	. . .
Buddhism disappeared from, between A.D. 634 and 1017	,,	237	. . .
Site of Huvishka's monastery at—	,,	238	. . .
	XVII	107	. . .
Statues of Buddha at—	I	240	. . .
Statue of dancing girl at—	,,	,,	XL.
Buddhist railings at—	,,	241	. . .
	III	23	VIII—X.
	XVII	110	XXXI.
Group supposed to represent Silenus, &c., from— .	I	242	. . .
Greek influence shown in sculpture from— . .	,,	243	. . .
Excavations in 1871 at—	III	13	I.
Græco-Bactrian coins found at—	,,	14	. . .
Copper celt found at—	,,	16	II.
Jain and other remains from Kankálí mound at— .	,,	19	V—VII.
Dress of female figures at—	,,	25	VI, VII, XI.
Wall ornaments at—	,,	27	XII.
24 inscriptions at—	,,	16, 30	XIII—XVI.

* It has not been thought necessary to refer to every passage that mentions masons' marks.

	Vol.	Page.	Plate.
Mathurá in Mathurá District, N.-W. P.—*contd.*			
Abundant Jain remains of early date at— . .	III	45	. . .
Suggested identification of sites at—	,,	28	. . .
	XX	31, 45	II.
The manufactory for Buddhist sculpture . . .	XI	75	. . .
Named Islámábad by Aurangzeb	XX	39	. . .
Changes in course of Jumna at—	,,	31	. . .
Sculptures in museum at—	,,	34	III, IV.
Short inscriptions at, dated 57 and 62 S.	,,	36, 37	V.
Series of ancient coins found at—	,,	37	. . .
Muhammadan persecutions at—	,,	38	. . .
Sculpture of Herakles strangling Nemæan lion found at—	XVII	109	XXX.
Discussion of Hwen Thsang's topography of— . .	,,	111	. . .
Mathurá District—			
Early history of—	XX	3—5	. . .
Matsya-desa—			
Extent of—	II	244	. . .
	XX	2	. . .
Mauas—			
See **Moga, King.**			
Maukharí—			
Tribal name of Varmma kings of Magadha .	XV	165	. . .
Perhaps the same as Maurya	,,	166	. . .
Maukharí dynasty of Magadha—			
Opposed to later Guptas	XVI	78, 80	. . .
Maurya dynasty—			
Alluded to by Euphorion and Hesychius . . .	I	Intr. XLI.	. . .
Relations between Antiochus the Great and— . .	II	41	. . .
Máyána (Máyápura) in C. I.—			
Inscribed *satí* pillar at—	,,	302	. . .
Máyápura, *or* **Máyúra**—			
An ancient town close to Haridwár in Sahâranpur District, N.-W. P.	,,	232	. . .
Mayúradhwaja—			
A king of Ayodhya and Srávastí	I	329	. . .
	XI	98	. . .
Gives name to a fort in Rohilkhand	I	330, *Note*	. . .
See **Moradhwaj, Rájá.**			

	Vol.	Page.	Plate.
Medi, *or* Med tribe—			
Probably a branch of the Su or Abár horde	II	53	. . .
Settled along the Hydaspes (Jhelam) in time of Peutingerian Tables, *i.e.*, before 250 A.D.	"	52, 53	. . .
In tenth century settled in Sindh	"	53	. . .
= Modern Mer tribe of Aravali Range, Kathiáwár, and Beluchistán	"	"	. . .
Seem to have been the first Indo-Scythian conquerors of the Panjáb	"	54	. . .
Probably followers of King Moga *or* Moas	"	"	. . .
Mediæval Brahmanical period—			
Remains of—	III	5	. . .
Medo-Scythians—			
Probably preceded Aryans in N.-W. India	IX	160	. . .
Megallæ of Pliny—			
Perhaps represented by Meos	XX	28	. . .
Megarsus R. of Dionysius Periegetes—			
= Satlaj R.	II	12	. . .
Megasthenes—			
Mentions tumuli as Indian form of sepulchre	I	76, *Note*	. . .
Mega—			
A tribe in the Jammú hills, Panjáb	II	11—13	. . .
Probably = Mekei of Arrian	"	11	. . .
Seem originally to have been located on Satlaj	"	13	. . .
Mekala—			
The mountain range in which the Narbadá rises	XVII	85	. . .
Mekhala, Kingdom of—			
Kshemavatí capital city of, identified with Khemrájpur ruins in Bastí District	XII	183	. . .
Menander, King—			
Advanced to Ganges	II	41	. . .
Meo race—			
Forms bulk of population of Mewát	XX	22	. . .
Of Hindu origin	"	"	. . .
Sub-divisions of—	"	23	. . .
Connected with aboriginal Mínas	"	25, 27	. . .
Customs and legends of—	"	25—29	. . .

	Vol.	Page.	Plate.
Meo race—*contd.*			
Todar Mal belonged to—	XX	26	. . .
May represent the Megallæ of Pliny	"	28	. . .
Turbulent character of—	"	29	. . .
Cruelties of Muhammadan rulers to—	"	29, 30	. . .
Meteorite—			
Worship of—	XVI	32	. . .
Mewát—			
Described by Bábar	XX	19	. . .
Formed by Akbar into the Sarkárs of Alwar and Tejára	"	21	. . .
Meos form bulk of population of—	"	22	. . .
Pacified by English Government	"	30	. . .
Tejára and Sarhata, capitals of—	"	117, 118	. . .
History of—	"	10—22	. . .
Invaded and ravaged by Ulúgh Khán (Balban) in A.H. 658	"	13, 29	. . .
Severities of Fíroz Tughlak in—	"	14	. . .
Mhau-maidán in Rájputána—			
An ancient city	II	293	. . .
Mihirkul (Mihirakula)—			
King of Sangala, contemporary with Báláditya II. of Magadha	"	197	. . .
Milinda—			
Yavana, King of Sangala, and opponent of the Buddhist Nágasena	"	"	. . .
Mill, Dr.—			
Translated several important inscriptions	I	Intr. VII	. . .
Mills—			
Sometimes inscribed	III	IX	. . .
Míná race—			
Former extent of power of—	VI	113	. . .
Formerly intermarried with Meo race	XX	25, 27	. . .
Minár—			
One only, to each early mosque	IV	IX	. . .
Minnagara of the Erythræan Periplus—			
Probably = Thatha in Sindh	II	47	. . .
Perhaps = Calamina of Saint Thomas legend	"	60	. . .

	Vol.	Page.	Plate.
Mithabel in Gorakhpur District, N.-W. P.—			
An ancient site	XVIII	52	...
Mithila *or* Videha—			
Comprised Champáran District and greater part of Darbhangá	XVI	34	...
Janakpur ancient capital of—	"	"	...
Mitra dynasty—			
One coin of, found at Bairát in Alwar State	II	249	...
Coins of, found at Kosam in Alláhábád District	X	4	II.
found at and near Bhuilá Dih in Bastí District	XII	153, 165, 169	...
from Bairánt in Benares District	XXII	115	...
Modern Brahmanical period—			
Remains of—	III	6	...
Moga (Muga, Moa, Moas, Mauas) King—			
According to tradition was a Saka	II	54	...
Perhaps first established Indo-Scythian rule in Panjáb	"	59	...
Succeeded by Vonones, Azes, &c.	"	54	...
Coins of,	"	59, 187	...
Founded Mong (Mung, Mog) his chief mint city	"	187	...
Mentioned in Taxila inscription of the Satrap Liako Kusulako	"	134, 187	LIX.
Also known as Rájá Sankhár	"	187	...
Mogalána, Mahá—			
Born at Kulika (= Jagdíspur), near Nálanda	I	29	...
Mogaliputra—			
Distinguished from Mogalána	"	Intr. XXXIX	...
Presided at Buddhist synod in reign of Asoka	"	" "	...
Mokand-dwára in Kotá State, Rájputána—			
Early temples and short inscriptions at—	XXIII	131	...
Mon (Motan, Mowa)—			
Names of the Kunet race	XIV	127	...
Mong (Mung) in Gujrát District, Panjáb—			
Founded by Rájá Moga *or* Muga	II	187	...
= Nikaea	"	184, 187	...
Coins of the 'nameless king' very abundant at—	"	187, *Note*	...
Mongír (Monghyr, Mungír)—			
Ancient names of—	XV	15	...
Speculations as to derivation of modern name	"	18	...

	Vol.	Page.	Plate.
Mongír Monghyr, Mungír—*contd.*			
Identified with Hwen Thsang's *I-lanna-Po-fa-to* .	XV	16	. . .
Legends of Karna and Vikrama at— . . .	"	"	. . .
Mongír District—			
Hot springs at—	"	App.	. . .
Morá Mountain, near Buddha Gayá—			
Contains Prágbodhi cave of Hwen Thsang . .	III	105	. . .
Morá Town, in Jaypur State—			
An ancient site	VI	227	. . .
Morá Village, near Mathurá—			
Inscription of son of Satrap Rajubul at— . . .	XX	48	. . .
Moradhaj (Mayúradhwaja), in Bijnor District, N.-W. P.—			
Great Fort at—	II	237	. . .
Ruins of (?) *stúpa* at—	"	238	. . .
History unknown of—	"	"	. . .
Moradhwaj, Rájá—			
Traditions of—at Haswá in Fatehpur District . .	XVII	98	. . .
Rájputána traditions of—	VI	227	. . .
See **Mayúradhwaja.**			
Mori—			
A Rájput clan in Mewár	"	208, 232, 234	. . .
Moriyas, City of—			
Identified with Rájdhání or Updhaolia in the Gorakhpur District	XVIII	31	II.
Morví inscription dated in Gupta era—	XXII	3, 7	. . .
Discussed	IX	16	. . .
Mubárak Sháh—			
Tomb of, near Delhi	XX	153	XXXV.
Mubárakpur (Kotila), near Delhi—			
Tomb of Mubárak Shah at—	"	"	. . .
Muga—			
See **Moga, King.**			
Mughal (Early) architecture—			
Described	III	12	. . .

	Vol.	Page.	Plate.
Mughal (Late) Architecture—			
Described	III	12	. . .
Mugháls—			
Resemblance of traditions of, to those of the Gonds .	IX	158	. . .
Muhámmád Tughlák, Emperor—			
Tomb and Forts of, at Delhi	I	217	. . .
Multai, N.-E. of Jabalpur—			
Perhaps = Malaita of Ptolemy	XXI	93	. . .
Multán in Multán District, Panjáb—			
Topography of—	V	114	XXXVI.
= Meu-lo-san-pu-lo (Mulasthánipura) of Hwen Thsang.	"	115	. . .
Captured by Raja Chach of Sindh	"	114	. . .
Ditto by Muhammad bin Kásim	"	115	. . .
Temple of Sun at—	"	115—120	. . .
Captured by Mahmúd of Ghazní	"	217	. . .
Coins of—	"	121	XXXVII.
Stone rings at—	"	125	. . .
Buildings of, were built of brick	"	126	. . .
Archæological well at—	"	127	. . .
Was the capital city of the Malli	"	129	. . .
Temple of Pahládpuri at—	"	"	. . .
Ancient name of, was Kasyapapura, = Kaspapuros of Hekataeus, = Kaspaturos of Herodotus, and Kaspeira of Ptolemy	II	69	. . .
	V	129	. . .
Muhammadan tombs at—	"	130	. . .
Rokn-i-Alam tomb at—	"	132	XXXVIII.
Legends and customs of—	"	133—136	. . .
Tile mosaics of—	"	133	XXXIX.
Munde—			
A name of the Tákarí character	II	9	. . .
Munga—			
See **Umga (Munga) in Sháhábád District.**			
Mungír—			
See **Mongír.**			
Murmárí in Bhandárá District, C. P.—			
Worship of deceased English lady at—	XVII	2	. . .
Murpar in Ráipur District, C. P.—			
Temples at—	VII	147	. . .

N

	Vol.	Page.	Plate.
Nabhakas and Nabhamatis, *or* Nabhapantis—			
Peoples mentioned in Asoka's edicts	V	20	. . .
Náchná *or* Kúthará in Ajaygarh State, Bundelkhand—			
Site of an ancient city	XXI	95	. . .
Curious Gupta temple at—	,,	96	XXV, XXVI.
Inscription of Prithiví Sena and Vyaghra Deva at— .	,,	97	XXVII.
Temple of Mahadeva at—	,,	98	. . .
Nadolá in Jodhpur State, Rájputáná—			
Legend of—	XXIII	92	. . .
Late temples at—	,,	94	. . .
Early *Khetla-ká-sthán* temple at—	,,	95	XIX.
Nadubandagar of Ptolemy—			
Perhaps = Narwár	XXI	58, 92	. . .
Nága—			
Synonymous with Karkota and Takshaka . .	VI	167	. . .
See **Snake-worship.**			
Nágar *or* Karkota Nágar in Jaypur State, Rájputána—			
Said to have been founded by Rájá Machchhakanda .	,,	162	. . .
Probably at one time held by Nágas . . .	,,	166	. . .
Legend of destruction of—	,,	168	. . .
Traces of volcanic action at—	,,	170	. . .
Description of 6,000 ancient coins found at— . .	,,	165, 173-183	. . .
Gems and miscellaneous antiquities found at— . .	,,	183	. . .
Description of site of—	,,	184	XXII.
Short mediæval inscriptions at—	,,	185	. . .
Temples at—	,,	186	XX, XXII.
Ancient embankments at—	,,	190	. . .
Traditional extent of—	,,	195	. . .
Thousands of Málavána coins obtained at— . .	XIV	150	XXXI.
Nágar—			
An ancient site in Bastí District	XII	83	. . .
Nágarí *or* Támbavatí Nagarí, near Chitor, in Mewár—			
Founded by Rájá Hari Chand	VI	196	. . .
Great numbers of punch-marked coins found at— .	,,	198	. . .

	Vol.	Page.	Plate.
Nágari *or* **Támbavatí Nágari, near Chitor, in Mewár**—*contd.*			
Stúpa at—	VI	198	XXIV.
Analysis of 145 ancient coins found at—	„	200	. . .
Madhyamikáya coins of Sibi country found at—	„	201	. . .
	XIV	146	XXXI.
Probably the Takshak-Nagara of Tod	VI	208	. . .
Extent of ruins of—	„	210	. . .
Nágárjuna—			
Controversy between King Milinda and—	II	197	. . .
Mongol legend of residence of, in a cave in Magadha	VIII	43	. . .
Nágárjuni Hills in Gayá District, Bengal—			
Described	I	44	XVIII.
Three caves in—	„	„	XIX.
Inscriptions of Dasaratha, grandson of Asoka, &c., in the caves of—	„	49	XX.
Minor pilgrims' records of Gupta and later age in caves of—	„	50	XX.
Caves of, successively occupied by Buddhists and Brahmans	„	51	. . .
Variation in names of the caves of—	„	52	. . .
Legends relating to—	„	43	. . .
Nagarkot—			
Another name for Kángrá fort	V	155	. . .
Nágas, dynasty of nine—			
Reigned at Padmávatí = modern Narwár	II	307	. . .
Date of—	„	309	. . .
Extent of dominions of—	„	308	. . .
List of—	„	310	. . .
Six coins of, found at Nágar in Jaypur State	VI	178	. . .
Nágaudh (Nágod) State, in Bághelkhand—			
Also called **Uchahara**, *q.v.*	IX	5	. . .
Probably = Sagabaza of Ptolemy	XXI	92	. . .
Nágaur in Jodhpur (Márwár) State, Rájputána—			
Legends of—	XXIII	50	. . .
Walls of—	„	53	. . .
Fountain of Akbar's reign, and other buildings in fort at—	„	55	. . .
Temples of Mahádeo and Murlídhar, and of Barmáyan at—	„	56—58	XIII, XIV.
Cave at—	„	58	. . .
List of temples at—	„	60	. . .

	VOL.	PAGE.	PLATE.
Nágaur, in Jodhpur (Márwár) State, Rájputána—*contd.*			
List of mosques at—	XXIII	61	. . .
Inscribed private houses at—	"	"	. . .
Tanks at—	"	63	. . .
Minor inscriptions at—	"	64	. . .
Shams mosque at—	"	65	XII.
Gateway of Atarkin at, with inscription dated A.H. 630	"	69	XI.
Nagor in Sántál Parganas, Bengal—			
Great fort of—	VIII	146	. . .
Nágpur, capital of C. P.—			
Antiquities in museum at—	VII	115—118	. . .
Náin in Jáypur State, Rájputána—			
An ancient Mína stronghold	VI	109	. . .
Nákodár in Jálandhar District, Panjáb—			
Tombs of time of Sháh Jahán and Jahángír at— .	XIV	59	XX.
Nala Rájá—			
Narwár legend of—	VII	95—101	. . .
Nálanda—			
Said to have been residence of Bimbisára . .	I	28	. . .
Certainly = Barágaon in Patna District, Bengal .	"	"	. . .
Description of ruins of—	"	29	XVI.
Sáriputra and Mogalána, born near—	"	"	. . .
Great temple of Báláditya at—	"	34	. . .
	III	94	. . .
'Nameless king,' the—			
Speculations concerning identity of—	III	39, 44	. . .
Coins of, abundant at Mong	II	187, *Note*	. . .
Nanaguna R. of Ptolemy—			
= Taptí R.	IX	151	. . .
Nándchánd, 40 miles E.-N.-E. of Damoh in C. P.—			
Temples at—	XXI	160	XL, XLI.
Nandinagara—			
A town mentioned in Sánchi inscriptions . . .	X	59	. . .
Nara Singha Deva, King of Chedi—			
Inscription in Rewá State of—	XXI	114	XXVIII.

	Vol.	Page.	Plate.
Nára Sinha, town, of Hwen Thsang—			
= Ránsi, 25 miles west of Lahore, Panjáb . . .	II	202	. . .
	XIV	47	. . .
Naráyana city—			
Capital of ancient kingdom of Bairát . . .	II	243	. . .
Naráyana Kanwa, King—			
Perhaps = Vishṇu Tushára	V	140	. . .
Náráyana temple, of Hwen Thsang—			
Perhaps = Naráyanpur in Gházípur, N.-W. P.—	XXII	76	. . .
Naráyanpur in Ráipur District, C. P.—			
Temples at—	VII	193	XIX.
Statues at—	"	194	. . .
Narbadá R.—			
Legends connected with—	IX	74	. . .
Narendra Gupta, King—			
Another name of Sasángka	"	157	. . .
Nárnaul in Patiála State, Panjáb—			
Early Muhammadan buildings at—	XXIII	27	. . .
Narod—			
See **Ranod in Central India.**			
Narwár in Gwáliár State, Central India—			
Ancient Padmávatí, capital of Nága Kingdom . .	II	307	. . .
Perhaps = Nadubandagar of Ptolemy . . .	XXI	58, 92	. . .
Coins of Nága Kings found at—	II	309	. . .
Inscription dated S. 1177 = A.D. 1120 at— . .	"	312	. . .
Held by Rájá Cháhada Deva in 1251 A.D.. . .	"	314	. . .
List of Rájás of—	"	316	. . .
Held by Tomar dynasty of Gwáliár from A.D. 1398 to A.D. 1506	"	317	. . .
Afterwards held by Kachhwáhas of Amber . . .	"	"	. . .
Described by Bhávabhúti in eighth century A.D. .	"	308, 318	. . .
Description of fortress of—	"	319	. . .
Roman Catholic chapel and cemetery at— . . .	"	322	. . .
Large mutilated inscription at—	"	323	. . .
Inscribed 'column of victory' at—	"	324	. . .
Inscribed *Báorí* and *Satí* pillars at—	"	"	. . .
Iron works at—	"	325	. . .
Bridges at—	"	"	. . .
Gipsy legend at—	"	327	. . .
Legend of Rájá Nala at—	VII	95—101	. . .

	Vol.	Page.	Plate.
Náthdwára in Udaipur (Mewár) State, Rájputána—			
Great temple of Náthjí at—	XXIII	100	. . .
Navadevakula of Hwen Thsang—			
= Newal and Bángarmau in Oudh	XI	47	. . .
Nawagaon in Ráipur District, C. P.—			
Group of temples at, built of materials from Arang	XVII	22	XII, XIII.
Nephthalites—			
= Ephthalites, = **White Huns,** *q.v.*			
Ner in Gayá District, Bengal—			
Ruined temple at—	VIII	65	. . .
Newal and Bángarmau in Cawnpore District, N.-W. P.—			
= Navadevakula of Hwen Thsang	XI	47	. . .
Legend of—	„	48	. . .
Sites of Buddhist and Brahmanical buildings at—	„	50	. . .
Terra-cotta figures from—	„	52	XVIII.
Nikumbha race—			
Identical with Raghuvansí race	XX	9, 10	. . .
Early history of—	„	8—10	. . .
Founded Alwar	„	120	. . .
Nímsár (Nímkhár) in Sítápur District, Oudh—			
Ancient fort at—	I	350	. . .
Nímtor in Rájputána—			
Temple and inscription dated S. 1027 at—	XXIII	124	. . .
Nirgrantha Jnáti putra—			
Proper name of Mahavíra the last Jain hierarch	XI	170	. . .
Nirvána—			
Great *stúpa* of, at Kasiá	XVIII	63, 73, *seqq.*	V, VI.
Date of, discussed	VIII	34	. . .
Nirvána, era of—			
Inscription at Gayá dated in—	I	1, 3	. . .
	III	126	XXXV.
Nográm—			
See **Ránígat.**			
Nongarh in Mongír District, Bengal—			
Perhaps = Lo-in-ni-lo of Hwen Thsang	„	160	. . .
Stúpa and statue at—	„	161	XLVII.
	VIII	118, 119	. . .

	Vol.	Page.	Plate.
Norris, Mr.—			
Deciphered Sháhbázgarhi Inscription of Asoka . .	V	8	. . .
Numerals, ancient Indian—			
Deciphered by Stevenson, Bháu Dájí and Cunningham	I	Intr. xxxiii xlii	. . .
Suhaniya slab showing—	II	401	. . .
In Arian alphabet in Yusufzai	V	61	. . .
Núrábád, near Gwáliár, C. I.—			
Muhammadan buildings at—	II	397	. . .
Núrmahal in Jálandhar District, Panjáb—			
Sarai built by Núr Jahan at—	XIV	62	. . .
Núrpur Tahsil in Kángrá District, Panjáb—			
Anciently named Dahmeri or Dahmbeori, = Audumbara	,,	116	. . .
Pathánkot (Pratishthána) was capital of— . . .	,,	,,	. . .
Rájás of—	,,	118	. . .

O

	Vol.	Page.	Plate.
Obelisks, sculptured—			
In Málwá, Mirzápur District, and Central Provinces .	XI	132	. . .
At Daraulí in Sháhábád District	XIX	25	. . .
Obolus, coin—			
Represented by Indian *boddika*	XI	176	. . .
Obscene sculptures—			
On temples at Khajuráho	II	420	. . .
Odonbeores of Pliny—			
= People of Kachchh	V XIV	155 136	. . . . . .
Odumbara—			
See **Audumbara.**			
Ohind on Indus in Yusufzai (Peshâwar District), Panjáb—			
Said to have been founded by Alexander the Great .	II	95	. . .
Indo-Scythian coins found at—	,,	,,	. . .
= U-to-kia-han-cha, = Udakhanda, = Hund, = Hind, = Waihand, = (?) Orá, = Kárajáng, = Bithanda	,,	93	. . .

	Vol.	Page.	Plate.
Ohind on Indus in Yusufzai (Pesháwar District), Panjáb— *contd.*			
Was capital of Gándhára up to 1026 A.D.	XIV	93, 94	. . .
Probably = Embolima or Ekbolima of Greek writers	"	101—103	. . .
Sometimes called Ambar-ohind	"	103	. . .
Distinguished from Ohind on Jhelam	"	"	. . .
Inscription dated S. 61 from—	V	58	. . .
Okhala village near Delhi—			
Inscribed tombs of reign of Iltitmish formerly existing at—	XX	160	. . .
Ongari, a village in Patna District, Bengal—			
Inscription said to exist at—	VIII	74	. . .
Ooemo—			
See **Wema Kadphises, King.**			
Ophiolatry—			
In Káshmír	II	10	. . .
See **Nága** *and* **Snake.**			
Orai, in Jalaun District, N.-W. P.—			
Supposed site of battle between Parmál and Prithí Ráj	VII	20	. . .
Orissa—			
Sculptures of *Navagraha* common in—	XIII	119	. . .
Ancient sites in Native States of—	"	126	. .
Gupta dynasty of—	XVII	17, 85, 87	. . .
Otantapura—			
A name of Bihár city	VIII	75	. . .
	XI	185, 191	. . .
Oudh—			
See **Ayodhya, kingdom.**			
O-yu-to of Hwen Thsang—			
Perhaps = Pátan-Bihár in Unao District, Oudh	"	55	. . .
Ozoabis of Ptolemy—			
Perhaps = Asírgarh	IX	121	. . .

P

	Vol.	Page.	Plate.
Pachet, in Bánkurá District, Bengal—			
Inscriptions of 17th century at—	VIII	180	. . .

	Vol.	Page.	Plate.
Pachran, in Gonda District, Oudh—			
Copper-plate inscription found at—	XI	100	. . .
Padaraoná (Paraunâ), in Gorakhpur District, N.-W. P.—			
Perhaps = ancient Páwá	I	74	. . .
Remains of (?) *stúpa* at—	"	75	. . .
Pádham, in Mainpuri District, N.-W. P.—			
Series of coins from—	XI	38	XIII.
Padmávatí—			
Capital of Nága kingdom = modern Narwár . .	II	307	. . .
Described by Bhavabhúti in 8th century A.D. .	"	308—318	. . .
Pahárpur in Dinájpur District, Bengal—			
Ruins of great temple at—	XV	117	XXXII.
Painám—			
A name of **Sunárgáon**, *q.v.*	"	137	. . .
Paintings, rock—			
Of animals, &c., at Ginja Hill	XXI	119	XXX.
Inscription in, near Bank Ghát in (?) Chutiá Nágpur .	XIII	55	. . .
Pákbirra, in Singhbhúm District, Bengal—			
Jain remains at—	VIII	193—195	. . .
Also called Ponchá	"	198	. . .
Pakkalaoti—			
= **Pushkalávatí**, *q.v.*			
Pákna-Bihár in Farrukhábád District, N.-W. P.—			
Site of great monastery at—	XI	31	X.
Indo-Scythian inscription at—	"	32	XII.
Carved bricks and seals from—	"	35	XI, XII.
Pakores, king of S. Ariana and Sindh—			
Probably of Parthian origin	II	47	. . .
Pála dynasty of Magadha and Bengal—			
Rose in 8th or 9th century A.D.	III	135	. . .
	XV	148	. . .
Probably of Bhuinhár caste	"	116, 147	. . .
Professed Buddhism	III	119	. . .
Ruled from Benares to mouths of the Ganges . .	XVI	1	. . .
Genealogy of—	III	134	. . .
	XI	178	. . .
	XV	149	. . .

	Vol.	Page.	Plate.
Pála dynasty of Magadha and Bengal—*contd.*			
Corrected chronology of—	XI	181	. . .
Inscriptions of—	III	113—118,	
	XV	120, 121	. . .
		150	. . .
Vikrama Samvat used in only two inscriptions of— .	XI	177	. . .
Succeeded in Bengal by Sena dynasty in 11th century A.D.	III	134	. . .
	XV	155	. . .
Pálí, in Biláspur District, C. P.—			
Temples at—	VII	217	. . .
Inscriptions of Jájalla Deva at—	"	218	. . .
Pilgrim's record at—	"	"	. . .
Two inscriptions said to have existed at— . .	"	219	. . .
Pálí, in Gayá District, Bengal—			
Temple in Gupta style at—	VIII	61	. . .
	XVI	52	. . .
Pálí, in Jodhpur State, Rájputána—			
Hindu temples at—	XXIII	86	. . .
Naulakha Jain temple at—	"	89	XVIII.
Inscription at—	"	91, *Note*	. . .
Pálí Kherá, in Mathurá District, N.-W. P.—			
Bacchanalian group and other sculptures at— . .	XX	47	III.
Palibothra—			
The Greek form of **Pátaliputra**, *q.v.*			
Palodheri, in Yusufzai (Peshávar District), Panjáb—			
(?) = Po-lu-sha of Hwen Thsang	II	91	. . .
Scythian inscription in cave at—	"	92	. . .
Panassa of Ptolemy—			
Probably a town on Banás (Parnása) R. in C. P. .	IX	57	. . .
Panchála (Northern) kingdom—			
Ahichhatra, capital of—	I	255	. . .
Ditto (Southern) kingdom—			
Kampil, capital of—	XI	11	. . .
Pándrá, in Mánbhúm District, Bengal—			
Mediæval temples at—	VIII	155	VI, XIV.
Panduá (Chhotá), in Húglí District, Bengal—			
Muhammadan buildings at—	XV	123	XXXV.
Mínár at—	"	126	. . .

	Vol.	Page.	Plate.
Panduá (Hazrat), in Máldah District, Bengal—			
A capital of the Muhammadan kings of Bengal .	XV	79	. . .
Also named Fírozábád	,,	80, *Note*	. . .
Abandoned by Mahmúd I	,,	81	. . .
Now in deep jungle	,,	,,	. . .
Four groups of ruins at—	,,	82	. . .
Description of buildings and inscriptions at— . .	,,	82—94	XXIV—XXVI.
Pandya (Panda) country—			
Mentioned in Sháhbázgarhi inscription . . .	V	20	. . .
Pánini, grammarian—			
Born at Sálátura	II	95	. . .
Panj Pahárí, near Patna—			
=Hill of Upagupta	VIII	IX	. . .
Panjáb—			
Ethnology of—	II	2	. . .
Turanian tribes of—	,,	6, 22	. . .
Aryan tribes of—	,,	13	. . .
Greek art in—	V	5	. . .
Ancient cities on banks of great rivers of— . .	,,	5	. . .
Capital of, at Taki or Asarur, *q. v.*, in A. D. 633 .	III.	200	. . .
Finally annexed to Ghaznavite empire, A. D. 1026 .	,,	42	. . .
Tákari alphabet largely used in—	,,	9	. . .
Panjkara R. in Yusufzai—			
=Garaios R. of Arrian	V	3	. . .
Panjor (Panchapura) in Patiála State, Panjáb—			
Notices of, by Muhammadan historians . . .	XIV	70	. . .
Inscriptions at—	,,	71	XXII.
Panjpír, a hill in Yusufzai—			
A possible position for Aornos	II	106	. . .
Panjtar in Yusufzai—			
Inscription dated 122 from—	V	61	. . .
Panná State, Bundelkhand—			
Legend of diamond-mines in—	VII	49, 50	. . .
Pantaleon, King—			
Coins of, copied from Indian originals . . .	XIV	19	X.

	Vol.	Page.	Plate.
Párá, in Mánbhúm District, Bengal—			
Inscriptions and temples at—	VIII	162—166	. . .
Formerly the seat of local chiefs	„	167	. . .
Parainí on Ken R.—			
Statue of boar at—	XXI	158	. . .
Paramárddi Deva (Parmál) Chandel, King—			
History and traditions of—	II	455	. . .
Kálanjar inscription of—	XXI	36	. . .
Páranagar, in Alwar State, Rájputána—			
Ancient capital of Bargújar Rájás	XX	124	. . .
Colossal rock-cut figure at—	„	„	. . .
Temple of Nílkanth Mahádeo at—	„	126	XXIX.
Inscription dated S. 1010 = A.D. 953 at—	„	„	. . .
Paraoli, in Cawnpore District, N.-W. P.—			
Early brick temple at—	XI	46	. . .
Parapiotæ of Ptolemy—			
A people in Central India	XXI	93	. . .
Parasnath	XIII	73	
Parasuá kot, in Pílibhít District, N.-W. P.—			
Ruins of great temple at—	I	357	. . .
Parasuráma, Rájá of Maháthán—			
Legend of—	XV	106	. . .
Paraunâ—			
See **Padaraona.**			
Parávalí, 16 miles N. of Gwáliár, Central India—			
More than 100 temples near—	XX	107	XXIV.
Fine early Hindu temple at—	„	108	XXV.
Sundry short inscriptions at—	„	109	. . .
Temple of Gupta period and *Chaua-kuá* at—	„	„	XXVI.
Inscription of the Tomara Rájá Kírtti Sinha Deva, dated Samvat 1528 = A.D. 1471, at—	„	110	. . .
Description of minor temples near—	„	„	XXVI.
Short inscription dated Samvat 1107 = A.D. 1050 at—	„	112	. . .
Párbatí, near Giryek, in Patna District, Bengal—			
Identified with Hwen Thsang's 'pigeon monastery'	XV	7	V.
Seals and seal mould found at—	„	10	VI.

	Vol.	Page.	Plate.
Parihár clan—			
= Poruari of Ptolemy	IX	5, 57	. . .
	XXI	93	. . .
Claim to have preceded the Chandels and Baghels in Bundelkhand and Rewá	IX	5	. . .
Parihár Rájás of Gwáliár—			
List of—	II	378	. . .
Parkham, in Mathurá District, N.-W. P.—			
Colossal inscribed statue of 3rd century B.C. at— .	XX	40	VI.
Parnása R.—			
= Banás R.	VIII	15	. . .
Pároli in Gwáliár State—			
Small temples in late Gupta style at—	XX	105	XXIII.
Imperfect inscriptions of about 10th century A.D. at—	"	"	. . .
Famous sandstone quarries at—	"	106	. . .
Parsarur, in Siálkot District, Panjáb—			
Coins of Apollodotus, Zoilus, and Indo-Scythians found at—	XIV	47	. . .
Parsháwar—			
Of early Muhammadans = **Pesháwar**, *q.v.* . . .	II	87	. . .
Parthian—			
Tribes confounded in Erythræan Periplus with Sus or Sakas	"	47	. . .
Names of Indo-Scythian Kings, Vonones, &c. . .	"	47, 59	. . .
Parvatí—			
See **Daryápur Párvatí.**			
Pasupati, King of Gwáliár—			
Date of—	"	311	. . .
Patainí Deví, near Uchahara—			
Temple of (?) Gupta age at—	IX	31	VI.
Patál Gangá—			
A sacred stream in Barábár hills	I	42, 53	. . .
Pátaliputra—			
= Modern Patna, and was also named Pushpapura and Kusumapura	VIII	1	. . .

	Vol.	Page.	Plate.
Pátaliputra—*contd.*			
Was situated on tongue of land between Ganges and old course of the Sôn	VIII	VI	. . .
Founded about 450 B.C., either by Ajátasatru or Udayáswa	,,	2	. . .
	XI	151	. . .
Greek and Roman accounts of—	VIII	4, 27	. . .
	XI	152	. . .
Chinese ditto	,,	153	. . .
Mentioned in Gupta inscriptions at Garhwá and Udayagiri	III	56	. . .
	X	51	. . .
Probably deserted at time of the fall of the early Gupta dynasty	XI	153	. . .
Confluence of five rivers at—	,,	163	. . .
Changes of river-beds near—	,,	154	. . .
Probably has been for most part cut away by the Ganges	VIII	24	. . .
Restored as Patna by Sher Sháh	,,	,,	. . .
	XI	156	. . .
Identification of sites at—	VIII	27	. . .
	XI	157	XLI.
Position of Asoka's pillar at—	,,	159	. . .
Pátan-Bihár, in Unao District, Oudh—			
Perhaps = O-yu-to of Hwen Thsang	,,	55	. . .
Pathánkot in Kángrá District, Panjáb—			
A very ancient site	V	153	. . .
Coins of Zoilus, Vonones, &c., and of Audumbara found at—	,,	154	. . .
	XIV	116	. . .
Pathárí, in Bhopál Agency, Central India—			
Extensive ancient remains at—	VII	64	VIII—XI.
	X	69	. . .
Monolithic pillar inscribed in Gupta character at— .	VII	67	. . .
	X	70	. . .
'Gadarmal' temple near—	VII	69—75	. . .
Statue of Máyá Deví and infant Buddha at— . .	,,	70	. . .
Sundry ruins near—	,,	76—80	. . .
	X	71	. . .
Patna, in Patna District, Bengal—			
= The ancient Pátaliputrapura, also named Pushpapura and Kusumapura	VIII	1	. . .
Founded on present site by Sher Sháh	,,	28	. . .
	XI	156	. . .
Mosque of Sher Sháh at—	VIII	28	. . .

	Vol.	Page.	Plate.
Patna in Patna District, Bengal—*contd.*			
Two other mosques at—	VIII	29	. . .
Ruined citadel of—	,,	31, 33	. . .
High mounds in the fort of—	,,	,,	. . .
Named Azímábád by Muhammadans	,,	34	. . .
Seals, gems, &c., found in Ganges under—	XI	155	. . .
	XV	. . .	III.
Buddhist stone stools found at—	XI	163	. . .
	XV	3	III.
Akbar's visit to—	XI	162	. . .
Identification of ancient sites at—	,,	157	XLI.
Two colossal Buddhist statues from, in grounds of Asiatic Society of Bengal	XV	I	II
Patna State, attached to Sambalpur District, C. P.—			
Ancient remains in—	XIII	126	. . .
Pattharghatta, in Bhágalpur District, Bengal—			
Hindu rock sculptures at—	XV	36	. . .
Paundra-Desa—			
A name of Eastern Gauda or Varendra, *q.v.*	,,	III.	. . .
Paundra Varddhana of Hwen Thsang—			
Identified with Mahásthán in Bogra District	,,	102, 110	. . .
Derivation of name	,,	112	. . .
Capital of Paundra-Desa = Varendra = Eastern Gauda, = Mahá Kántára	,,	111, 112	. . .
Under a petty Rájá at end of 8th century A.D.	,,	. . .	. . .
Pauravas—			
Anciently occupied valley of Ganges above Delta—	II	15	. . .
Name of, probably preserved in classical Porus—	,,	17	. . .
Páwá, site of a relic *Stúpa* of Buddha—			
Identified by Cunningham with Padaraona in Gorakhpur District, N.-W. P.	I	74	. . .
Identified by Carlleyle with Fázilnagar and Chetiyaon in same District	XVIII	102	. . .
Páwá (Páwápuri, *or* Apápapuri) in Patna District, Bengal—			
The burial-place of the Jain hierarch Mahávíra	VIII	77	. . .
	XI	170	. . .
Peacock—			
Emblem of the Sáraswatí R.	IX	70	. . .
On Gupta and Saurashtran silver coins	,,	22	. . .

	Vol.	Page.	Plate.
Pehoa (Prithudaka) in Ambála District, Panjáb—			
Inscription of Rájá Bhoja .Deva, dated Samvat 276, = probably A.D. 882, at—	II	224	. . .
Other inscriptions at—	”	225	. . .
	XIV	101	. . .
Places of pilgrimage near—	”	102	. . .
Peppé, Mr.—			
Photographed antiquities in Bihár	VII	63	. . .
Persian architecture—			
Compared with Indo-Persian	V	187	XLV.
Persian Empire—			
N.-W. India a satrapy of, under Darius	V	185	. . .
Pesháwar City, in Pesháwar District, Panjáb—			
Little Yuchi kingdom of, in 5th century A.D. . .	II	64, 73	. . .
First mentioned by Fa-Hian in A.D. 400 as Fo-leu-sha	”	87	. . .
Noticed by Sung-Yun in A.D. 520	”	”	. . .
Described by Hwen Thsang as Pu-lu-sha-pu-lo .	”	”	. . .
Mentioned by Masúdi, Abú Rihán, and Bábar as Parsháwar	”	”	. . .
Present name of, given by Akbar	”	”	. . .
Stúpa of the alms-bowl of Buddha at— . . .	”	”	. . .
Great *stúpa* and monastery of Kanishka at— . .	”	88, 89	. . .
Pesháwar District—			
Ancient sites in—	XIX	92	. . .
Inscriptions said to exist in neighbourhood of— . .	”	95	. . .
Peukelaotis—			
= **Pushkalávatí**, *q.v.*	II	90	. . .
Phraates, King of Taxila—			
Mentioned by Apollonius of Tyana . . .	”	83, 113	. . .
Phullitæ of Ptolemy—			
= 'Leaf-clad' Gonds	IX	151	. . .
Probably = Savara tribe	XVII	124	. . .
	XXI	93	. . .
Piáwan in Rewá State, Baghelkhand—			
= Jhirná of Mr. Garrick	XXI	113	. . .
Pillars—			
Usual number of, in Hindu temples	I	177	. . .

	Vol.	Page.	Plate.
Pilo-molo, capital of Gurjara in time of Hwen Thsang—			
= Bálmer in Jodhpur State	II	70	. . .
Pi-lo-shan-na of Hwen Thsang—			
Identified (wrongly) with Atranjí Kherá . . .	I	269	. . .
= Bilsar in Etá District, N.-W. P. . . .	XI	15	. . .
Pimprama of Alexander—			
= Modern Asarur, *q.v.*	II	200	. . .
Pír Khána, S. of Lahore, Panjáb—			
Old Muhammadan buildings at—	XXIII	1	. . .
Pithaora in Uchahara (Nágaudh) State—			
= Prishtapuraka of Samudra Gupta . . .	IX	10	. . .
Pithora Rái			
See **Prithí Ráj Chauhán.**			
Pitinka people—			
Mentioned in Sháhbázgarhi inscription . . .	V	20	. . .
Plaster statues—			
At Sháhdheri (Taxila)	V	69	. . .
From Rokarí in Bannú District	XIV	29	XIV.
Pliny—			
Sources of information recorded by, are obscure . .	II	83	. . .
Po-lu-sha of Hwen Thsang—			
Identified with Palodherí in Yusufzai . . .	II	91	. . .
Identified with Sháhbázgarhi in Yusufzai . . .	V	15	. . .
Ponchá—			
See **Pákbirra.**			
Poruari of Ptolemy—			
= Parihár clan	IX	5, 57	. . .
	XXI	93	. . .
Porus, King—			
Site of battle between Alexander the Great and— .	II	173—187	LXVII.
Po-shi-po of Hwen Thsang—			
Identified with Bhásu-Bihár in Bogra District . .	XV	102	. . .
Pottery, glazed—			
Found at Bhilsá and other ancient sites . . .	III	51	. . .

	Vol.	Page.	Plate.
Prabhákara Vardhana—			
Father of King Harsha Vardhana	IX	154	. . .
Prabodha Chandrodaya of Krishna Misra—			
Refers to Kírtti Varmma Chandel and Karna Deva, King of Chedí	II	453	. . .
Mentions Brahman mediæval persecution of Buddhism	XX	104	. . .
Prayág—			
Ancient name of Alláhábád, *q.v.*	I	296, 300	. . .
Pret-Silá, near Buddha Gayá—			
A place of pilgrimage	,,	4	. . .
	XVI	50	. . .
Rude stone circles at—	VIII	66	. . .
Prinsep, James—			
Archæological discoveries of—	I	Intr. VII, XVIII	. . .
Prishtapuraka of Samudra Gupta—			
= Pithaora in Uchahara	IX	10	. . .
Prithí Ráj (Prithiví Rájá) Chauhán—			
Was son of Someswara, and grandson of Arnna .	X	99	. . .
Celebrated in Chand Ráesa	I	159	. . .
Defeated Parmál Chandel	II	455	. . .
Fort at Delhi of—	I	160, 183	. . .
Prithiví Sena of Vákátaka—			
Inscription of—	XXI	97, V	XXVII.
Prithudaka—			
See **Pehoa.**			
Ptolemy—			
Geographical work of, dates between 140 and 169 A.D.	II	83	. . .
Identification of localities mentioned by— . . .	XXI	90	XXIV.
Pudumyi and Yadnya Srí—			
Date of inscriptions of—	I	Intr. XXIII	. . .
Pujáripali, in Sarangarh State, C. P.—			
Undeciphered inscription at—	XVII	68	. . .

	Vol.	Page.	Plate.
Pulinda people—			
Mentioned in Sháhbázgarhi Inscription	V	20	. . .
In Kathá-Sarita-Ságar synonymous with Savara and Bhilla	XVII	139	. . .
Punáwa, in Gayá District, Bengal—			
Budhokhar and Káramár tanks at— . . .	I	13	XII.
Buddhist remains of *circa* A.D. 1000 at— . .	"	14	. . .
Punch-marked coins—			
See **Coins, punch-marked.**			
Puralya, in Mánbhúm District, Bengal—			
Ruined temples at—	VIII	182	. . .
Púrna Varmma, King of Western Magadha—			
Last descendant of Asoka, renewed *Bodhi-drúm* about 610 A.D.	III	81, 135	. . .
Purushadata—			
Coin of, found at Bhuilá Dih	XII	164	. . .
Pushkalávatí—			
= Peukelaotis, = part of Hashtnagar on Swát R. in Yusufzai	II	90	. . .
	V	2	. . .
Great *stúpa* of the 'eyes-gift' built by Asoka at— .	II	90	. . .
Pushpamitra, King of Magadha—			
Persecuted Buddhists of Sákala	I	Intr. xxxi	. . .
	II	41	. . .
Pushpávatí—			
Former name of Bilharí, in C. P.	IX	34	. . .
Pushapuran—			
A name of Pátaliputra	VIII	1	. . .
Púta—			
Ancient name of citadel of Jhelam	II	18, 174	. . .
Putwár—			
The region between the Indus and Jhelam . .	II	153	. . .

R

	Vol.	Page.	Plate.
Ráát—			
A misspelling for **Ráth,** *q.v.*			
Raghuvansí race—			
Identical with Nikumbha	XX	9, 10	. . .

	Vol.	Page.	Plate.
Ráhatgarh, in Ságar District, C. P.—			
Fort, &c., at—	VII	60—62	. . .
Inscription of Jaya Varmma Deva, dated 1312 S. at—	X	31	. . .
Ráhilya, near Mahobá, in Hamírpur District, N.-W. P.—			
Temple at—	II	441	. . .
	VII	26	III.
Railings, Buddhist—			
At Buddha Gayá	I	10	VII—XI.
	III	86, 98	XXVI, & XXVIII—XXX.
Described	„	23	VIII—X.
At Sháhdheri (Taxila)	II	135	. . .
	V	75	. . .
Ráipur (Ráyapura), in Ráipur District, C. P.—			
Fort and temples at—	VII	165	. . .
Tanks and sculptures at—	„	166	. . .
Inscriptions in Museum at—	„	167	. . .
Places with ancient remains near—	„	168	. . .
Genealogy of Haihaya Rájás of—	XVII	80	. . .
Early copper-plate inscriptions from— . . .	„	55—59	XXVI, XXVII.
Rájágriha—			
= Modern **Rájgír**, *q.v.*, in Patna District, Bengal .	I	20	. . .
Called Kuságarapura by Hwen Thsang	„	21	. . .
= 'Girivraja', the capital of Jarásandha	„	„	. . .
The second city of, built by Bimbisára	„	23	. . .
Was capital of Saisunága dynasty	III	140	XLI.
Identification of Sattapáni cave at—	„	141	XLIII.
Vaibhára cave and Jarásandha's house at— . . .	„	142	XLII.
Chinese pilgrims' topography of, ...	I	22	. . .
	VIII	90	. . .
Rájam—			
See **Rájim, in Ráipur District, C. P.—**			
Rajaona, in Mongír District, Bengal—			
Probably = Lo-in-ni-lo of Hwen Thsang . . .	III	153	. . .
Buddhist and Hindu statues and inscriptions at— .	„	154	XLV.
Rajaori (Rájápuri) State in Panjáb—			
History and Rájás of—	XIV	106	. . .
Rájapodor in Orissa—			
Temples at—	XIII	120	. . .

	Vol.	Page.	Plate.
Rájápur, in Gwáliár State, Central India—			
Nearly perfect *stúpa* at—	XXI	178	. . .
Rájavásiní—			
Old name of Rásin, in Bándá District, N.-W. P. .	XXI	16	. . .
Rájdháni, or Updhaolia, in Gorakhpur District, N.-W. P.—			
Identified with the city of the Moriyas	XVIII	31	II.
	XXII	3, 7	. . .
Ruins at, described	XVIII	34—40	III, IV.
Rájgarh, in Alwar State, Rájputána—			
Said to have been founded in S. 202 = A.D. 145 .	XX	121	. . .
Jain statues at—	"	122	. . .
Rájgarh, in Chhatarpur State, Bundelkhand—			
Fort, &c., at—	VII	42—45	. . .
Rájgarh, in Chándá District, C. P.—			
Saiva temple at—	IX	141	XXVII.
Rájgír, in Patna District, Bengal—			
Five hills surrounding	I	21	. . .
Identification of Baibhár (Webháro) hill and of Son-bhandár and Sattapáni caves at—	"	21, 25	. . .
	VIII	VIII, XIV,	. . .
		91—99	. . .
Other caves at—	"	XVI, 86	. . .
		89	. . .
Hot springs at—	I	27	. . .
Existing remains not numerous at—	"	24	. . .
Site of Asoka's *stúpa* at—	"	"	. . .
Another *stúpa* and statues at—	"	26	. . .
Passage into *stúpa* at—	"	27	. . .
Small *stúpa* at—	VIII	XVIII	. . .
Inscriptions of Son-bhandár cave at—	I	25	XIII.
Inscription dated 1007 Samvat in well at— . .	VIII	86	. . .
Long rock inscription in shell characters at— . .	"	"	. . .
Great lines of walls at—	"	87—89	XXII.
Artificial lake near	"	99	. . .
Legend of the Kahárs at—	"	100	. .
See **Rájágriha.**			
Rájim in Ráipur District, C. P.—			
Legends of—	XVII	7	. . .
Principal group of temples at—	VII	148	. . .
	XVII	9	IV.

	Vol.	Page.	Plate.
Rájim in Ráipur District, C. P.—*contd.*			
Peculiar plan of oldest temples at—	XVII	9	. . .
Bais Rájpút attendants at great temple of— . .	"	"	. . .
Temple of Rájiva-lochana at—	"	10	V.
Minor temples at—	"	13	. . .
Inscription mentioning Mahárája Bhoja at— . .	"	15	. . .
Probable origin of name of—	"	17	. . .
Copper-plate inscription of Rájá Tivara Deva at— .	"	"	VI—VIII.
Long inscription mentioning Prithiví Rájá at— .	"	18	IX.
Inscription of Jaga or Jagat Pála at— . . .	"	"	. . .
Pilgrims' inscriptions at—	"	19	X.
Rajjána (Rajjhána *or* Rajjaona), in Mongír District, Bengal—			
Identified with Lo-in-ni-lo of Hwen Thsang . .	XV	15	. . .
Buddhist statues at—	"	14	. . .
Inscribed statue of Párvatí at—.	VIII	118	. . .
Rájputána—			
Boundaries and divisions of—	XX	1	. . .
Rájputána, Eastern—			
Geography of—	VI	1	I.
	XX	. . .	I.
Summary of General Cunningham's tour in— . .	"	I—VI	. . .
Rajubul (Ranjubula), Buddhist Satrap—			
Probably father of Saudása	III	40	. . .
	XII	43	. . .
Two classes of coins of—	III	40	. . .
Extent of dominions of—	"	41	. . .
Inscription of son of, at Mora, near Mathurá . .	XX	48	. . .
Coins of, found at Sankisa	XI	25	. . .
found at Pádham	"	38	. . .
13 coins of, from Sultánpur in Jálandhar District .	XIV	57	. . .
Rájya Pála, Prince of Kanauj—			
Grant dated S. 1199 = A.D. 1142 of, from Gagahá in Gorakhpur District	XXII	59	. . .
Rájyasrí—			
Sister of King Harsha Varddhana	IX	155	. . .
Rájya Varddhana—			
Brother of King Harsha Varddhana, killed by Gupta King of W. Gauda	"	"	. . .
Rákshí R.—			
= Ancient Drishadvatí R.	XIV	88	. . .

	Vol.	Page.	Plate.
Rámadata, Buddhist Satrap—			
Coins of—	XII	43	
Rámagráma, site of relic stúpa of Buddha—			
Identified with Koraun Dih in Bastí District . .	"	217	. . .
Rámpur Deoriya in Bastí District .	XVIII	4	. . .
	XXII	2, 111	II.
Ráma-ká-dheri, in Ráwal Pindi Distrcit, Panjáb—			
Site of the blood-offering *stúpa*	XIV	7	. . .
Probably burnt by Mahmúd of Ghazní . . .	"	8	. . .
Rámánand, Hindu reformer—			
Date of—	II	296	. . .
Rámáyana, story of—			
Partly based on Buddhist Játakas	XXI	11	. . .
Rámgarh, in Kotá State, Rájputána—			
Undescribed remains at—	XXIII	137	. . .
Rámgarh Hill, in Sirguja State, Chutiá Nágpur, Bengal—			
Rock sculptures at—	XIII	34	. . .
Inscription of Asoka's age at—	"	~~31~~ 40	. . .
Temple at—	"	35	. . .
Scratched inscription at—	"	41	. . .
Identified by Mr. Beglar with the Chitrakúta of Rámáyana	"	50	X.
Rámnagar, in Barelí District, N.-W. P.—			
See **Ahichhatra.**			
Rámnagar, in Mandlá District, C. P.—			
Inscription dated S. 1724 = A.D. 1667, giving genealogy of Gond Rájás at—	VII	106	. . .
	XVII	46	. . .
Rámpurwa, in Tarái of Champáran District, Bengal—			
Edict pillar of Asoka discovered by Mr. Carlleyle at—	XVI	VIII, 110	XXVIII.
	XXII	51	VI, VII.
Rámtek, in Nágpur District, C. P.—			
Inscription at—	VII	112	. . .
Hindu and Jain remains at—	"	113	. . .
Ruins at, ascribed to Hemádh Pant	"	114	. . .
Ancient names of, Sinduragiri and Tapogiri . .	"	"	. . .
Ránígat, in Yusufzai, Panjáb—			
Ruined fortress at, described	II	107—111	LV, LVI.
	V	55	. . .

	Vol.	Page.	Plate.
Ránígat in Yusufzai, Panjáb—*contd.*			
Also called Nográm *or* Nowagrám *or* Bagrám . .	V	55, 56	. . .
Identified by some with Aornos	II	96—111	. . .
	V	56	. . .
Ránípur-Jurál, in Patna State, C. P.*—			
Great group of ancient temples at—	XIII	128—137	XI—XVI.
Ranjubula—			
See **Rajubul, Buddhist Satrap.**			
Ranod, in Gwáliár State—			
Ancient palace with inscription of Rájá Somesvara at—	II	304	LXXXV.
Inscription dated S. 1234 = A.D. 1177 at— . .	”	306	. . .
Rúpmatí of Málwa—			
Songs composed by—	”	289	. . .
Ránsi, 25 miles west of Lahore, Panjáb—			
= Ancient Nara Sinha	”	203	LXXI.
	XIV	47	. . .
Coins of Gondophares found at—	”	48	. . .
Rár in Cawnpore District, N.-W. P.—			
Early brick temples at—	XI	46, 47	. . .
Rárh (Rádha) province—			
Boundaries and chief cities of—	XV	37, 146	. . .
Rasálu, Rájá—			
Panjáb legends of—	II	153	. . .
	XIV	49	. . .
Ráshtrakúta dynasty—			
Intermarried with Kalachuris	IX	80	. . .
Rásin, in Bándá District, N.-W. P.—			
Extensive ruins at—	XXI	15	VI, VII.
Two short inscriptions at—	”	18	XIV, XVII.
Ratanpur in Biláspur District—			
Sculptures and inscriptions from—	VII	214	. . .
Capital of northern section of Chedí . . .	XVII	72	. . .
Genealogy of Haihaya Rájás of—	”	78	. . .
Ráth, in Hamírpur District, N.-W. P.—			
Hindu pillars at—	VII	22	. . .

* In the Introduction this place is said to be in the Karund (Korond or Káláhandí) State.

	Vol.	Page.	Plate.
Ráthor dynasty of Kanauj—			
Founded by Chandra Deva	I	150	. . .
Ráwal Pindi, in Ráwal Pindi District, Panjáb—			
= Ancient Gajnípur *or* Gájípur	II	20, 152	. . .
Remains of *stúpas* at—	„	151	. . .
Bactrian, Roman, and Indo-Scythian coins at— . .	„	148, 152	. . .
Oil lamp of classical shape with Ario-Pálí inscription found at—	„	152	. . .
Ráyapura (Ráypur)—			
See **Ráipur in C. P.—**			
Ráypur, in Kothi State, Baghelkhand—			
Inscription at—	XXI	76, 156	. . .
Reparí, in Agra District, N.-W. P.—			
Idgáh of Alá-ud-dín Khiljí at—	IV	217	. . .
Rewá (Ríwá) city in Rewá State, Baghelkhand—			
Ancient sculptures from Gúrgí-Masáun at— . . .	XXI	144	XXXVI—XXXVII.
Kalachuri and Chandel copper-plate inscriptions at— .	„	145	. . .
= Ptolemy's country of the Bolingæ	„	92	. . .
Early history of—	„	103, 153	. . .
Chroniclers' list of Baghel Rájás of— . . .	„	106	. . .
Later history of—	„	107	. . .
Known to Muhammadan historians as Bhath, Bhattah, *or* Bhath-ghorah	„	110, 154	. . .
Rise of Baghel dynasty of, in 12th century A.D. .	IX	113	. . .
Rishis' caves in Bándá District, N.-W. P.—			
Described	XXI	7	. . .
Rithi, in (?) Damoh District, C. P.—			
Temples at—	„	160	. . .
Rithorá, in Bándá District, N.-W. P.—			
Small early temples at—	„	4	. . .
Ríwá—			
See **Rewá.**			
Roads, ancient—			
Importance of tracing	VII VIII	140 48	. . .
In Bihár	„	48—51	. . .
Leading to port of Tamralipti (Tamlúk)	„	50	. . .
In Central Provinces	VII	140	. . .

	Vol.	Page.	Plate.
Rohilkhand—			
Formerly named Katehar	I	352, 356	. . .
	XI	1	. . .
Rohiní river of Buddhist tradition—			
Identified with Rawái river in Bastí District . .	XII	190, 207	. . .
Rohtak, in Rohtak District, Panjáb—			
Ancient sites near—.	XVI	136, 139	. . .
Rohtás (Rohtásgarh), in Sháhábád District, Bengal—			
Rock-cut seal of Sasángka at—	VII	VI	. . .
Rokn-i-álam tomb—			
At Multán	V	132	XXXVIII.
Rokri, in Bannú District, Panjáb—			
Buddhist plaster figures from—	XIV	29	XIV.
Rudra Sinha (Sena) Swámi, Satrap of Suráshtra—			
Discussion of date of—	X	127	. . .
	XV	30	. . .
Rudrapur, in Gorakhpur District, N.-W. P.—			
Identified with the town of Hwen Thsang's hospitable Brahman	XVIII	41	. . .
General Cunningham's objections to this identification	"	42	. . .
Great fort of Sáhankot No. II at—	"	44	. . .
Ruins nearly all Brahmanical at —	"	46	. . .
Short inscription, dated 1161 Samvat at— . .	"	48	. . .
Rúpbás in Bharatpur State, Rájputána—			
Deserted town near—	VI	17	. . .
Monoliths near—	"	18	. . .
	XX	98	. . .
Colossal statues at—	VI	20	. . .
Rúpnáth, in Jabalpur District, C. P.—			
Edict of Asoka at—	VII	59	. . .
	IX	38	. . .

S

	Vol.	Page.	Plate.
Sabanna of Ptolemy—			
= Town of Zhobi, west of Indus	II	32	. . .
Sabaræ of Ptolemy—			
= Saura (Savara) tribe	XVII	125	. . .

	Vol.	Page.	Plate.
Sabasarnes—			
An *alias* of Abisares	II	32	. . .
Sadan—			
A hill tribe east of the Jhelam	,,	13	. . .
Saddo in Suwát—			
Mutilated inscription at—	V	62	. . .
Sádhora (Sádhaura) in Ambála District, Panjáb—			
Mosques, &c., at—	XIV	73	XXIII.
Sagabaza of Ptolemy—			
Probably = Nágaudh in Baghelkhand	XXI	92	. . .
Sagala *or* Euthymedia—			
***See* Euthymedia.**			
Ságar in Ságar District, C. P.—			
Perhaps = Agara of Ptolemy	,,	93	. . .
Ságar Dih in Champáran District, Bengal—			
Stúpa, &c., at—	XVI	19	VI, VII.
Sageda metropolis of Ptolemy—			
Probably = Chitrangadapura, ancient capital of Chedí, = Sirpur, or Srípura in C. P.	XVII XXI	69, 70 93	. . . . . .
Sáhankot, No. 1—			
Part of the Rájdhání group of ruins in south of Gorakhpur District, N.-W. P.	XVIII	40	. . .
Sáhankot, No. 2—			
At Rudrapur, in Gorakhpur District	,,	44	. . .
Saharia tribe in Gwáliár—			
Identified with Saura (Savara) tribe	XVII	113	. . .
Sahaspur in Biláspur District, C. P.—			
Inscription dated Chedí S. 934 = A.D. 1183 at— .	,,	43	XXII.
Sahegarh in Alígarh District, N.-W. P.—			
Mounds at—	XII	9	. . .
Indo-Scythian coins found at—	,,	11	. . .

	Vol.	Page.	Plate.
Sáhet-Máhet in Gonda District, Oudh*—			
= Srávastí, *q.v.*	I	330	L.
Extent of ruins at—	"	331	. . .
Identification of sites at—	"	337	. . .
Colossal inscribed statue of Buddha of Indo-Scythian period at—	"	339	. . .
	XI	84, 86	. . .
Jetavana monastery at—	"	79	XXIV.
Further excavations at—	"	82	XXV—XXX.
Seals of various kinds found at—	"	89	XXVIII.
Buddhist creed inscription of 7th or 8th century A.D. at—	"	92	. . .
Octagonal well at—	"	93	XXIX.
Named Chandrikapuri about 800 A.D.	"	98	. . .
Sahri-Bahlol in Yusufzai, Panjáb—			
Ruins at—	V	36—45	XI, XII.
Statue of Buddha at—	"	37	. . .
Dhamámi tope at—	"	39, 43, 46	. . .
Sculptures, &c., in Lahore Museum from— . .	"	42	. . .
= ? City of Rishi Ekasringa of Hwen Thsang . .	"	23, 42	. . .
Inscribed bowl found at—	"	44, 63	. . .
Coins found at—	"	45	. . .
Sahria race—			
See **Savara race.**			
Sáhsarám (Sásserám) in Sháhábád District, Bengal—			
Inscriptions of Asoka and Pratápa Dhavala at— .	XI	133	. . .
Tombs of Sher Sháh and his family at and near— .	"	"	XXXIX.
Saidpur-Bhitarí—			
See **Bhitarí in Gházípur District, N.-W. P.**			
Saka era—			
Speculations as to origin of—	III	45	. . .
Sákala (*or* Sángala)—			
Capital of the Báhikas in time of Mahábhárata . .	V	149	. . .
See Sángala.			
Sakas—			
Alleged battle at Kahror between Sáliváhana and— .	II	21	. . .
Apparently = Su horde of Chinese writers . . .	"	45	. . .
= Abár tribe	"	48	. . .
Sakastene—			
= Parts of Kipin, or Drangiana and Arachosia . .	"	45, 51	. . .

* Sáhet-Máhet is partly in the Gonda and partly in the Bahraich District.

	Vol.	Page.	Plate.
Sáketa—			
Early Hindu name of **Ayodhya City,** *q.v.*	I	317	. . .
Sakhrabastí—			
= Modern Sakhra or Sakha, 24 miles N.-W. of Jhelam	II	172	. . .
Perhaps = Udinagar of tradition, and Euthymedia or Sagala of Ptolemy	,,	153	. . .
Sakri R. in Patna District, Bengal—			
(?) = Saktimatí R. of Mahábhárata	VIII	125	. . .
Formerly flowed past Rájgír	,,	127 *Note*	. . .
Saktimatí R. of Mahábhárata—			
(?) = Sakri R., in Patna District, Bengal . . .	,,	125	. . .
Sákya maidens—			
Legend of massacre of—	I	332, 347	. . .
Supposed site of massacre of, near Bhuilá Dih . .	XII	172	. . .
Sálár Masaúd—			
Fanatical expedition of—	I	330 *Note*	. . .
Sálátura (So-lu-to-lo)—			
= Láhor, 4 miles N.-W. of Ohind, in Peshâwar District, Panjáb	II	95	. . .
The birth-place of Pánini	,,	,,	. . .
Sales Rájá—			
Legend of—	XVI	28	. . .
Salímgarh—			
A part of old Delhi	I	223	. . .
Sáliváhana (Satawáhana), Rájá—			
Panjáb and Jesálmer traditions of—	II	21, 22	. . .
Capital of, at Sálbáhanpur = Siálkot	,,	,,	. . .
Rasalu, son of—	,,	,,	. . .
Bais Rájputs claim descent from—	,,	280	. . .
Perhaps = Gotamiputra Satakarni	V	20	. . .
Temple at Sonátapan, near Bánkurá ascribed to— .	VIII	201	. . .
Salt Range in Panjáb—			
Called Mount Júd by early Muhammadans . . .	V	79	. . .
Antiquities of—	,,	79—85	. . .
	XIV	33	. . .

	Vol.	Page.	Plate.
Salt Range in Panjáb—*contd.*			
Coins found in—	V	93	...
Tributary to Káshmír in 631 A.D.	,,	83	...
Sáma-Játaka—			
The basis of legend of Sarwan	XXI	42, 44	...
Sámanta Deva, King of Gándhára—			
Coins of, common in Yusufzai and elsewhere	V	45, 83	...
Samatata province—			
Also known as Bágdi or Bháti	XV	146	...
Sambhal in Morádábád District, N.-W. P.—			
Jámi Masjid with inscription of Bábar at—	XII	IV, 26	III, IV.
Sambhalpur (Sambalpur), in Sambalpur District, C. P.—			
Sarabhapura, probably ancient name of—	XVII	57	...
Inscription of Mahásu Deva Rájá from—	,,	,,	...
Legends of—	,,	59	...
Samráon (Simráun *or* Samangarha), in Champáran District, Bengal—			
Former capital of Tirhút, taken by Emperor of Delhi 1324 A.D.	XVI	2, 3	...
Mr. Hodgson's description of ruins of—	,,	,,	...
Samudra Gupta, King—			
Was sovereign of **Mahá Kántára**, *q.v.*	XV	112	...
Long inscription of, at Eran	X	89	...
Mathurá inscription giving genealogy of—	III	15, 37	XXI.*
Corrections in readings of Alláhábád pillar inscription of—	IX	10	...
Supposed copper-plate inscription of, formerly at Benares	XIX	60	...
Samvat—			
See Era.			
Sanabares, King—			
Preceded Gondophares	II	61	...
Sanakánika—			
Name of the country round Bhílsá in Gupta period	X	50	...
Sanchánkot (Sujánkot) in Hardoí District, Oudh—			
Fort and *stúpa* at—	XI	53	...

* This inscription belongs to the reign of Chandra Gupta II., successor of Samudra Gupta.

	Vol.	Page.	Plate.
Sánchárí—			
Ancient name of **Máchárí**, *q.v.*	VI	77	. . .
Sánchi in Diwánganj Tahsíl of Bhopál State, C. I.—			
Date of buildings at—	I	Intr. XXIII	. . .
.	V	189	. . .
Inscribed Buddhist railing at—	"	57, 58	. . .
Inscriptions of Chandra Gupta II., dated Samvat 93,			. . .
and of Hariswámí, dated S. 131 at—	"	59	. . .
Pillar of Swámí Gosura at—	"	62	XXII.
Sanctum—			
Excentric in brick temples at Konch and Buddha			
Gayá	VIII	67	. . .
stone temples at Pathári and Gyárispur .	"	"	. . .
Sandal wood—			
Material of statues of Buddha at Kosámbi and Srá-			
vastí	I	340	. . .
Sandrabatis of Ptolemy—			
Probably = Chandrávatí in Kota (Kotah) State, Ráj			
putána	II	264	. . .
Perhaps = Jejákabhukti, = Bundelkhand. . .	XXI	58, 91	. . .
Sandracottus of Greek writers—			
= Chandra Gupta Maurya	I	Intr. I	. . .
Sanga, Rájá—			
Great battle between Bábar and—	XX	93	. . .
Sangabhadra—			
Monastery of, at Mandáwar	I	250	. . .
Sángala (Sákala, Ságal) of Alexander—			
= Sángla-wála Tiba, in Jhang District, Panjáb . .	II	192	LXVIII.
In ruins in Hwen Thsang's time	"	193	. . .
Stúpa of Asoka at—	"	195	. . .
Was the capital of the Madras (*or* Jártikas, *or* Báhikas,			
according to Mahábhárata)	"	"	. . .
Buddhist legends of—	"	197	. . .
Was capital of Yavana King Milinda)	"	"	. . .
Later subject to Mihirkul	"	"	. . .
Noticed by Arrian, Curtius, and Diodorus . . .	"	"	. . .
Wrongly placed by Arrian and Curtius	"	192, 200	. . .
Sánkara in Alígarh District, N.-W. P.—			
Sundry remains at—	XII	15, 24	II.
Inscription said to exist at—	"	24	. . .

	Vol.	Page.	Plate.
Sankaráditya, King—			
Date of—	III	95	. . .
Sankaragana—			
Name of two kings of Chedí	IX	80, 85	. . .
Sankhár Rájá—			
A Panjáb name for Vikramáditya, and also for Moga	II	173, 187	. . .
Sankisa in Farrukhábád District, N.-W. P.—			
A famous place of Buddhist pilgrimage	I	271	. . .
Nága's tank at—	,,	274	. . .
Elephant pillar at—	,,	277	XLVI.
Brahman settlement at—	,,	279	. . .
Discovery of base of Asoka pillar at—	XI	22	. . .
Traditions of—	,,	24	. . .
Series of coins from—	,,	25	. . .
Seals and carvings from—	,,	26	IX.
Sankshoba, Rájá of Uchahara—			
Inscriptions of—	IX	7	IV.
Santáls—			
Known as Sauras in Rájmahál	XVII	122	. . .
Sántí Varma—			
A misreading for **Isána Varma**; *q v.*			
Santípur—			
An old name of Vijayamandirgarh	VI	54	. . .
Sapaleizes—			
Indo-Scythian silver coin of—	II	30	. . .
Saparnus R. of Arrian—			
= Either Zhobi or Gomal R. to west of Indus	,,	32	. . .
Sápharan (Supharan), *or* Subanrikha R. in Chutiá Nágpur, Bengal—			
Perhaps = Kirna Suvarna of Hwen Thsang	VIII	189, 191	. . .
Sapt-Rishi Kál—			
A synonym of Lok-kál used in Káshmír	XXI	136	. . .
Sarabhapura—			
Probably ancient name of Sambhalpur, C. P.	XVII	57	. . .

	Vol.	Page.	Plate.
Sárangarh State, C. P.—			
Ruins in—	XIII	143	. . .
Saranges R. of Arrian—			
Probably = Satlaj R.	II	11	. . .
Sárangpur-Khokra in C. I.—			
Ancient punch-marked and cast coins found at—	"	288	. . .
Story of Báz Bahádur and Rúpmatí of—	"	289	. . .
Sáraswatí R.—			
Peacock, the emblem of—	IX	70	. . .
Sárdula Varmma, King of Magadha—			
Placed Hindu images in Barábár caves	I	52	. . .
Sarhata in Alwar State, Rájputána—			
Capital of Mewár before Muhammadan conquest	XX	118	. . .
Mosque at—	"	119	XXVIII.
Sarhind (Sirhind) in Patiála State, Panjáb—			
Made capital of a district by Fíroz Tughlak, A.D. 1360	II	205	. . .
The most easterly possession of Brahman kings of Kábul	"	206	. . .
Legends concerning—	"	"	. . .
Prosperous in Muhammadan times till A. D. 1709	"	208	. . .
The scene of murder of family of the Sikh Guru Govind	"	"	. . .
Destroyed by Sikhs in 1763, but now recovering	"	209	. . .
Muhammadan buildings at—	II	209, 212	. . .
Chiefly Muhammadan coins found at—	"	212	. . .
Sáriputra—			
Mentioned in inscription at Kasiá	XVIII	68	. . .
Born at Kalapináka near Nálanda	I	29	. . .
Sárnáth—			
See **Benares (Sárnáth)** *and* **Dhamek.**			
Sárongarh, in Champáran District, Bengal—			
An ancient Dusád fort	XVI	26	. . .
Sarsáwa—			
See **Sirsáwa in Sahéranpur District, N.-W.P.**			
Sarvanáth, Rájá of Kári-Taláí—			
Inscriptions of—	IX	9	IV.

	Vol.	Page.	Plate.
Sarwan and Sánwal—			
Legend of—	XXI	41	. . .
Sasan, King—			
A relative of Gondophares, reigned in Panjáb . .	II	61	. . .
Coin of, found in No. 15 mound at Mánikyála . .	„	167	LXV.
Sasángka, King—			
Ruled country named Kirna Suvarna . . .	VIII	191	. . .
Destroyed *Bodhi-drúm* about 600 A.D. . . .	I	5, 10	. . .
	III	80	. . .
Gold coins of—	„	138	. . .
Called Narendra Gupta in Jain books . . .	IX	157	. . .
Seal of, on a rock at Rohtás	VII	VI	. . .
Tank named after, at Bhásu Bihár, in Bogra District, Bengal	XV	102	. . .
Sasángka, King (II)—			
Perhaps a late Chandel or Baghel prince . . .	XXI	88, 156	. . .
Sassanian coins—			
See **Coins, Indo-Sassanian.**			
Sásserám—			
See **Sáhsarám, in Sháhábád District, Bengal.**			
Sástrí era—			
A synonym for Lok-kál of Káshmír	„	136	. . .
Satadru R.—			
= Satlaj R.	II	12	. . .
Satanwára, in Gwáliár State, C. I.—			
Satí pillar, dated 1016 Samvat, at—	VII	94	. . .
Sati—			
A hill tribe west of the Jhelam	II	13	. . .
Satí pillars—			
Historical value of—	III	10	. . .
Usually face the east	XXI	101	. . .
After 9th century sculptured on one face only . .	X	75	. . .
Very early inscribed, at Bálod	VII	137	. . .
Satlaj R.—			
Probably = Zaradrus R. of Ptolemy	II	12	. . .

	Vol.	Page.	Plate.
Satmás in Agra District, N.-W. P.—			
Sepulchral cairns near—	VI	33	. . .
Satrap—			
A title frequently used in India	I	Intr. XL	. . .
Satraps—			
Of Taxila	II	113, 133	. . .
Satraps, Buddhist—			
Coins of, at Indor Kherá	XII	41—43	. . .
See **Sandása, Rajubul, = Manigal,** *and* **Jíhonia.**			
Sattapáni cave—			
Probably = Son-bhandár cave at Rájgír	VIII	VIII, XIV	. . .
Scene of first Buddhist synod	III	142	. . .
Satya, *or* **Saya Mitra—**			
Coins of, found at Bhuilá Dih	XII	171	. . .
Saudása, a Buddhist Satrap—			
Son of Rajubul	III	40	. . .
	XII	43	. . .
Mathurá inscription and coins of—	III	39	XIII.
Coins of, follow same type as a didrachm of Azilises .	„	39, 40	. . .
found at Sankisa	XI	25	. . .
Pádham	„	38	. . .
Saura (Savara) race—			
Extension of eastern section of—	XVII	119	. . .
Known as Suirs, Seories, and Suirai	„	118	. . .
Vocabulary of—	„	122	. . .
= Sabarai and Soræ Nomades of Ptolemy, = Suari of Pliny	IX	157	. . .
	XVII	125	. . .
	XXI	94	. . .
Perhaps = Phullitæ of Ptolemy	„	93	. . .
In Rájmahál identified with Santáls	XVII	122, 125	. . .
		136	. . .
Mentioned in Aitareya Bráhmana	IX	157	. . .
	XVII	125	. . .
Mentioned by Varáha Mihira, &c.	„	127	. . .
Probably the dominant race of aborigines both west and east	„	131	. . .
Apparently of same race as Bhuiyás, Musahars, and Rájwars, also cognate to Kurkús and other Kolarian tribes	XVII	117, 133	. . .

	Vol.	Page.	Plate.
Saura (Savara) race—*contd.*			
Estimated numbers of, and of cognate tribes . .	XVII	137	. . .
Habits and religion of—	„	„	. . .
Name of, in early writers seems to include all Kolarian tribes	„	139	. . .
Name of, in Kathá Sarita Ságara used vaguely as synonymous with Pulinda and Bhilla . . .	„	„	. . .
Extension of, westward	„	112	. . .
Identified with Saharias of Gwáliár	„	113	. . .
	XX	102	. . .
Estimate of numbers of western section of— . .	XVII	114	. . .
Physical characteristics of ditto . .	„	117	. . .
Personal names of ditto . .	„	118	. . .
According to Varáha Mihira conquered Cheros (Kols) in Sháhábád and Benáres, A.D. 499, and ruled to 989 A.D.	„	131, 132	. . .
Very few now in Sháhábád	„	„	. . .
Photographs of eastern specimens of—	„	132	XXXII, XXXIII
Buildings in Sháhábád and Bihár ascribed to— . .	„	„	. . .
Saural, in Lalitpur District, N.-W. P.—			
Temple	XXI	170	. . .
Saurâth, in Darbhangá District, Bengal—			
An ancient site	XVI	94	. . .
Sauvira—			
= Plains between Indus and Jhelam	II	14	. . .
Savara (Sabara) race—			
See **Saura (Savara) race.**			
Savaripura—			
Ancient name of Sirpur in C. P.	VII	168	. . .
Sáwal-Dher in Yusufzai—			
Rut—	V	55	. . .
Sayyidpur—			
See **Saídpur-Bhitarí.**			
Sculpture—			
Art of, introduced into India by Greeks . .	III	97	. . .
Seal—			
From Harapá in Montgomery District, Panjáb, engraved with foreign characters	V	108	. . .
Of black earthenware found at Lauriyá-Navandgarh .	I	71	IX.
Seals—			
Found at Taxila	XIV	14, 15	. . .

	Vol.	Page.	Plate.
Seals, Buddhist—			
Findspots of—	IX	4	. . .
Found at Bakror	I	12	. . .
Buddha Gayá and Kiyul	III	158	XLVI.
Giryek	I	17	. . .
Kasiá	XVIII	70	. . .
Pákna-Bihár	XI	35	XII,
Sáhet-Máhet	"	89	XXVIII.
Sankisá	"	26	IX.
Sárnáth	I	119, 129	. . .
Sehwá in Ráipur District, C. P.—			
Group of temples at—	VII	145	. . .
Inscribed slab at—	"	146	. . .
Sena dynasty of Bengal—			
Capital of at Gaur (Lakhnautí)	XV	39	. . .
Succeeded Pála dynasty	"	156	. . .
Three inscriptions known of—	"	"	. . .
Bábu Rajendralála Mitra's errors in chronology of—	"	157 *seq.q.*	. . .
Initial year of Lakshmana Sena era used by—	"	158 "	. . .
According to tradition kings of, belonged to Vaidya caste	"	162	. . .
Probably descended from Áditya Sena Deva of Magadha	"	163	. . .
In religion staunch Brahmanists	"	"	. . .
Genealogies of—	"	167	. . .
Ended about 1300 A.D.	"	168	. . .
Seopur in Mirzápur District, N.-W. P.—			
Ruined temple at—	XXI	130	. . .
Seorí—			
Another name of the Saura (Savara) tribe	XVII	118	. . .
Seorí- (Savarí) Náráyan in Biláspur District, C. P.—			
Probably = Sora Arcati Regis of Ptolemy	XXI	94	. . .
A place of pilgrimage	VII	196	. . .
Inscribed statue dated 898 Kalachuri Samvat at—	"	197	. . .
Long inscription dated 979 ditto at—	"	199	. . .
Brick temple with sanctum on circular plan at—	"	"	. . .
Seosarra, in Bastí District, N.-W. P.—			
Inscribed copper-plate said to exist at—	XVIII	27	. . .
Serpent—			
See **Snake.**			

	Vol.	Page.	Plate.
Serpent worship—			
Mr. J. Fergusson's erroneous theory of—	I	Intr. xxiv	. . .
Sha-chi of Fa-Hian—			
= Ayodhya City	”	117	. . .
Sháhábád District, Bengal—			
Anciently called Kárusha Desa	III	70	. . .
	XV	155	. . .
Dominion of Cheros and Sauras in—	XVII	131, 132	. . .
Three famous shrines in—	XVI	59	. . .
Sháhbázgarhi in Yusufzai, Panjáb—			
Ancient and modern names of—	V	9, 15, 18	. . .
Ruins at—	”	10—18	III, IV.
Edict inscription of Asoka at—	”	8, 18—22	V.
Sháhdheri (Deri-Sháhán) in Ráwal Pindi District, Panjáb—			
= Ancient Taxila, *q.v.*	II	112 *seqq.*	. . .
	V	66	. . .
Ruins at, or near, comprise at least 55 *stúpas*, 28 monasteries and 9 temples	II	112, 151	LIV, LVII.
	XIV	. . .	V
Six distinct divisions of ruins at—	II	116	. . .
Ario-Pálí inscriptions on vase from tope No. 13 and on copperplate from tope No. 14 at—	”	124—5	LIX.
on gold plate from—	”	130	LIX.
of Satrap Liako Kusuluko from—	”	132	LIX.
	V	67	. . .
on silver plate from—	II	135, *Note*	. . .
Valuable gold plate found at—	”	131	. . .
Great *stúpa* of Sháhpur at—	”	123	LVIII.
Broken inscribed monolith at—	”	126	. . .
Burnt clay colossal statues at—	”	127	. . .
	V	74	. . .
Attic column found at—	II	129	. . .
Buddhist railings at—	”	135	. . .
	V	75	. . .
Anomalous building at—	”	74	XIX.
'Tiger' monastery and *stúpa* at—	”	”	XX.
Buddhist temple (*vihár*) of Ionic order at—	”	68, 69, 190	. . .
Second Ionic temple, probably of sun, at—	XIV	9	VII.
Ruins of large *vihár* on Little Jhandiála mound at—	”	11	VI.
Monasteries, &c., on Meri hill at—	”	12	VII.
Seals and minor antiquities from—	”	14	VIII, IX.
Lapis lazuli found at—	II	117	. . .
Thousands of coins found at—	”	”	. . .
	XIV	16	X.

	Vol.	Page.	Plate.
Sháhdheri (Deri-Sháhán) in Ráwal Pindi District, Panjáb— *contd.*			
Only three gold coins of, known	XIV	16	x.
Square copper coins of, current with those of Agathokles and Pantaleon	„	18	. . .
Symbol, probably of city, on coins of—	„	19	. . .
Bilingual inscribed coins of—	„	20	. . .
Small coins found at—	„	21	. . .
Detailed description of coins found at—	„	21—24	. . .
Etymology of names of cities Sirkap and Sirsukh included in ruins at—	„	8	. . .
Sháhi—			
A title of Indo-Scythian kings	III	42	. . .
Sháhjahánábád *or* **modern Delhi—**			
Described	I	224	. . .
Sháhpur, near Bihár, in Patna District, Bengal—			
Hindu images at—	XV	11	. . .
Inscription of King Áditya Sena Deva dated S. 55 (?)at—	„	12, 164	XI.
	XVI	60, 79	. . .
Sháhpur at Delhi—			
Identified with Siri	I	207	. . .
Inscription dated 753 A.H. = 1353 A.D. at— . .	XX	153	XXXI.
Sháhpur, near Sháhdheri in Ráwal Pindi District, Panjáb—			
Part of the ruins of Taxila—	II	123	. . .
Sharkí dynasty—			
Mosques built at Jaunpur, Kanauj, Benares, and Etáwah by—	XI	102	. . .
Shell characters—			
See **Alphabet, ancient Nágrí.**			
Sher Sháh, Emperor—			
Tombs of himself and family at Sáhsarám . . .	XI	133	XXXIX.
Refounded Patna and built a mosque there, 1541 A.D.	VIII	28	. . .
	XI	156	. . .
Conquered Bengal in A.D. 1537-38	XV	177	. . .
Shergarh at Delhi—			
Described	I	221	. . .
Shergarh, *or* **Kábar in Barelí District, N.-W.P.—**			
Named after Sher Sháh	„	359	. . .

	Vol.	Page.	Plate.
Sherghàti in Bihár—			
Remains at, described by Kittoe	VIII	64	. . .
Shorkot in Jhang District, Panjáb—			
Ancient fort of—	V	97	. . .
Legends of—	„	98	. . .
Coins found at—	„	99	. . .
= (?) Alexandria Soriane	„	„	. . .
History in Muhammadan times of—	„	„	. . .
Inscribed bricks at—	„	102	. . .
Siálkot, in Siálkot District, Panjáb—			
= Sálbáhanpur according to Panjáb tradition	II	21	. . .
Legends of—	XIV	45	. . .
Coins of Greek Kings, Philoxenes, &c., found at—	„	„	. . .
Sibi country—			
Between Lahore and Multán	„	145	. . .
Also territory round Chitor	„	146	. . .
Jayatura capital of latter	VI	205	. . .
Coins of, from Chitor	„	204	. . .
	XIV	146	XXXI.
People of, called Sobii by Quintus Curtius	„	145	. . .
Siddhrámpur in Patna District, Bengal—			
= Siddhásrama, the hermitage of Viswámitra	VIII	v, 11	. . .
Sikandar Lodí, Emperor—			
Built fort of Agra	IV	xiv	. . .
Báradarí of, at Agra	„	99	XI.
Probably buried at Delhi	„	„ *Note*	. . .
Mosque of reign of, at Khairpur, near Delhi	XX	155	XXXVI.
Destroyed temples at Narwár, &c.	II	353	. . .
certain Sharkí buildings at Jaunpur	XI	115, 117	. . .
Sikandra in Bharatpur State, Rájputána—			
Old gate at—	VI	74	. . .
Mosques at—	XX	79	XVIII.
Sikka—			
A fort opposite old Multán	V	114	. . .
Silabhadra—			
A Buddhist teacher, A.D. 600	XVI	47	. . .
Silabhadra monastery of Hwen Thsang—			
Probably = Kauwá Dol in Gayá District, Bengal	VIII	40	. . .

	Vol.	Page.	Plate.
Siláo in Patna District, Bengal—			
Probably = Vikramasila	VIII	75, 84	...
Said to have been founded by Vikramáditya	"	"	...
Silenus—			
Group at Mathurá supposed to represent	I	242	...
Simga in Ráipur District, C. P.—			
Old *satí* monument at—	XVII	33	...
Simra in (?) Damoh District, C. P.—			
Temples and early *satí* monument at—	XXI	101, 159	...
Simraun—			
See **Samraon in Champáran District.**			
Sindh—			
Ták race in—	II	8	...
King of, in A.D. 641 a Súdra, perhaps of **Bála** tribe	"	34	...
Kings of, Brahmans from A.D. 642 to 711	"	34	...
Occupied by Zaths (probably = Játs) and Meds in 7th century A.D.	"	55	...
Singhapura (Seng-ho-pu-lo) of Hwen Thsang—			
= Mallot in Salt Range, *q.v.*	"	192	...
	V	35	...
Singhbhúm District, Bengal—			
Find of Roman gold coins at Bámanghatí in—	XIII	72	...
Singorgarh (Singaurgarh) in Jabalpur District, C. P.—			
Fort at—	IX	48	...
Pillars of victory at—	"	49	...
History of—	"	50	...
Singror in Alláhábád District, N.-W. P.—			
An old site and scene of defeat of Khán Zamán	XI	62	...
Perhaps = Ayumukha of Hwen Thsang	"	69	...
Sirhind—			
See **Sarhind.**			
Siri fort at Delhi—			
Identified with Sháhpur	I	207	...
Sirkap—			
A portion of the ruins of Taxila	II	119	...
Sirpur (Srípura) in Ráipur District, C. P.—			
Probably = Chitrangadapura, = Sageda metropolis of Ptolemy	XVII	69, 70	...
	XXI	93	...
Anciently named Savaripura	VII	168	...

	Vol.	Page.	Plate.
Sirpur (Srípura) in Ráipur District, C. P.—*contd.*			
Extensive ruins at—	VII	168	. . .
	XVII	23	XIV.
Six inscriptions of Siva Gupta, &c., at—	VI	169, 185	. . .
	XVII	25	XVIII, XIX.
Buildings and sculptures in Gupta style at—	VII	174	XVI.
	XVII	28	XV—XVII.
Only one Buddhist sculpture found at—	"	31	. . .
Legends of—	VII	171, 192	. . .
	XVII	29, 31	. . .
Sirsá in Sirsá District, Panjáb—			
Ancient fort at—	XXIII	8	. . .
Sikh relics at—	"	9	. . .
Ancient tank and sculptures at—	"	10	. . .
Sirsáwa (Sarsáwa) in Sahâranpur District, N.-W. P.—			
Notices of, in Muhammadan authors	XIV	79	. . .
Worship, and legend of Gugá Chauhán at—	"	80	. . .
Sirsukh—			
A portion of theruins of Taxila	V	67	. . .
Sisupála, Rájá—			
A legendary king of Chedí	IX	76	. . .
Sítá-Kund in Champáran District, Bengal—			
Fort and other remains at—	XVI	22	VIII.
Sítámarhi Cave in Gayá District, Bengal—			
Described	VIII	106	V.
Siva, temples of—			
Often originally dedicated to Vishnu	II	266, 278	. . .
Siva Gupta, King—			
Mentioned in certain inscriptions from C. P.	VII	VI	. . .
	XVII	17, 85, 87	. . .
Siva Sinha Deva, Rájá of Tirhút—			
Copper-plate inscription, dated Saka 1321 = A.D. 1399 of—	XVI	4, 96 and Pref. VI	. . .
Siwálik country—			
Extent of—	VI	205	. . .

	Vol.	Page.	Plate.
Skanda Gupta, King—			
Description of silver coins of—	IX	24	V.
Inscription on Bhitarí pillar relating to— . . .	I	38, *Note* 97—99, 101	XVII, XXX.
at Bihár probably of—	"	38	. . .
of, at Garhwá, dated 140	X	11	V.
Translation of inscription of, at Indor Kherá, dated 146	XII	38	. . .
Skanda Gupta, General—			
An officer of Harsha Vardhana	IX	155	. . .
Snake—			
Ancient cast coins from W. Panjáb with figure of— .	II	10	. . .
	VI	167	. . .
Kept by King Abisares in time of Alexander . .	II	23	. . .
Worship of, at Bhándak in C. P.	IX	131	. . .
in Káshmír	II	10	. . .
Traces of worship in Rájputána of—	VI	208	. . .
See **Nága** *and* **Serpent worship.**			
Soamus R. of Arrian—			
= Suhán R. in Panjáb	II	23	. . .
Sobii of Curtius and Diodorus—			
= Sibæ of Strabo, = people of Sibi in Panjáb . .	"	27, 37	. . .
	XIV	145	. . .
Probably also called Sabæ, Ibæ, Chobia, and Silei .	II	39, 40	. . .
Sohágpur in Rewá State, Baghelkhand—			
Inscribed Jain statue at—	VII	240	. . .
Large temple at—	"	240—243	XX, XXI.
Extensive Jain and Hindu remains at—	"	244, 245	. . .
Sohdara in Gujránwála District, Panjáb—			
Minár of time of Mahmúd of Ghazní, formerly existing at—	XIV	44	. . .
Sohna in Gurgaon District, Panjáb—			
Hot springs at—	XX	135	. . .
Mosques and tomb at—	"	136	. . .
Sohrí Dal, Rájá—			
Oudh traditions of—	I	329	. . .

	Vol.	Page.	Plate.
Son R.—			
Identical with Erannoboas of Pliny and Arrian . .	VIII	VI, XIII	. . .
Cunningham's views on changes in course of— . .	"	V	. . .
Mr. Beglar's views on ditto . . .	"	X—XIII and 5—26	. . .
Punpun and Murhar rivers in old course of— . .	"	8	. . .
Course of, when the Rámáyana and Mahábhárata were composed	"	9—13	. . .
Not mentioned by Hwen Thsang	"	20	. . .
Described in 'Mudra Rákshasa'	"	"	. . .
Probably adopted present course shortly before Muhammadan conquest	"	23	. . .
Effect on Ganges of change in course of— . . .	VIII	XII, 23	. . .
Rises at Son Mundá in Bilárpur district, C. P. . .	VII	236	. . .
Sonabhadra—			
An old name of the Son R.	VIII	V, 7	. . .
Sonárgaon—			
See **Sunárgáon in Dhákka District.**			
Sonátapan in Bánkurá District, Bengal—			
Brick temple at—	"	200	. . .
Temple ascribed to Sáliváhan at—	"	201	. . .
Old name of, was Hamíradángá	"	"	. . .
Son-bhandár cave at Rájgír—			
Probably = Pi-po-lo cave of Chinese writers . .	I	21, 25	. . .
Inscriptions of—	"	25	XIII.
= Saṭṭapáni cave	III	140	. . .
	VIII	VIII, XIV	. . .
Sonitapura of Vishnu Purána—			
Identified with Devíkot, near Dinájpur	XV	100	. . .
Sonmayi in Patna district, Bengal—			
Remains at—	VIII	X	. . .
Son Mundá, near Amarkantak in Bilárpur District, C. P.—			
Is true source of Son R.	VII	236	. . .
Sopeithes, King—			
The Kathæi, probably subjects of—	II	35	. . .
Territory of, included the Salt Range	"	36	. . .
Capital of, on the Hydaspes (Jhelum), probably at or near Bherá	"	" 38	. . .
Silver coins of—	"	38 *Note*	. . .
Perhaps = Rájá Chobnáth	"	40	. . .

	Vol.	Page.	Plate.
Sophagasenas, Maurya King—			
Made a treaty on Indus with Antiochus the Great .	II	41	. . .
Sophites—			
See **Sopeithes.**			
Sora Arcati Regis, town of Ptolemy—			
Probably = Seorí-Náráyan in C. P.	XXI	94	. . .
Soræ Nomades of Ptolemy—			
= Savara tribe	"	"	. . .
Sorar in Ráipur District, C. P.—			
Temple of 'Kalal' Rájá at—	VII	137	. . .
Inscribed *satí* pillar at—	"	142	. . .
Soron (Súkara-Kshetra) in Etah district, N.-W. P.—			
Pilgrims' inscriptions at—	I	267	. . .
Srávastí—			
= **Sáhet-Máhet, in Gonda district, Oudh,** *q.v.* . .	"	330	. . .
Early history of—	"	332	. . .
Chinese pilgrims' accounts of—	"	333	. . .
Jetavana and connected buildings at—	"	334	. . .
Purvárâma monastery of Visákhá at—	"	345	. . .
Vikramáditya, king of, according to Hwen Thsang .	XI	96	. . .
Buddhist revival at, probably in reign of Harsha Varddhana of Kanauj	"	98	. . .
Mayúra-dhwaja, &c., kings of—	"	"	. . .
Srenika, King—			
= **Bimbisára, King,** *q.v.*			
Sringi Rishi (Singi Rikhi) in Mongír district, Bengal—			
Buddhist creed and inscription dated S. 35 at— . .	XV	20	XI.
rughna, Kingdom—			
Position of—	I	246	. . .
Described by Hwen Thsang	II	227	. . .
= Kuninda (Kulinda)	XIV	134	. . .
Srughna, Town—			
= Sugh *or* Sughan, in Ambálá District, Panjáb .	II	222	LXXI.
Mostly in ruins in Hwen Thsang's time— . . .	"	"	. . .
Great forts at—	"	228	. . .
Ancient Hindu coins numerous at—	"	229	. . .
Included city of Mandar or Mandalpur, which (?) = Mandir *or* Manduli of Ferishta	"	229—230	. . .

	Vol.	Page.	Plate.
Stevenson, Dr. J.—			
Translated inscriptions in caves of W. India . .	I	Intr. xxxi	. . .
Deciphered some ancient forms of numerals . .	"	" xxxiii	. . .
Erroneously supposed Vikramáditya to be referred to in Násik inscriptions	"	" xxxii	. . .
Stone—			
Art of cutting, according to General Cunningham known to Hindus two centuries before Asoka . .	XXII	iv	. . .
Ditto, according to Mr. Beglar, introduced into India by the Greeks	VIII	123	. . .
Early examples in Bihár of Indian buildings in— .	III	143	XLII
Stone circles—			
At Deosá in Jaypur State	VI	104	XII
Constructed in Rájputána for playing the game of *táhar* or *ewáro*	XXIII	49	. . .
See **Circles, rude stone.**			
Stone implements—			
Found at Deosá and Dhand in Jaypur State . .	VI	107, 161	. . .
Masaon Dih in Ghazípur district . .	XXII	100	. . .
From Bairánt, in Benares district	"	116	. . .
Found in many places in Northern India . . .	"	117	. . .
Stools, stone—			
Found at Patna and other Buddhist sites . . .	XI XVII	163 4	. . . . . .
Found at Bithá in Alláhábád district	III	52	. . .
Straton, King—			
Coins of, imitated by Satrap Rajubul, and found with his coins	"	40	. . .
Stúpas, Buddhist—			
Age of, determined by proportion of height to diameter	II	288	. . .
Additions frequently made to—	I	116	. . .
Erected sometimes as a memorial only . . .	"	112	. . .
Originally meant 'mound of earth'	"	69	. . .
Of stone or brick in Asoka's time	"	"	. . .
Specimens of earthen, only at Lauriyá-Navandgarh .	"	"	* . .
Small votive, at Jamálgarhi and in Burma . .	V	48	. . .
Su, a Scythian horde—			
Driven from Jaxartes by Yuchi in 163 B.C., and from Sogdiana in B.C. 126	II	44	. . .
Identical with the Sakas, and Abárs	"	45, 48	. . .

* But see references under "Tumuli, or earthen barrows."

	Vol.	Page.	Plate.
Suari of Pliny—			
= Saura (Savara) tribe	XVII	125	. . .
Suastos R. of Arrian—			
= Suwát R.	V	3	. . .
Súba-Bihár—			
= **Tusáran-Bihár**, *q.v.*			
Also Muhammadan name of Bihár city (Dand-Bihár)	VIII	75	. . .
Subhegarh, in Muzaffarpur district, Bengal—			
Ancient fort at—	XVI	30	IX.
Legends of—	„	31	. . .
Sudána, *alias* **Sudatta—**			
See **Wessantara.**			
Sudhanwan, King—			
Persecuted Buddhism	XX	103	. . .
Súdras—			
Probably represent Medo-Scythians conquered by Aryans	IX	160	. . .
Sue-Bihár—			
See **Tusáran Bihár.**	XI	31	. . .
Sugh *or* **Sughan in Ambálá district, Panjáb—**			
= Ancient **Srughna**, *q.v.*	II	227	LXXI.
Suhán R. in Panjáb—			
Soamus R. of Arrian	„	23	. . .
Suhaniya near Gwáliár, C. I.—			
An ancient city	„	399	. . .
Great temple at—	„	400	. . .
Sundry inscriptions at—	„	401	. . .
Slab with numerical figures from—	„	„	. . .
Suir S(uirae)—			
Other names of the Soura (Savara) tribe, *q.v.*	XVII	118	. . .
Suktimati R. Mahabhareta—			
= Mahánadí R.	„	69	. . .

	Vol.	Page.	Plate.
Sultánganj, in Bhágalpur District, Bengal—			
Ruins of monastery at—	XV	25	. . .
Colossal copper statue of Buddha at—	X	127	. . .
	XV	26	. . .
Other antiquities found at—	XV	27	. . .
Excavation of *stúpa* at—	„	28	X.
Coins of Chandra Gupta II. and Swámí Rudra Sinha found together at—	X	127*	. . .
	XV	29	. . .
Sultánkot—			
The Muhammadan name of Bayána, *q.v.*	XX	62	. . .
Sultánpur in Sultánpur District, Oudh—			
= Kasapura or Kusapura of Hwen Thsang . .	I	313	. . .
Held by a Bhar Rájá in time of Alá-ud-dín Khiljí .	„	314	. . .
Sultánpur (Dallá), in Jálandhar District, Panjáb—			
Site of the Támasavana monastery	XIV	55	XIX.
Fort at, founded by Daulat Khán Lodí, in reign of Ibráhím Lodí	„	„	. . .
Early coin with name of Buddha from—	„	57	. . .
Short Muhammadan inscription at—	XXI	134	. . .
Sumer Singh—			
Mentioned in tradition as a Chandel Raja of Mahoba .	X	66	. . .
Sun—			
Images of, rare after 9th century A.D.	XIII	63	. . .
Temple of, at Taxila—	II	114	. . .
Gwáliár	„	342, 353	. . .
Gayá	III	110, 112	XXXIII.
Multán	V	115—120	. . .
Greek and Hindu representations of—	III	97	XXVII.
Multán coins of—	V	121	XXXVII.
Worship of, at Indor Kherá in time of Skanda Gupta .	XII	38, 68	. . .
by Káthi tribe in Panjáb	II	34	. . .
in Sháhábád district	XVI	72	. . .
Sunárgáon (Sonárgáon), in Dhákka District, Bengal—			
Said to have been residence of one of the 12 Bhuinhár chiefs	XV	135	. . .
Capital of E. Bengal under Muhammadan rule . .	„	„	
Also known as Painám	„	137	. . .
Map of—	„	„	XXXIII.
Ruined muslin factory of East India Company at— .	„	139	. . .
Tombs and mosques at—	„	139—144	XXXV.

* In text the coin is erroneously referred to Chandra Gupta I., and the Swámí's name is given as Rudra Sena.

	Vol.	Page.	Plate.
Sunit (Sunet) in Ludhiána District, Punjáb—			
Extensive remains at—	XIV	65	. . .
Analysis of 576 coins from—	"	"	. . .
Legend of—	"	66	. . .
Sung-Yun and Hwui-Seng—			
Travelled in Kábul valley and W. Panjáb in A.D. 502	II	84	. . .
Suprabuddha, Rájá—			
Residence of, identified in Bastí district	XII	211	. . .
Surahar, in Lalitpur District, N.-W. P.—			
Temple at—	XXI	176	. . .
Súrajpur—			
A name of Baṭesar in Agra District	IV	222	. . .
Surasena people—			
Belonged to Jádava or Jádovansi race	XX	2	. . .
Described by Greek writers	"	"	. . .
Generally adopted Buddhist and Jain religions in Indo-Scythian times	"	3	. . .
Early history of—	"	4	. . .
Extent of territory of—	"	2	. . .
Suráshtra, satraps of—			
Silver coins of—	IX	22	. . .
Suror on Ken R.—			
Old *satí* pillar at—	XXI	158	. . .
Susima—			
Elderbr other of Asoka—	II	112	. . .
Suvarna coins—			
Mentioned in inscription at Gaṛhwá—	X	11	. . .
Suwát in Yusufzai—			
Rich in ancient remains	V	1	. . .
Suwát R.			
= Suastos R. of Arrian	"	3	. . .
Swámí Gosura—			
Pillar of, at Sánchi	X	62	XXI.

	Vol.	Page.	Plate.
Swetámbara Jains—			
Legendary origin of—	X	55	. . .
Syálapati Deva, King of Gándhára—			
Also named Kallár—	V	83	. . .
Coins of, common in Yusufzai	,,	45	. . .
Synod, Buddhist—			
First held by Ajátasatru at Sattapáni cave at Rájagriha	III	143	. . .
Second held at Vaisáli	I	63	. . .
T			
Tadaka forest—			
Near Bihár, in Sháhábád District, Bengal	VIII	12	. . .
Tadwa (Tanda), in Bahraich District, Oudh—			
=To-wai of Fa-Hian	I	348	. . .
Remains of *stúpa* containing body of Kásyapa, &c., at—	,,	349	. . .
	XI	71, 77	XXI—XXIII.
Tagma, metropolis of Ptolemy—			
Probably = Mahásthán, *q.v.*	XV	114	. . .
May = Dhákka (Dacca)	,,	127	. . .
Tahangarh, in Karauli State, Rájputána—			
Captured by Muhammad bin Sám in A.H. 592 = A.D. 1196	XX	88	. . .
Foundation of, ascribed to the Yádava Rájá Tahan Pála	,,	90	. . .
Called Islámábád in inscription, dated A.H. 925 = A.D. 1519	,,	91	XIX.
Inscription of Islám Sháh, dated A.H. 953 at— .	,,	,,	,,
Táhar—			
A game played in Rájputána with stone circles .	XXIII	49	. . .
Tahora, of Peutingerian Tables—			
Probably = Attak	II	7	. . .
Táj Mahal at Agra—			
Date and cost of—	IV	159	. . .
Ták—			
An aboriginal race in Sindh	II	8	. . .

	Vol.	Page.	Plate.
Tákari alphabet—			
An ancient form of Nágrí used in Panjáb . . .	II	8	. . .
Used in coins and inscriptions of Káshmír and Kángra, and in Rájá Taranginí	,,	9	. . .
	V	182	. . .
Also called 'Mund' or 'Lunde'	II	9	. . .
Takht-i-Bahi, in Yusufzai—			
Ruins at—	V	23—36	VI—X.
Inscription of Gondophares, dated 103 Samvat at— .	,,	59	. . .
Taki (Tse-kai) of Hwen Thsang—			
= Asarur, in Gujránwálá District, Panjáb . . .	,,	113	. . .
Takka race—			
Probably gave their name to Taxila (Takkasila) .	II	6	. . .
'Takkadesa,' country of, annexed to Káshmír *circa* 900 A.D.	,,	8	. . .
Present social position of—	,,	10	. . .
Takkál-Bábá, in Pesháwar District, Panjáb—			
Great *stúpa* at—	XIX	133	. . .
Takshak-Nagara of Tod—			
Probably Nágarí in Mewár	VI	208	. . .
Takshaka—			
Synonymous with Nága	,,	167	. . .
Talao, in Alwar State, Rájputána—			
Saiva temple at—	XX	123	XXIX.
Legend of the lake at—	,,	,,	. . .
Tamasis of Ptolemy—			
Perhaps = Kálanjar	XXI	58, 91	. . .
Tambavatí—			
An ancient name of Chátsú in Jaypur, and of Nágarí in Mewár	VI	197	. . .
Tameræ of Ptolemy—			
Perhaps inhabited **Varendra,** *q. v.*	XV	113	. . .
Tamraliptí (Tamlúk)—			
Ancient routes to—	VIII	50, 142	. . .
Tandwá—			
See **Tadwa (Tanda), in Bahraich District, Oudh.**			

	Vol.	Page.	Plate.
Tánsen, musician—			
Akbar's favourite	II	370	. . .
Sent to Akbar from Rewá	XXI	110	. . .
Tápti R.—			
= Nanaguna R. of Ptolemy	IX	151	. . .
Táráxgarh—			
A fort near Ajmer	XXIII	39	. . .
Tarnáwa near Sháhdheri (Taxila)—			
Buddhist ruins at—	II	147	. . .
Taylor, Colonel Meadows—			
On the Prehistoric Archæology of India	I	Intr. xxx	. . .
Mistakes of, about Pushpamitra	„	„ xxxi	. . .
Taxila—			
Perhaps named from the Takka tribe	II	6	. . .
Situated in Amanda district, according to Pliny . .	„	6, 112	. . .
Wealth and splendour of, as described by Arrian, Pliny, Strabo, and Philostratus	„	112, 113	. . .
Rebelled against king Bimbisára of Magadha . .	„	112	. . .
Reduced to submission by Asoka, after failure of Susima	„	„	. . .
Resided in by Asoka and his son Kunála . . .	„	113	. . .
Formed part of the dominions of Eukratides . .	„	„	. . .
Conquered by Su or Abár Indo-Scythians B.C. 126 .	„	„	. . .
Kushán Indo-Scythians (Kanishka), and administered by Satraps *circa* 26 A.D.	„	„	. . .
Apparently visited by Apollonius of Tyana A.D. 42—45	„	„	. . .
Called Chu-sha-shi-lo (Chutyasira) by Fa-Hian A.D. 400, and visited by Sung-yun A.D. 502 . .	„	114	. . .
Called Ta-cha-shi-lo (Takshasila) by Hwen Thsang A.D. 630 and 643	„	„	. . .
Monasteries at, mostly ruinous in Hwen Thsang's time	„	115	. . .
Mentioned in vase and copper-plate inscriptions .	„	125, 133	. . .
Identified with modern **Sháhdheri**, *q.v.*	„	112, 125, 135	. . .
	V	66	. . .
The name (= Takshasila) of, proves that art of stone-cutting was known to Hindus before Alexander .	II	111	. . .
	XXII	IV	. . .
Tejára (Tijára), in Alwar State, Rájputána—			
Great tomb of Aláuddín Álam Sháh at—	XX	115	XXVII.
Other Muhammadan buildings at—	„	117	. . .
Early history of—	„	„	. . .

	Vol.	Page.	Plate.
Tej Karan, prince of Gwáliár—			
Romantic story of—	II	376	. . .
Teládha in Patna District, Bengal—			
Identified with Ti-lo-tse-kia of Hwen Thsang . .	VII	34	. . .
	XI	105	. . .
Site of monastery at—	„	166	XLII.
Inscriptions at, giving name of town	„	168	„
Mosque with inscription of Sher Sháh's reign at— .	„	169	. . .
Appears to have given name to the Telís of Magadha .	„	165	. . .
Telí dynasty—			
In Uchahara preceded Parihárs	IX	6, 7	. . .
Telkupi on Dámuda R. (Dámodar) in Chutiá Nágpur—			
Numerous temples at—	VIII	169—178	. . .
Miniature „	„	175	. . .
Santál custom at—	„	177	. . .
Temple—			
Parts of mediæval Hindu	II	359	. . .
Terahí in Gwáliár State, C. I.—			
Temples and inscriptions at—	XXI	177	. . .
Terra-cotta—			
Largely used for ornament in N. India . . .	XI	42	. . .
at Indor Kherá	XII	50	. . .
Statuary at Bhuilá Dih	„	162	. . .
Statuette of Buddha at Kasiá	XVIII	67—100	. . .
Tetráwa in Patna District, Bengal—			
Buddhist ruins at—	I	39	. . .
	XI	182	XLIV.
Colossal statue of Buddha at—	„	183	. . .
Short inscriptions from—	I	39	. . .
	XI	183	. . .
Tewar (Tripura) in Jabalpur District, C. P.—			
The ancient capital of Chedí	IX	54, 77	. . .
	XVII	72	. . .
Probably mentioned by Hwen Thsang	IX	55	. . .
Identified with Sageda, Metropolis of Ptolemy . .	„	56	. . .
Old city of Karanbel close to—	„	57	. . .
Sculptures at—	„	58	. . .
Thakkiya (Takiya)—			
A district in E. Panjáb	„	103	. . .

	Vol.	Page.	Plate.
Thánegáon in Chándá District, C. P.—			
Temple at—	VII	126	. . .
Thánesar (Stháneswara) in Ambála District, Panjáb—			
Buddhism declining at, in A.D. 634	II	221	. . .
? = Batan-Kaisara of Ptolemy	,,	212	. . .
Situated in Kuru-Kshetra *or* Dharma-Kshetra, the 'holy-land' of the legend of the Pándus	,,	213-219	. . .
Great lake at, mentioned by Varáha Mihira in A. D. 500	,,	217-218	. . .
Further explorations to be made at—	,,	221	. . .
Muhammadan remains at—	,,	222	. . .
Tháru tribe—			
Mr. E. Colvin's account of—	XII	136	. . .
Thatha in Sindh—			
= Binagara of Ptolemy, and Minnagara of Erythræan Periplus	II	46	. . .
Thoda in Jaypur State, Rájputána—			
History of—	VI	126	. . .
Temples at—	,,	128,132	XIV, XV.
Tholobana of Ptolemy—			
= Bahuriband in C. P.	IX	57	. . .
	XXI	93	. . .
Thomas, Mr. E.—			
List of principal publications of, to 1871	I	Intr. xxviii	. . .
Settled chronology of Muhammadan kingdoms of Ghazní, Delhi, and Bengal	,,	,, ,,	. . .
'Note on the excavations at Sárnáth' by—	,,	124, 126	. . .
Contributions to history of Bengal by—	XV	165	. . .
Thomas, Saint—			
Legends of death of, at Calamina in India	II	60	. . .
Alleged mission of, to Parthia, Persia, and India	,,	,,	. . .
	V	,,	. . .
Tigawá in Jabalpur District, C. P.—			
Ruined temples of Gupta age at—	IX	42	IX.
Standing Gupta temple at—	,,	45	X, XI.
Inscription of 8th century at—	,,	46	. . .
Tiládaka—			
See **Teládha —**			
Tile mosaics—			
A Multán	V	133	XXXIX.

	Vol.	Page.	Plate.
Ti-lo-tse-kia of Hwen Thsang—			
= Teládha in Magadha	VIII	VII, 34	. . .
Tilsanda of Muhammadan historians—			
= Bilsar in Etah District, N.-W. P.	XI	15	. . .
Tipágarh in Chándá District, C. P.—			
Fort, &c., at—	VII	130-133	. . .
Tiranda—			
A name of **Bhatinda**, *q.v.*—	XXIII	2, 7	. . .
Tirhút (Tírabhukti)—			
Derivation of name	XVI	1	. . .
Included in dominions of Pála dynasty of Magadha .	"	"	. . .
Map of—	"	"	1.
Local dynasty of—	"	2	. . .
Rájá Siva Sinha Deva, the greatest of local dynasty of—	"	4	. . .
Included in dominions of Sharkí kings of Jaunpur .	"	5	. . .
Submitted to Sikandar Lodí, A.D. 1499-1500 . .	"	"	. . .
Titaráwa—			
See **Tetráwa in Patna District,** Bengal —			
Tittagarh in Patna State, C. P.—			
Ruins near—	XIII	137-140	. . .
Tivara Deva, king of Kosala—			
Copper-plate inscription of—	XVII	18	. . .
Tochari tribe—			
Of Strabo, &c., = Great Yuchi	II	43, 64	. . .
Gold and silver coins of, in Hwen Thsang's time .	"	79	. . .
Coinage of, same as that of Bamiyan	"	"	. . .
Todar Mal—			
Was a Meo by birth	XX	26	. . .
Tomar dynasty of Delhi—			
Lists of—	I	148	. . .
Identical with Tomar dynasty of Kanauj . . .	"	150	. . .
Tomar Rájás of Gwáliár—			
List of—	II	382	. . .
Topra (Tobra), in Ambála District, Panjáb—			
Is the place from which Fíroz Shah removed Asoka's pillar to Delhi	XIV	78	. . .

	Vol.	Page.	Plate.
Toramána, King of Málwa—			
Dates of silver coins of—	II	311	...
	IX	21, 26	V.
Cannot be identified with Toramána of Káshmír	"	27	...
Translation of inscription of, at Eran	X	84	...
Tornáwa, N.-E. of Sháhdheri (Taxila)—			
Buddhist remains at—	II	147	...
Tortoise—			
Symbol of Jumna river—	X	49	...
Trailokya Varmma, Chandel King—			
Copper-plate inscription of—	XXI	147	...
probably of, under name of Trailokya Malla	"	148	...
Trigartta *or* **Traigartta-desa—**			
= Jálandhar district	V	148	...
Coins of—	"	152	...
Troilchan Pál—			
King of Gándhára in 11th century A.D.	"	82	...
Tripura *or* **Tripuri—**			
Ancient name of **Tewar** in **Jabalpur District,** *q v.*	IX	54	...
Tughalk-Pathán architecture—			
Described	III	9	...
Tughlak Sháh—			
Death of, at Multán	V	134	...
Tomb of, at Delhi	I	213, 215	...
Tughlakábád fort at Delhi—			
Described	"	"	...
Tuksán, in Alígarh District, N.-W. P.—			
Mounds of ruins at—	XII	2	...
Tulamba, in Multán District, Panjáb—			
Fortress of—	V	111	XXXV.
Also called Kulamba (Kulambha)	"	112	...
Muhammadan attacks on—	"	"	...
Moulded bricks at—	"	"	...
Tumaula, in Mathurá District, N.-W. P.			
Statue of Buddha at—	XX	53	...

	Vol.	Page.	Plate.
Tumuli, *or* Earthen barrows—			
None probably later than 400 A.D.	I	326	. . .
At Lauriyá-Navandgarh	„	69—72	XXIV.
	XXII	37, 49	. . .
At Kasiá in Gorakhpur	I	76—79	. . .
	XVIII	94	. . .
At Bhuilá Dih	XII	143, 153	. . .
Mentioned by Megasthenes as the Indian form of sepulchre	I	76, *Note*	. . .
Turkí Kings of Kábul—			
= Yuchi Indo-Scythians	II	66	. . .
Turtipár in Balliá District, N.-W. P.—*			
Khairá Dih ruins at	XXII	107	. . .
Turturia, in Biláspur District, C. P.—			
Early Buddhist and Brahmanical remains at— . .	XIII	146, 152	XVII.
Priestesses at—	„	147	. . .
Turushka—			
= Turk, = Tochari	II	74	. . .
Tusáran-Bihár (Súba-Bihár), in Partábgarh District, Oudh—			
Derivation of name of—	XI	64	. . .
Map of—	„	„	XIX.
Indo-Scythian sculpture at—	„	65	XX.
coins from—	„	67	. . .
Bhar legends of—	„	„	. . .
Probably = Ayumukha or Hayamukha of Hwen Thsang	„	68	. . .
Tushám, in Hissár District, Panjáb—			
Two inscribed rocks at—	V	136	. . .
Four minor inscriptions at—	„	138	. . .
Ruins at—	„	137	. . .
Inscription at, supposed to mention Ghatotkacha of Gupta dynasty	„	139	XL.
Named originally 'Tushárárámа'	„	140	. . .
Description of hill at—	XXIII	19	VIII.
Enormous bricks in ruins at—	„	20	IX.
Position and condition of great inscription at— . .	„	21	XXVIII.
Tushára dynasty—			
=? Kanwa dynasty of Puranas	V	140	. . .

U

	Vol.	Page.	Plate.
Uchahara, *or* Nágaudh State, in Baghelkhand—			
An ancient Parihár principality, formerly named Barme	IX	5	. . .
The seat of a Teliyá Ráj	„	6	. . .
Perhaps = Udyáraka of Samudra Gupta . . .	„	10	. . .

* In the text Turtipár is erroneously stated to be in the Gházípur District.

	Vol.	Page.	Plate.
Udakhanda—			
= Ohind on the Indus, and not Attak	II	93	. . .
Udal—			
See **Alhá and Udal.**			
Udamnagar—			
See **Udinagar.**			
Udandapura—			
= Bihár City	VIII	75	. . .
	IX	185	. . .
Udandapura Desa—			
= Magadha	"	"	. . .
Udayagiri, in Bhopál State, C. I.—*			
Sculptures of descent of Ganges and Jumna and of Varáha Avatár at—	X	48	XVIII.
Description of caves in—	"	46, 52	XVI.
Jain inscription, dated 106 of Gupta era at— . .	"	54	XIX.
Hindu, Buddhist, and Jain remains at—	"	55	. . .
Lion pillar at—	"	56	. . .
Udayagiri, in Purí District, Orissa—			
Notes on caves at—	XIII	91—95	. . .
Udáyana, King—			
Kosámbi, capital of—	I	301	. . .
Buddhist accounts of—	"	302	. . .
Jain form of legend of—	III	47	. . .
Udáyáswa, King—			
Founded Pátaliputra, according to the Puráṇas . .	XI	151	. . .
Udaypur, N. of Bhilsá, in C. I.—			
Ruins at—	VII	81	. . .
Great temple dated S. 1116 at—	"	82—87	VI, VII.
Legends of—	"	83	. . .
	X	65	. . .
Numerous unpublished inscriptions at—	VII	82	. . .
	X	69	. . .
Temple, with circular ground-plan, at—	VII	v	V—VII.
Bedi, or hall for reading the Vedas, at—	X	69	. . .
Udi, Rájá—			
See **Hudi, Rájá.**			

* The Imperial Gazetteer places Bhílsá and Udayagiri in the Bhopál State. Mr. Fleet informs me that both places are in the Iságarh District of Scindia's dominions, or the Gwáliár State.

	Vol.	Page.	Plate.
Udaingar (Udamnagar)—			
A name applied to at least three places	II	186	. . .
Probably ancient name of Sakhrabastí (Sakhra)	"	153	. . .
Ancient name of Dilâwar (Dárápur) on Jhelam R.	"	175	. . .
of Asarur	"	200	. . .
Udyána—	V	64	. . .
Described by Sung-Yun in A.D. 519	"	4	. . .
Udyáraka of Samudra Gupta—			
Probably = Uchahara	IX	10	. . .
Ujjain (Ujain), in Gwáliár State, C. I.—			
Copper coins with name of city	XIV	148	XXXI.
Ujjain, in Tarái District, N.-W. P.—			
Probably = Govisana	I	252	. . .
Ukala-Kshetra—			
Said to be an old name of Soran, in Badaon District, N.-W. P.	"	266	. . .
Ulúgh Khán (Balban)—			
Ravaged Mewát in A.H. 658	XX	13, 29	. . .
Defeated Dalaki-wa-Malaki in A.D. 1247	XXI	105	. . .
Umbrellas, stone—			
Found at Sárnáth	I	125	. . .
Small votive, at Jamálgarhi and in Burma	V	48	. . .
Umgá (Mungá) in Sháhábád District, Bengal—			
Ruins at, described by Kittoe	VIII	63	. . .
Temple and inscription of Rájá Durdama at—	XI	140	. . .
Upagupta—			
Panj Pahárí near Patna, = hill of	VIII	IX	. . .
Site of monastery of, at Mathurá	I	234	. . .
	XX	32	. . .
Upátikya—			
Coin of, found at Mathurá	III	14, 39	. . .
Updhaolia—			
See **Rájdhání in Gorakhpur District.**			
Urai—			
See **Orai.**			

	Vol.	Page.	Plate.
Urasa, N. of Taxila—			
= Varsa Regio of Ptolemy, and modern Rash . .	II	29	. . .
Uruvilwá forest of Buddhist legend—			
= Urel near Buddha-Gayá	XI	VI, 147	. . .
Usun—			
A Scythian tribe, hostile to the Yuchi	II	62, 63	. . .
Utrám, near Páli in Gayá District, Bengal—			
Remains at—	VIII	62	. . .
Uttama-datta—			
Coin of, found at Sunit, near Lúdiána	XIV	65	. . .
Uttara Kosala—			
See **Kosala, Uttara.**			
V			
Vaidyanáth—			
See **Baijnáth.**			
Vairáta—			
See **Bairát.**			
Vaisáli—			
Ruins of, described in 1834, by Mr. Stephenson . .	I	55	. . .
Map of—	,,	. . . .	XXI.
The scene of the second Buddhist Synod . . .	,,	63	. . .
Buddha resided in Kutágára hall at— . . .	,,	,,	. . .
Included modern Besárh and Bakhra . . .	,,	56	. . .
Fort and *stúpa* at—	,,	,,	. . .
Vihár and other *stúpas* at—	,,	57	. . .
Hindu and Buddhist sculptures at—	,,	58	. . .
The Lion Pillar of Bakhra near—	,,	59	XXII.
Inscription in shell characters of 7th or 8th century A.D. on Lion Pillar near—	,,	60	. . .
Inscribed statue of Buddha at Bakhra near— . .	,,	61	. . .
Identification of Asoka's *stúpa* at—	,,	62	. . .
Was the capital of the Lichchhavi family . . .	,,	63	. . .
Was capital of the country of the Vrijis . . .	XVI	34	. . .
Numerous tanks at site of—	,,	6	II.
History of Buddha's almsbowl formerly kept at— .	,,	8	III.
Ancient inkstand inscribed with Gupta characters found at—	,,	12, 90	IV.

	Vol.	Page.	Plate.
Vajra Varáhi—			
A goddess of the later Buddhists	I	14	. . .
Images of, at Nálanda	„	35, 36	. . .
Vákátaka—			
= Ptolemy's country of the Bettigi	IX	56	. . .
	XXI	94	. . .
Boundaries of—	IX	121, 137	. . .
= Chándá, Nágpur, and Seoni Districts, C. P.	XVII	69	. . .
Inscriptions of Rájás of—	XXI	97	. . .
Sena Rájás of, perhaps identical with Kailakila Yavanas	XVII	84, 86	. . .
Valabhi—			
Captured by barbarians (? Gújars) in A.D. 523	II	70	. . .
Ruled by a Kshatriya King in A.D. 641	„	„	. . .
Types of coinage of—	IX	31	V.
Valabh era—			
Discussion of relation between Gupta era and—	„	20	. . .
	X	App.	. . .
Vara, Rájá—			
A legendary prince of the Panjáb	II	97	. . .
Varáha (Boar)—			
Images of, rare after 10th century A.D.	XIII	64	. . .
Avatár, as described in Puránas	X	49	. . .
is supposed to have occurred at Bárah Chhetra, in Bastí District	XII	213	. . .
Varáha Coins—			
Described	I	329	. . .
Found at Bághera, in Jaypur State	VI	137	. . .
Varendra—			
A province in Bengal, synonymous with Eastern Gauda and Paundra-desa, and probably also with Mahá Kántára	XV	40, 111, 112	. . .
Boundaries and chief cities of—	„	145	. .
Varmma *or* Maukhari dynasty of Western Magadha—			
Inscriptions and historical notices of—	III	135	. . .
List of—	„	137	. . .
Chronology and genealogy of—	XV	164—166	. . .
Varsa Regio of Ptolemy—			
= Urasa, = modern Rash	II	29	. . .

	Vol.	Page.	Plate.
Varusha—			
See Palodheri.			
Vasubandhu, Buddhist saint—			
A disciple of Manorhita	I	333	. . .
Taught at Pesháwar in first century A.D. . .	II	89	. . .
Vásudeva, Indo-Scythian King—			
Mathurá inscriptions of—	III	32	XV.
Reasons for including, in the Indo-Scythian dynasty .	,,	41	. . .
Identified with Vásudeva Kanwa of the Purános .	,,	43	. . .
Vásudeva, King of Multán—			
Coins of—	V	123	. . .
Vatsa-pattana—			
A name of **Kosámbi,** *q.v.*	I	302	. . .
Vena, Chakravarttí, Rájá—			
See **Ben, Rájá.**			
Venka Deva—			
The last of the Little Yuchi or later Indo-Scythian princes	XIV	41	. . .
Ventura, General—			
Explored Buddhist ruins in Panjáb	II	145, 159	. . .
Vespasi, Satrap—			
Mentioned in Kanishka inscription at Mánikyála .	,,	163	. . .
Videha—			
See **Mithila.**			
Vigraha Pála, King of Magadha—			
Coins ascribed to—	XI	174, 176	. . .
Date of—	,,	181	. . .
Vijaya Chandra, Rájá of Kanauj—			
Inscription at Jaunpur, dated S. 1225, = A.D. 1168, of—	,,	117, 125	XXXVII.
Vijayamandirgarh, in Bharatpur State, Rájputána—			
Santípur, ancient name of central citadel of— . . .	VI	54, 81	XX.
History of—	,,	55	. . .
Fortifications of—	,,	56	. . .
Mínár at—	,,	56, 65, 83	VII, XX.

	Vol.	Page.	Plate.
Vijayamandirgarh in Bharatpur State, Rájputána—*contd.*			
Monolith with inscription of Vishnu Vardhana Varíkin, dated S. 428, at—	XV	59, 81	VIII, XX.
Erection of fort ascribed to Rájá Pála, S. 1100, at— .	XX	81	. . .
Inscription of Auhád Khán, dated A.H. 820 = A.D. 1414, at—	,,	82	XVII.
Inscriptions of Dáúd Khán, dated A.H. 861, at— .	,,	86	. . .
of Khán Khánán at—	,,	,,	. . .
Inscription of Bábar at—	,,	88	. . .
See also **Bayána.**			
Vikrama era—			
Perhaps an Indo-Scythian era made current by Kanishka	II	68, *Note*	. . .
Earliest known inscription dated in, is of S. 811 = A.D. 754	,,	68	. . .
Speculations as to origin of—	III	39, 45	. . .
Reckoned in Mithila and Rangpur as 134 years before Saka	XV	160	. . .
Termed Vikrama Saka in inscription at Boram Deo, C. P.	XVII	40	. . .
Vikramáditya, of Ujjain—			
Suggested identity of, with Sáliváhana . . .	I	139	. . .
Sometimes known in Panjáb as Rájá Sankhár . .	II	173	. . .
Speculations as to identity of, with Wema-Kadphises .	III	44	. . .
King of Srávastí, according to Hwen Thsang . .	XI	96	. . .
Ayodhya, according to Táranáth . . .	,,	97	. . .
Ujjain, and restorer of Ayodhya, according to tradition	,,	,,	. . .
Suggested identity of, with Chandra Gupta I. . .	,,	,,	. . .
Connected by Oudh traditions with Samudra Pála and Chandra Pála, who probably are meant for Samudra Gupta and Chandra Gupta	,,	99	. . .
Vikramáditya, Chálukya—			
Defeated Harsha Vardhana	I	281	. . .
Vikramasila, in Magadha—			
Mentioned in Táranáth's history of Tibet . . .	VIII	75	. . .
Probably = Silao, near Bihár	,,	75, 84	. . .
Vimala Mitra, Buddhist teacher—			
Legend of—	I	250	. . .
Víra Deva of Magadha—			
Attended Kanishka's monastery at Peshávar in 9th or 10th century A.D.	II	89	. . .

	Vol.	Page.	Plate.
Víra Sena—			
Probably Satrap of Mathurá under Kanishka . .	XII	41	. . .
Víra Varmma Deva, Chandel King –			
Kálanjar inscription of—	XXI	38	. . .
Dahi copper-plate inscription of—	"	74	. . .
Virát—			
See **Bairát.**			
Virudhaka, King of Srávastí—			
Legends of—	I	332, 347	. . .
Visákhá city, of Hwen Thsang—			
= **Ayodhya city,** *q.v.*	"	317	. . .
Visákhá maiden—			
Buddhist legends of—	"	318, 345	. . .
Visákhá Datta—			
Coins of, found at Ayodhya	"	319	. . .
Vísala Deva Chauhán, Rájá of Ajmer—			
Captured Delhi in A.D. 1151-52	"	156	. . .
Inscription of, dated S. 1220 = A.D. 1163, on Asoka's 'Golden Pillar' at Delhi	"	166	. . .
Was grandfather of Prithí Ráj, and founded Vísalpur in Jaypur State	VI	152	. . .
Vísalpur in Jaypur State—			
Temples with inscriptions of time of Prithí Ráj Chauhán at—	"	154	XVII, XXI.
Vishnu—			
Temples of, frequently converted to worship of Siva .	II	266, 278	. . .
Worship of, prevailed from 7th to 10th century A.D. .	IX	149	. . .
Vishnu, King (?)—			
Perhaps the same as Náráyana Kanwa of the Puránas	V	140	. . .
Vishnu Gupta, King—			
Gold coins of—	I	40, *Note*	. . .
Vishnu Varddhana, King—			
Inscription dated S. 428 of—	VI	59	VIII.
	XX	81	. . .

	Vol.	Page.	Plate.
Vonones, King—			
Probably a Scythian from frontiers of Parthia . .	II	47, 59	. . .
Vrijis—			
Vaisáli, the capital of country of—	XVI	34	. . .
Tumuli at Lauriyá-Navandgarh are the *chetiyas* of the—	XXII	49	. . .
Vrishadarbha—			
The ancient name of part of the Panjáb . . .	II	14	. . .
Vyághra—			
17 coins of, found at Sunit, near Lúdiána . . .	XIV	65	. . .
Vyághra Deva of Uchahara—			
Inscription of—	XXI	v, 97	XXVII.
Vyághrapura (Koli) of Buddhist tradition—			
Identified with Báráh Chhetra in Bastí District, N.-W. P.	XII	213	. . .
The residence of Rájá Suprabuddha, father of Máyá Deví	"	213	. . .
According to Brahmans, the site of Varáha Avatár of Vishnu	"	213	. . .

W

	Vol.	Page.	Plate.
Waihand—			
See **Ohind.**			
Wairágarh, in Chándá District, C. P.—			
Various ruins at—	VII	127	XIII.
Diamond mines at—	"	129	. . .
Wardak in ? Afghánistán—			
Inscription of Kanishka from—	II	67	. . .
Webharo mountain of Pálí annals—			
≡ Baibhár hill at Rajgír	I	21	. . .
Wells—			
Square, used formerly by Buddhists in India, as now in Burma	V	94	. . .
Octagonal, used by Buddhists	XI	16, 93	. . .

	VOL.	PAGE.	PLATE.
Wema Kadphises, King—			
Perhaps = Chinese Yen-kao-Ching	II	67	. . .
Speculations as to his identity with Vikramáditya and the 'nameless king'	III	39, 44	. . .
Find-spots of coins of—	"	45	. . .
Approximate date of—	V	187	. . .
Perhaps = Rájá Ben	XII	37	. . .
Wepullo mountain of Pálí annals—			
= Vipula hill at Rájgír	I	22	. . .
Wessanagara—			
= **Besnagar**, *q.v.*	X	37	. . .
Wessantara, *alias* **Sudána,** *alias* **Sudatta—**			
Legends of—	V	14, 199	. . .
White Huns—			
Broke the power of the Yuchi in 5th century A.D.	II	63	. . .
Distinct from Little Yuchi	"	75	. . .
Also known as Ephthalites or Nephthalites; wrongly called Cidaritæ by Priscus	"	75, 76	. . .
Chinese accounts of—	"	75, 78	. . .
Opposition to inroads of, in 5th and 6th centuries A.D.	III	137	. . .
Wijásan—			
See **Bhándak, in Chándá District, C. P.**			
Wilford, F.—			
Essay on Comparative Geography of India by—	I	Intr. II	. . .
Value of work of—	"	" XVIII, *Note*	. . .
Wilkins, Charles—			
Translated several inscriptions	"	" II	. . .
Wilson, H. H.			
'Ariana Antiqua' and other works of—	"	" V	. . .
Sketch of the history of the kingdom of Pandya by—	"	" VII, *Note*	. . .
Erroneous opinions of, concerning date of Bhílsá topes and cave temples of W. India	"	" XXXIX, XL	. . .
Readings of Sháhbázgarhi inscription by—	V	21	. . .
Wood—			
Used in roofs at Taxila (Sháhdheri)	"	73	. . .
The material of the walls of Pâṭaliputra according to Greek authors	VIII	27	. . .
Temples in Chamba State built of—	XIV	110	. . .

	Vol.	Page.	Plate.
Y			
Yádava race—			
Legendary accounts of—	II	14	. . .
Yáduvansí race—			
Now represented by the Hindu Jádons of Karaulí and Sabalgaṛh, and the Musalman Meos and Khánzádas	XX	5	. . .
Real history of, begins with Dharma Pála *circa* A.D. 800	„	6	. . .
List of Rájás of, in Karaulí and Bayána . . .	„	1	. . .
Yakshas—			
Colossal statues of, from Patna	XV	1	II.
Yama—			
Unique temple dedicated to, at Márkanda, C.P. .	IX	148	. . .
Yasah Karna Deva, King of Chedí—			
Mentioned in inscriptions	.	88, 109	. . .
Yaso Varmma, King of Kanauj			
Notices and date of—	III	135	. . .
Coins of—	II	159	. . .
	III	138	. . .
Appears to have re-built the great *stúpa* at Mánikyála	II	160	. . .
Yaso Varmma Deva, Chandel King—			
Inscription giving history of reign of—	XXI	83	. . .
Yaso Varmma pura—			
A name of Bihár City	III	135	. . .
	VIII	76	. . .
Yaudheya tribe—			
= Johiyas of Baháwalpur	XIV	140	. . .
Provenance of coins of—	II	14	. . .
	XIV	140	. . .
Description of coins of—	„	141	XXXI.
Perhaps = Adraistæ of Arrian, and Aráshṭras of Mahábhárata	„	142	. . .
Coins of Bráhmaṇa Deva, chief of—	„	143	. . .
Bhánu Varmma, probably a chief of— . .	„	144	. . .
Yavanas (Greeks)—			
Fought Agnimitra, and under Menander advanced to Ganges	II	41	. . .

	Vol.	Page.	Plate.
Yavanas, Kilakila—			
See Kilakila Yavanas.			
Yen-kao-ching, King of the Yuchi—			
Was son of Khieu-tsieu-ki, and probably = Wema (Hima) Kadphises	II	63, 67	. . .
Yojana of Hwen Thsang—			
= 40 Chinese *li*, = nearly 7 miles	I	270	. . .
	III	77, *Note*	. . .
Yona nation—			
Mentioned in Sháhbázgarhi inscription	V	20	. . .
Yuchi—			
Comprised Great and Little Yuchi	II	62	. . .
Yuchi, Great—			
Occupied Káshgár, Yárkand, and Kotan in B.C. 163, and Sogdiana and Tahia in B.C. 126	"	44, 63	. . .
Divided into 5 tribes, which were united by Khieu-tsieu-ki	"	43, "	. . .
= Tochari of Strabo, &c.	"	" 64	. . .
Ruling tribe of, known as Kuei-shwang, Gushán, Khushan, Korano, &c.	"	" "	. . .
= Túrkí rulers of Kábul mentioned by Abú Rihán	"	66	. . .
Kanishka belonged to—	"	67	. . .
Probably = Kaspeiræoi of Ptolemy, &c.	"	68	. . .
Titles of kings of—	"	69	. . .
Perhaps represented by modern Gújars	"	70	. . .
Conquests in Kábul, Ariana, Gándhára, and India by Khieu-tsieu-ki and Yen-kao-ching, kings of—	"	63--67	. . .
Still powerful in 1st century A.D.	"	63	. . .
Weakened in 222 A.D. by attacks of other tribes	"	63, 68	. . .
Finally overthrown by White Huns in 5th century A.D.	"	"	. . .
Kitolo of Gándhára, last known king of—	"	63	. . .
Little Yuchi kingdom of Pesháwar, founded by the son of Kitolo King of—	"	64	. . .
Yuchi, Little (early)—			
Entered Tibet in second century B.C.	"	62	. . .
Yuchi, Little (late)—			
Held the kingdom of Pesháwar in 5th century A.D.	"	64, 73	. . .
Adopted name Kitolo or Kator, still preserved by the Chief of Chitral	"	73	. . .
Not identical with the Ephthalites or White Huns	"	75	. . .

	Vol.	Page.	Plate.
Yusufzái country—			
Boundaries of—	V	1	. . .
Yusufzái country (British) in Peshâwar District, Panjâb—			
Map of—	"	. . .	II.
= Ancient Pushkalávatí or Peukelaotis	"	2	. . .
Formerly thickly populated	"	"	. . .
Described by Dr. Bellew	"	5	. . .
Principal ruins in—	"	"	. . .
Sculptures in, chiefly Buddhist of early date	"	6, 7	. . .
Coins, Greek, Scythian, &c., found in—	"	6	. . .
Brahmanism introduced early into—	"	7	. . .
Few Muhammadan remains in—	"	8	. . .
Stone, the material of buildings in—	"	95	. . .
Bas-reliefs in Indo-Persian style in—	"	187	. . .
List of 165 statues of kings and other sculptures from—	"	197	. . .
Arian character only used in inscriptions from—	"	7	. . .
Collection of Arian inscriptions from—	"	57—64	XVI.
Great caves in—	XIX	111	. . .
Yuvarájá—			
Name of two kings of Chedí—	IX	112	. . .
Z			
Záhir Pír—			
See **Gugá Chauhán.**			
Zamániá in Ghâzípur District, N.-W. P.—			
Formerly called Madan-Banáras	III	63	. . .
Zanthii of Strabo—			
Perhaps = Ját tribe	II	55	. . .
Zaoou (*Gen.*) on coins—			
= Scythian title Shaowu	III	44	. . .
Zaradrus R. of Ptolemy—			
Probably = Satlaj R.	II	12	. . .
Zaths of Sindh in 7th century A. D.—			
Probably = Ját tribe	"	55	. . .
Zeda in Yusufzái country, Panjáb—			
Kanishka inscription found at—	V	57	. . .
Zeionises, Satráp—			
See **Jihonia, Satrap.**			

	Vol.	Page.	Plate.
Zhobi, town W. of Indus—			
Probably = Sabanna of Ptolemy	II	32	. . .
Zíb-un-nissa, daughter of Aurangzeb—			
Tomb of, at Delhi	I	230	. . .
Zoilus, King—			
Coins of, found at Pathánkot in Kángra District, Panjáb	XIV	116	. . .

GLOSSARY.

N.B.—The words are defined only in the senses in which they are used in the Reports.

A

Abhisheka—
Inauguration; coronation.

Abjad—
A. B. C.; notation of numerals by letters of Arabic alphabet.

Áchárya—
Hindu religious teacher.

Ádhiráj—
Sovereign (an epithet of kings.)

Ák—
A plant (*Asclepias gigantea*, Roxb.)

Akhárá (Akhádá)—
Place for wrestling in.

Akshay—
Imperishable.

Alláh—
God.

Amalaka—
(1) The fruit of the *aonlá* tree (*Phyllanthus emblica*, Roxb.)
(2) The ornament on the top of the steeple of a temple.

Ambá (ám)—
Mango.

Ámm (ám)—
Public.

Anár—
Pomegranate.

Antarála—
Antechamber of a temple.

Arddha-mandapa—
Entrance-hall of a temple.

Argha—
= Yoni, *q.v.*

Arháí—
Two and a half.

Arhat—
A Buddhist saint.

Ásan—
Seat; throne.

Ashta (áth)—
Eight.

Asthán—
A Hindú shrine.

Asura (asur)—
Demon.

Aswamedha—
The sacrifice of the horse, performed by claimants to universal sovereignty.

Átá (atta)—
Flour.

Aundhá—
Upside down.

Avatár—
Incarnation, especially of Vishnu.

Azán (izán)—
The Muhammadan summons to prayers, generally proclaimed from the minarets of a mosque.

B

Babúl—
A tree (*cacia arabica*).

Bachchhá—
Cub; the young of an animal.

Badi—
The waning moon fortnight of a month in the Hindú calendar.

Bádsháh—
King; emperor.

Bágh (باگھ)—
Tiger.

Bágh (باغ)—
Grove.

Báharí—
Outer.

Bahú—
Daughter-in-law.

Bairágí—
A class of Hindú ascetics.

Baithak—
Sitting-room; summer-house; seat.

Ban (vana)—
Grove.

Bándh (band)—
Embankment.

Banghy (Bahangí)—
A pole with two baskets for carrying loads.

Baniyá—
Tradesman; shopkeeper, especially a dealer in grain.

Banyan (Banian)—
A kind of fig-tree (*Ficus indica*).

Báolí (Báorí)—
A large well, with steps leading to the water.

Bará—
Great; large.

Báradarí—
An open hall, properly one with twelve doorways; a summer-house.

Bárah—
Twelve.

Bárát—
Marriage procession.

Bat—
Banyan tree (*Ficus indica*).

Battís—
Thirty-two.

Báwan—
Fifty-two.

Begam—
A title of noble Musalman ladies.

Bel—
A fruit-tree (*Ægle marmelos*).

Bhádon—
A Hindú month, August-September.

Bhaktin—
Priestess.

Bhándár—
Treasury; store-room.

Bháshá—
Hindi vernacular.

Bhikshu (*fem.* **Bhikshuni**)—
Mendicant.

Bhisá—
Mound.

Bhítarí—
Inner.

Bhúsá—
Straw.

Bhút—
Ghost; evil spirit.

Bíbí—
Lady (the word is generally applied to Muhammadans).

Bíghá (Bígah)—
A land measure of varying extent, but in many places = ⅝ths of an acre.

Bihár—
See "**Vihára.**"

Bíjak—
Inscription.

Bíná (víná)—
Indian lute.

Bír—
Ghost.

Biyáh—
Marriage.

Bodhi—
Knowledge, especially the perfect knowledge attainable by a Buddha.

Bodhisatwa—
Buddhist sage.

Búrhá (Búdhá)—
Old.

Burj—
Tower; bastion.

But—
Idol.

C

Chabutrá—
Platform; dais.

Chádar—
Sheet.

Chaitra (Chait)—
A Hindú month, March-April.

Chaitya—
A Buddhist chapel.

Chakkí—
Millstone.

Chakra—
Quoit (*discus*, an emblem of Vishnu).

Chakravartí—
Universal (*scil.* sovereign).

Chakwá—
The so-called "Bráhmaní duck" (*Anas casarca*).

Chandana—
Sandal-wood.

Chándmárí—
Artillery or rifle range.

Chapátí—
Cake of unleavened bread.

Chár diwálí—
Square enclosure.

Charan—
Foot-print.

Chaturbhuj—
Four-armed (a title of Vishnu).

Chaturmukh—
Four-faced.

Chaukí—
(1) Station; stage; outpost.
(2) Cell.

Chaukídár (chowkídár)—
Watchman.

Chaumukhí—
Four-faced.

Chaunsath—
Sixty-four.

Chaupar—
A game, played with dice.

Chaurásí—
Eighty-four.

Chaurí (Chaunrí)—
Fly-whisk.

Chawar (chaur)—
A broad water-course; swamp.

Chelá—
Disciple.

Chhattís—
Thirty-six.

Chhatr—
Umbrella; canopy.

Chhatrí (chatri)—
Canopy; kiosk.

Chhauní—
Cantonment.

Chhotá—
Small; little.

Chihal (chehel)—
Forty.

Chillá—
A rag hung on a tree as an offering.

Chirágh—
A native lamp.

Chor—
Thief.

Chuna—
A corruption of *chúná* = lime; lime-plaster.

Crore—
See "**Karor.**"

D

Dagoba (dahgopa)—
= Stúpa, *q.v.*

Dákait—
Brigand.

Dakhin—
India south of the Vindhya mountains.

Dálán (dallán)—
Verandah; corridor.

Dandá—
Stick; staff.

Darbár (durbár)—
Court of a prince.

Dargáh—
A Muhammadan shrine.

Darwán—
Door-keeper.

Darwáza—
Gate; gateway; entrance.

Das—
Ten.

Deolí—
Temple, especially a cenotaph sacred to the memory of a deceased Rájá.

Deorá—
Temple.

Des—
Country; region.

Deva—
(1) A male divinity.
(2) A certain class of minor divinities.
(3) A common element of royal names.

Deva-loka—
The abode of the 'devas.'

Devatá—
A class of minor divinities.

Deví—
(1) A female divinity.
(2) Siva's consort.

Dewal—
Temple.

Dháí—
Two and a half.

Dhák—
A tree (*Butea frondosa*).

Dharma—
Religion; religious merit; piety.

Dharma-chakra—
Buddhist sacred wheel.

Dharmsálá—
Rest-house.

Dharná—
A mode of extortion practised by Brahmans.

Dhenkí—
A rude machine for pounding grain.

Dhobí—
Washerman.

Dhol—
Drum.

Dhotí—
Waist-cloth.

Digambara—
'Sky-clad,' *scil.* (naked, the name of a Jain sect).

Dighá (dighí)—
Tank; pond.

Dih (dhi)—
Mound of ruins; old site.

Din—
Day.

Dínár—
A corruption of Latin *denarius.* In the Gupta period a gold coin corresponding to the *aureus.*

Díp—
Lamp.

Dípdán—
Lamp-post.

Díwán (Dewán)—
(1) Hall of audience; divan.
(2) Prime minister.

Doáb (Duáb)—
A tract of country between two rivers which meet.

Dol—
A swing.

Dopattá—
Shawl.

Drúm—
A tree.

Duáb—
See "**Doáb.**"

Dulhá—
Bridegroom.

Dulhin—
Bride.

Dúlí (dooly)—
A kind of litter.

Durbar—
See "**Darbár.**"

Durg—
Fort.

Durgah—
See "**Dargáh.**"

Dwápar-yug (jug)—
The third or 'brazen age' of Hindú mythology.

Dwárí (dwar)—
Door; opening.

Dwija—
'Twice-born,' *i.e.*, a Brahman, Kshatriya, or Vaisya, but especially a Brahman.

F

Fakír—
A Muhammadan ascetic.

Farang—
European.

Farmán—
A grant; letters patent.

Farsh (farash)—
Floor; pavement.

G

Gach—
Cement; mortar.

Gadádhar—
Mace-bearer; a title of Vishnu.

Gaddí (gadí)—
Cushion, especially the seat of a Rájá.

Gám (gaon)—
Village; town (*gráma*).

Ganj—
Market-place; bazaar.

Garbha-griha—
Sanctum of a temple.

Garh (garhí)—
Fort.

Garudá—
The man-faced eagle (emblem of Vishṇu).

Gauná—
Bringing a bride to her husband's house to consummate marriage.

Gaz (gaj)—
Yard-measure.

Genth—
A kind of fish.

Gerú—
Red ochre, *i.e.*, hæmatite.

Ghantá—
Bell.

Ghar—
House.

Ghár (غار)—
Cave.

Gharí—
A Hindú division of time, = 24 minutes.

Ghariyál (gariál)—
Alligator.

Ghát—
(1) A flight of steps leading to water.
(2) A mountain pass.
(3) A ferry.

Ghazal—
Ode.

Ghází—
Champion of the faith (Musalman).

Ghí (ghee)—
Clarified butter.

Giri—
Hill; mountain.

Gít—
Song.

Gosáin—
A kind of Hindú ascetic.

Gosirsha—
A kind of sandal-wood.

Got (gotra)—
A subdivision of a caste.

Gram—
A pulse (Cicer arietinum).

Grám-devatá—
Village deity.

Granth—
The holy book of the Sikhs.

Gridhra (gidha)—
Vulture.

Guhá—
Cave.

Gúlar—
A tree (*Ficus glomerata*).

Gumbaz—
Dome.

Guphá—
Cave.

Gur (goor)—
Unrefined sugar.

Guru—
Hindú religious preceptor.

Gurudwárá—
A Sikh monastery.

Gwálá—
Cowherd.

H

Hakím—
Physician.

Halwáí—
Sweetmeat-seller.

Hammám (hamam)—
Turkish bath.

Hansa—
Goose.

Háth—
Cubit

Háthí—
Elephant.

Hauz—
Reservoir; bath.

Hawelí (havelí)—
House; building.

Hazár—
A thousand.

Hínáyána—
Lesser vehicle, *scil.* the doctrine of a certain Buddhist sect.

Hindolá—
A swing.

Hiranya-báhu—
Golden armed.

Holí—
The Hindú Saturnalia.

Hom—
A kind of burnt-offering.

Hrada—
Tank; pond.

Hujra—
Chamber; pavilion.

I

I'dgáh—
Muḥammadan place of prayer.

Imámbárá—
Building used in the celebration of the Muḥarram.

Imlí—
Tamarind tree (*Tamarindus indica*).

Inám—
Rent or revenue-free; a grant of revenue-free land.

Intikháb—
Extract.

Izán—
See "**Azán.**"

J

Jádú—
Magic; juggling.

Jag (Yajnya)—
Sacrifice.

Jágír (Jághír)—
A grant of land made in reward for service.

Jáman—
Jambú—
A tree (*Sysygium jambolanum*).

Jámí (jáma)—
General; (public) applied to the chief mosque of a town).

Janeo (jeneu)—
The Brahmanical thread.

Jangal—
Jungle; undergrowth.

Janghiyá (jangia)—
Short drawers.

Játaka—
Buddhist sacred story.

Jaya—
Victory.

Jháu (jhao)—
The tamarisk (*Tamarix gallica*, var. *Indica*).

Jhíl—
A natural shallow sheet of water.

Jhoprá (jhoprí)—
Hut; shed.

Jhál—
Housings of horse or elephant.

Jizya—
Poll-tax imposed by Muhammadan rulers on non-conforming subjects.

Jogí—
A class of Hindú ascetics.

Jogini—
A kind of female demon.

Johar (jauhar)—
Self-immolation.

Júná—
Old.

Jyeshta (jeth)—
A Hindú month, May-June.

K

Ká (ke, kí)—
Of—

Káaba (Kábá)—
The holy of holies at Makká (Mecca).

Kabáb—
Roast meat.

Kabít—
A kind of Hindí poem.

Kachahrí (kacheri)—
Court-house; *anglice* 'cutcherry.'

Kachchhá (Kacha)—
Raw; incomplete; earthen; in all senses the opposite of *pakká*.

Káfir—
An unbeliever (*scil.* of Islám).

Kákiní—
A coin, $=\frac{1}{4}$ paṇa, $=20$ cowries.

Kála (Kál)—
Era; age

Kálá—
Black.

Kalama (Kalima)—
The Muhammadan creed—'There is no God but Alláh, and Muhammad is his prophet.'

Kalán—
Great; large.

Kalasa (Kalas)—
Pinnacle of temple steeple.

Kálíyug—
The present evil age.

Kánch—
Glass.

Kangura—
Battlement.

Kankar (Kunkur)—
Nodular limestone.

Káráhí (Karai)—
Iron pan.

Karan—
A kind of tree.

Karor (crore)—
Ten millions.

Kasái—
Butcher.

Katrá—
Market-place.

Kanwá—
A crow.

Kavit (kabit)—
A kind of Hindú poem.

Kendu (kend)—
A tree (*Diospyrus glutinosa*, Roxb.).

Khádim (kádim)—
Attendant at a mosque.

Khádir (khádar)—
Low-lying alluvial land.

Khajúr—
Wild date palm (*Phœnix silvestris*, (Roxb.).

Khambha (khambh, kambh)—
Pillar.

Khána—
House; dwelling; place.

Khand—
(1) a tract of country, *e.g.*, Bundelkhand.
(2) Canto of a poem, *e.g.*, Mahoba Khand of the Chand Ráesa.

Khángáh—
Shrine of Muhammadan saint.

Kháss (khás)—
Special; applied to distinguish a town from the surrounding tract of country bearing the same name.

Kherá—
Mound of ruins.

Khichrí (kichrí)—
A dish made of rice and pulse boiled together.

Khír—
Rice boiled in milk.

Khiráj—
Paying rent or land-revenue.

Khirkí—
Back-door; postern.

Kho—
Valley.

Khurpí (koorpie)—
A small spud used in scraping up grass.

Khutba—
The prayer for the sovereign in a mosque.

Kibla—
The niche in a mosque turned towards Makka (Mecca).

Kichrí—
See "**Khichrí.**"

Kiliá—
Fort.

Kiládár—
Governor of a fort.

Kodo—
A kind of grain (*Paspalum scrobiculatum*, Roxb.)

Kohna (kona)—
Old.

Koorpie—
See "**Khurpí.**"

Kos (kross)—
An Indian measure of distance, commonly equal to about two miles, but frequently more or less.

Kosha—
Disquisition.

Kot—
Fort.

Kothrí (Kotrí)—
Room; chamber.

Koti—
Ten millions.

Krís—
Nepalese curved sword.

Kshatrapa—
Satrap.

Kshatriya—
The second of Manu's four castes; Ráj-pút.

Kuá—
A well.

Kulhárí—
Axe.

Kumbha (kumbh)—
Water-jar.

Kund—
A small, deep, artificial reservoir.

Kusa—
A grass (*Poa cynosuroides*, Roxb.)

Kusala (Kusula)—
Happiness.

Kushak—
Palace; pavilion; kiosk.

Kutila—
A form of the Nagarí alphabet in use in 10th to 12th centuries, A D.

L

Lákh (lac)—
One hundred thousand.

Lakhaurá (lakhowr)—
Small native-made bricks.

Lál—
Red.

Lambardár (lumberdár)—
Headman of a village.

Langotí—
A small cloth worn by men to cover their nakedness.

Lashkar—
Camp.

Lát (láth)—
Pillar; monolith.

Li—
A Chinese measure of distance, equal to one-sixth of a mile.

Lingam (linga)—
The emblem of the male generative power; phallus.

Lohá—
Iron.

Lotá—
Brass water-pot.

M

Maafi—
See "**Muáfí.**"

Madhya—
Central; middle.

Madhya Mandapa—
Second chamber of a temple.

Madrasa—
College; school.

Magar—
Crocodile.

Mágha (Mágh)—
A Hindú month=January-February.

Mahá-mandapa—
Central hall of a temple; nave.

Mahájan—
Money-lender; merchant.

Mahal—
Palace.

Mahalla—
Ward of a town.

Mahanta (Mahant)—
Head of a Hindú monastery.

Mahárájá—
'Great king,' a higher title than Rájá.

Maháyána—
'Great vehicle,' *scil.* the doctrine of a certain Buddhist seet.

Mahuá (Mahwa)—
A tree (*Bassia latifolia*).

Makán—
House; building.

Makbara—
Tomb.

Málí (*fem.* **Málin**)—
Gardener.

Man (Mán)—
'Maund,' a weight which varies much, but the standard is 82 pounds.

Mandapa—
Porch of a temple.

Mandir—
Temple; palace.

Mansabdár—
A high army officer under the Mughal government.

Mantra—
A charm or spell.

Manzil (Manzal)—
Story or floor of a building.

Marh (Marhí)—
Temple.

Masjid—
Mosque.

Masuran—
A gold coin.

Math—
Temple; Hindú monastery.

Mátrá—
The head line in the Nágarí character.

Maund—
Anglo-Indian for 'man,' *q.v.*

Mauzá—
A townland, village with its lands.

Mayúra—
Peacock.

Mázína—
= Mínár, *q.v.*

Mendhi—
Henna dye.

Melá—
A fair.

Mihráb (Mehráb)—
Arch; the place in a mosque where the *mullá* pray with his face turned towards Mecca.

Mimbar—
Pulpit of a mosque.

Mínár—
Minaret; the pinnacle from which the *muassin* of a mosque calls the faithful to prayers.

Mishkal (Miskál)—
A weight = 4 *máshás* and 3½ ratís, *i.e.*, 35½ *ratís*.

Mlechchhá—
Barbarian, *scil.* a person out of the pale of Hindú caste.

Morhá—
Wicker-stool.

Motí—
Pearl.

Muáfí—
Free of land revenue or rent.

Muazzin—
The official of the mosque who utters the call to prayers.

Muharram—
Celebration commemorating the death of Hasn and Husain.

Muhr (Mohur)—
A gold coin equal in weight to the silver rupee.

Mukhannis (*pl.*— **ánán**)—
Eunuch.

Mullá (Mullah)—
Muhammadan religious teacher.

Muni—
Hindú saint.

Muríd—
Disciple.

Múrti—
Image; idol.

Musallá—
Carpet, or floor, for Muhammadans to pray on.

N

Nábdán—
A small drain.

Nadí—
A small river; a stream.

Nága (Nág), *fem.* **Náginí**—
(1) A snake, or dragon, especially a snake that is worshipped.
(2) Name of certain tribes.

Nagar—
Town.

Nágarí (Nágrí)—
The Sanskrit alphabet.

Nágína—
Gem.

Náhar—
Tiger.

Nakára—
Kettle-drum.

Nakshatra—
Lunar mansion, or asterism = 13° 20′, the twenty-seventh part of the zodiac.

Nakshawálá—
Painter.

Nálá (Nullah)—
A small watercourse; ravine

Nandi—
The bull of Siva.

Naogaja—
Lit. nine yards long; a giant.

Nat (*fem.* **Natní**)—
Gipsy.

Nau (Nao)—
Nine.

Navagraha—
The 'nine planets' of Indian astronomy.

Nílgái—
The 'blue bull' antelope (*Antelope picta*).

Ním (Nimb)—
A tree (*Melia azadiracta*, Roxb.)

Nirvána—
(1) The ideal goal of the Buddhist religion, which is variously explained.
(2) The death of Buddha.

Nohara—
Cattle pen.

Nullah—
See "Nálá."

Nyagrodha—
Banyan tree (*Ficus indica*).

P

Pachísí—
A game.

Pada (Pad)—
Foot ; footprint.

Paddy—
Unhusked rice.

Padma—
Lotus.

Pádsháh—
King ; emperor.

Pahár—
Hill ; mountain.

Pahárí—
Hill-man.

Pahlwán—
Wrestler.

Paisá—
A copper coin ; in the Government of India currency $= \frac{1}{4}$th of an anna, $= \frac{1}{64}$th of a rupee.

Pákar—
A kind of fig tree (*Ficus venosa*).

Pakká—
Complete ; perfect (of masonry. In all senses the opposite of *kachchhá*).

Pala—
Hindú division of time, $= \frac{1}{60}$th of a ghaṛi, *q.v.*

Palása—
A tree (*Butea frondosa*).

Pálkí (palkee)—
Palanquin.

Pán—
Betel leaf.

Paná—
A coin, = 80 cowries.

Pánch (panj, pancha)—
Five.

Pánda—
A class of Brahmans.

Páni (पाणि)—
Hand.

Pání (पानी)—
Water.

Pansal—
Leaf-roofed hut.

Páras—
Philosopher's stone.

Pardá—
Curtain ; screen.

Parvata (parbat)—
Hill ; mountain.

Parwáná—
A written order.

Patthar (pathar)—
Stone ; rock.

Paur—
Gate.

Pazáwá (pazáyá)—
Brick-kiln.

Phálgun—
Hindú month, = February-March.

Phaorá (phowra)—
Mattock.

Phátak—
Gate.

Pípal—
The sacred fig tree (*Ficus religiosa*).

Pír—
Muhammadan saint.

Pitri—
Ancestor to whom offerings are made.

Pokhar (pokhrí —
Pond ; tank.

Pol—
Gate.

Prásádá—
Temple.

Preta (pret)—
A ghost.

Pújá—
Ceremonial worship.

Pújárí—
Attendant at a temple.

Pul—
Bridge.

Puráná—
Old.

Putra (pút)—
Son.

Q

Qabar—
Tomb.

Qasbeh—
A small town.

R

Rahat—
= **Arhat,** *q.v.*

Rájá—
King; prince; Hindú nobleman.

Rákshasa—
A ferocious kind of demon.

Ramazán (Ramzán)—
The ninth Muhammadan lunar month, observed as a strict fast.

Rání—
Queen; the consort of a Rájá.

Rankiní—
Female demon.

Raoní—
Faussebraie, or outer line of fortification.

Rasoí (rasuí)—
Kitchen.

Ratí—
A weight = 1·825 of an English grain (Some authorities state the value differently.)

Rishi (rikhi)—
A Vedic saint.

Rolí—
A red colouring matter.

Roza (rauza)—
Mausoleum.

S

Ságar—
A large lake.

Sagparast—
A dog-worshipper.

Sáhib—
Mr.; a European.

Saikalgar (Siklegar)—
Polisher; armourer.

Sáís (syce)—
Groom.

Saiyid—
A person claiming descent from Muhammad.

Saka—
(1) Name of a tribe.
(2) Era (especially the era of Sáliváhána).

Sakti—
The personification of the female energy of a Hindú god.

Sál—
A tree (*Shorea robusta*).

Samádh—
Tomb of a Hindú ascetic or holy man.

Sámbar—
The so-called Indian elk.

Samvatsara (Samvat)—
Era; year. (In early inscriptions this word is used as equivalent to 'era' in general, but in later documents it usually means the era of Vikrama.)

Sangam—
Confluence.

Sangha—
The Buddhist assembly of the faithful; the Buddhist church.

Sanghoárámа—
A Buddhist monastery.

Sání—
Second.

Sankh—
Conch shell.

Sankránta—
The time of the sun's entrance into Aries

Sanyásí—
A class of Hindú ascetics.

Sarái—
Native inn.

Sárangí—
Indian guitar.

Sárí (Saree)—
A woman's wrapper or shawl.

Sarwar (Sarowar)—
Tank; pond.

Sás—
Mother-in-law.

Sasur—
Father-in-law.

Sát—
Seven.

Satáís—
Twenty-seven.

Satí—
A woman who burned herself alive after her husband's death.

Satyug (=jug)—
The 'golden age' of Hindú legend.

Sáwán (Sánwán)—
A kind of grain (*Panicum frumentaceum*, Roxb.)

Ser (Seer)—
A weight, normally equal to about two pounds, but it varies much.

Shahíd—
Muhammadan martyr.

Shahr-panáh—
City walls.

Sharíf—
Honourable; illustrious.

Sher (Shír)—
Tiger.

Shikár—
Hunting game.

Shikárgáh—
Hunting-ground.

Shish-mahal—
Hall of mirrors.

Sikhara, (sikar, sikri)—
Steeple of temple.

Siklegar—
See "**Saikalgar.**"

Silá—
A stone.

Singhásan—
Throne; pedestal.

Sinha (Singh)—
Lion; a Hindú cognomen.

Sipáhí—
Soldier; sepoy.

Sir—
Head.

Sirdár—
Headman; chief.

Siris—
A tree (*Mimosa sirissa*, Roxb),

Sitár—
Guitar.

Sivála (Shiwálá)—
Temple of Siva.

Sloka—
Couplet of Sanskrit poetry.

Solah (sola)—
Sixteen.

Soná—
Gold.

Srám—
A Buddhist disciple.

Srávakí (saraogí)—
A Jain.

Srí—
(1) Fortunate, an honorific prefix to personal names.
(2)=Lakshmí, consort of Vishnu.

Stambha—
Tower; pillar.

Sthán—
= **Asthá**, *q. v.*

Stúpa—
Buddhist dome-shaped tower built over relics, or as a memorial. The earliest *stúpas* were tombs.

Sudi—
The waxing moon fortnight of a month in the Hindú calendar.

Súdra—
The lowest of Manu's four castes.

Suráhí (surai)—
Water-bottle.

Surkh—
Red.

Surkhí (soorkey)—
Brick-dust, used as a component of mortar.

Surmá—
Antimony for painting eyebrows.

Súrya (súraj)—
The sun.

Sútra—
A verse, or clause, in a Hindú scripture.

Sutún—
Pillars.

Swástika—
The mystic cross.

Swetámbara, Swetavása—
White-robed, (a Jain sect).

T

Tahsíldár—
A revenue officer.

Táj—
(1) The projection at back of a mosque.
(2) The celebrated tomb at Agra, of which the proper name is Mumtáz Mahál.

Takht—
Throne.

Tál—
A lake, or large pond.

Támbapatra—
Copper plate.

Tamtam (tomtom)—
A kind of drum.

Tanká (tangka)—
A coin.

Tántrika—
In accordance with the Tántra system of religion.

Tapasya—
Penance.

Tappa—
= **Tola**, *q.v.*

Tarái—
The low country at the base of the Himálayas.

Tár (toddy)—
The toddy palm tree (*Borassus flabelliformis*), of which toddy (*tárí*) is the fermented juice.

Tasbíh-khána—
Place of prostration in a mosque.

Tathágata—
"Passed away," a title of Buddha.

Táwá—
Griddle.

Táziá—
The bier carried in the Muharram procession.

Tee—
The umbrella on top of a *Stúpa*.

Thákur (*fem.* **Thakuráin**)—
(1) a Rájpút.
(2) A god.

Thán—
= **Asthán**, *q.v.*

Thána—
Police station.

Thánadár—
Officer in charge of a police station.

Thára—
Rude cenotaph in Rájputána.

Thup, Thúpo—
= *Stúpa, q.v.*

Thupí—
A ruined *stúpa*.

Tibá—
A mound.

Tíká—
Mark on the forehead, made to indicate the sect of the wearer, or when a king is placed on the throne.

Tílá—
Mound; hillock.

Tilak—
= **Tíká**, *q.v.*

Tírath—
Place of Hindú pilgrimage.

Tolá—
Hamlet.

Top—
Cannon; artillery.

Tope—
(1) Anglicised form of *stúpa, q.v.*
(2) Grove; clump of trees.

Toran—
(1) Gateway of a temple or *stúpa*.
(2) A peg used in marriage ceremonies.

Tretá yug (jug)—
The second or 'silver age' of Hindú mythology.

Trisúl—
Trident, especially as a Buddhist symbol.

Tughra—
A form of Arabic writing.

Tulsí—
A plant (*Ocymum sanctum*, Roxb.) used in Hindú worship.

U

Udumbara—
A tree (*Ficus glomerata*).

Ustád—
Teacher.

V

Váhana (Váhan)—
Vehicle, (*scil.* of a Hindu deity).

Vajra—
(1) A thunderbolt, the emblem of Indra.
(2) Diamond.

Vana (ban)—
Forest; wood.

Vansa—
Family; lineage.

Varáha—
A boar, (especially the boar incarnation of Vishnu).

Vedí (bedí)—
Hall for reading the Vedas in.

Vihára (Vihár)—
A Buddhist monastery.

Vimána—
Central sanctuary of a temple.

Víná (bíná)—
Indian lute.

W

Walí—
A Muhammadan saint.

Y

Yaksha—
A class of minor divinities.

Yatí—
A Jain priest.

Yojana—
An Indian league, equal to 40 Chinese *li*, or nearly 7 English miles.

Yoni—
The emblem of the female reproductive power.

Yug (Jug)—
An age or dispensation in Hindú mythology.

Yuvarájá—
Heir-apparent of a kingdom.

Z

Zamíndár (Zemindár)—
Landholder; petty chief.

Zanana (Zenana)—
Female apartments.

Zarín—
Golden.

Ziárat—
Shrine of Muhammadan saint.

Zína—
Staircase.